IN THE BEST INTERESTS OF
THE GAME

IN THE BEST INTERESTS OF
THE GAME

DARRELL HAIR

HarperSports
An imprint of HarperCollins*Publishers*

Harper*Sports*
An imprint of HarperCollins*Publishers*

First published in Australia in 2011
by HarperCollins*Publishers* Australia Pty Limited
ABN 36 009 913 517
harpercollins.com.au

Copyright © Darrell Hair 2011

The right of Darrell Hair to be identified as the author
of this work has been asserted by him under the *Copyright Amendment
(Moral Rights) Act 2000*.

This work is copyright. Apart from any use as permitted under the
Copyright Act 1968, no part may be reproduced, copied, scanned, stored
in a retrieval system, recorded, or transmitted, in any form or by any
means, without the prior written permission of the publisher.

HarperCollins*Publishers*
Level 13, 201 Elizabeth Street, Sydney NSW 2000, Australia
31 View Road, Glenfield, Auckland 0627, New Zealand
A 53, Sector 57, Noida, UP, India
77–85 Fulham Palace Road, Hammersmith, London W6 8JB, United Kingdom
2 Bloor Street East, 20th floor, Toronto, Ontario M4W 1A8, Canada
10 East 53rd Street, New York NY 10022, USA

National Library of Australia Cataloguing-in-Publication data:

Hair, Darrell.
    In the best interests of the game / Darrell Hair.
    ISBN: 978 0 7322 9288 1 (pbk.)
    Subjects: Hair, Darrell. Cricket–Australia. Cricket–Umpiring–Australia.
796.3583092

Cover design by Heath McCurdy
Front and back cover images by Getty Images
Typeset in Bembo 12/18pt by Letter Spaced
Printed and bound in Australia by Griffin Press
70gsm Classic used by HarperCollins*Publishers* is a natural, recyclable product
made from wood grown in sustainable forests. The manufacturing processes
conform to the environmental regulations in the country of origin, Finland.

5 4 3 2 1   11 12 13 14

To Ron and Doreen

CONTENTS

FOREWORD	1
INTRODUCTION The Story of a True Believer	3

Part 1   Why Be an Umpire? 9
CHAPTER 1	Under the Sun and Over the Moon	11

Part 2   The Controversy 53
CHAPTER 2	The Oval	55
CHAPTER 3	The Aftermath	79
CHAPTER 4	The Ambush	91
CHAPTER 5	The Code of Conduct Hearing	110
CHAPTER 6	Humble Pie in Dubai	129
CHAPTER 7	Back on the Field and Back to Sydney	141
CHAPTER 8	The Tribunal	157
CHAPTER 9	Returning to Test Cricket	197

PART 3   DECISION MAKING 209
CHAPTER 10	The Controversial Umpire	211
CHAPTER 11	15 Degrees of Tolerance	228
CHAPTER 12	There Are Three Sides to Every Argument: The Decision Review System	245

Part 4   Inspirations 258
CHAPTER 13	Thanks, Miss Murray!	261
CHAPTER 14	It Wouldn't Happen in Mum's Backyard	274
CHAPTER 15	The Best of the Best	287

CAREER MATCHES	299
ACKNOWLEDGEMENTS	319

FOREWORD

What you will read in the pages of this book will be the truth, from the heart of an honest man, always ready to apply the Laws of Cricket as they were meant to be applied — without fear or favour. A fair, unbiased man who, when on the cricket field, could be absolutely relied on to give top-class assistance and support to the umpire at the other end, to work as part of a team for the benefit of the players, no matter what the level.

A man not everyone outside the world of umpiring (or even within its ranks) might understand or agree with, but a man who has the guts to do what he believes is right for the game's integrity, according to its laws, spirit and traditions. A man who, because of the ignorance and feebleness of those responsible for running cricket at its highest level, has suffered immeasurably. Those administrators will have much to answer for over the coming years given the ever-increasing burden on umpires, from the topmost level down to the grassroots of the game worldwide.

In writing this book Darrell Hair confirms that he has the courage of his convictions. His story is revealing in every sense of the word and I feel extremely privileged to have been asked by a man I respect and admire to introduce it.

Nigel Plews (1934–2008)

INTRODUCTION

THE STORY OF A TRUE BELIEVER

I was standing outside the umpires' changing room at The Brit Oval, Kennington, when my mobile rang. It was around 6.00 p.m. on 20 August 2006, a cloudy but unusually warm afternoon. I had umpired several matches on this ground before and enjoyed the atmosphere of the recently refurbished London ground, just south of the River Thames.

I had been thinking deeply about the day's events and was imagining how tumultuous the next few days would be. One team had clearly flouted the Laws of Cricket to gain an advantage. The umpires' job is simple — uphold the laws, ensure the offending side is penalised and, more importantly, ensure the other side is not disadvantaged as a result of unfair play by their opponents. The umpires today had made a decision they believed to be in the best interests of the game. That decision would, over the coming weeks, months and years, come to haunt one of those umpires. It would later seem as if his umpiring partner that day simply hadn't been there and to all intents and purposes no longer existed.

The ground was now almost empty of spectators – apart from a few rowdy patrons up in the hospitality boxes intent on wringing the last drop of entertainment from their day out. I gave no thought at that moment to how important some people in high places thought corporate cricket spectators were. I would find out much later about the hierarchy and mismatch of ideas that govern the modern game.

The only other people still evident were a hardy few up in the press box finishing their reports, which, as I was very soon to find out, would contain a stinging rebuttal of the umpires for their role in 'Cricket's Day of Shame', as one headline would read. Sadly, most, if not all, wrote their accounts without the knowledge that the match had already been awarded under the 'refusal to play' law and that there would be no play the next day.

Some of those journalists would later become public advocates of open cheating and would give evidence to that effect at an International Cricket Council (ICC) code of conduct hearing. Their evidence would be endorsed by an ICC referee, even though it was contradicted by the evidence of the four umpires on duty that day, as well as another ICC referee and a former Test umpire, that the ball in use had been tampered with.

But it was not the fault of the journalists that they did not know the full facts. That responsibility lay with cricket's administrators from both the England and Wales Cricket Board and the ICC who, in my view, by drip feeding incorrect information to the public, abysmally failed themselves, the organisations they represented and the general public.

I answered my phone. It was ICC chief executive Malcolm Speed calling from Dubai. After exchanging pleasantries, Speed asked me to give him a run-down on what had happened during the course of an afternoon that had culminated in Pakistan refusing to play on and the fourth Test of the series being awarded to England.

By the end of the call, which lasted some ten minutes, I can't say I felt either heartened or supported. That's the way with Malcolm Speed: he could make you feel ill at ease merely by walking into a room. Speed is a lawyer and did not enjoy a successful record of administration in sporting organisations and, more importantly, a record of failing to support umpires and referees. In the weeks ahead, my suspicions about the way in which he manages the game would be fully confirmed to me.

I always have doubts about any man who doesn't look you in the eye either when you meet or in conversation. Speed is such a man, at least with me. At no time during that first conversation did he acknowledge what a difficult job umpiring is, but this only conformed to past experience. Why should I expect anything to change now?

Speed asked many questions about the implementation of the law on ball tampering and whether the match had been correctly awarded to England. I assured him that both decisions were made jointly by Billy Doctrove and myself after following the correct procedures, and that we drew our conclusions based on the evidence before us.

As I packed my gear in readiness to leave for my hotel with the rest of the umpiring team, I reflected on Speed's phone call. He had been aware that meetings had already taken place in an attempt to get the match 'restarted', as he put it. I told him the match had been ended under the Laws of Cricket in one of the ways that a result is legitimately achieved, but that if he was considering overturning the decision, he should do so immediately, and publicly advise all concerned of his reasons for doing so.

Speed said he had been speaking to other stakeholders — conversations that had prompted him to intervene and try to get the umpires to alter their decision. I say 'umpires', but Speed apparently had decided against speaking to my fellow umpire, Billy Doctrove. Indeed, as he was later to admit in a sworn statement, he never made any attempt to do so.

I had no idea on this mild Sunday afternoon in London that my employer was about to set on the path to try and destroy my professional reputation. By the end of the coming week, I would slide from being a highly respected umpire, ranked number two in the world by the ICC's own assessment, to being burnt in effigy in Pakistan, with my reputation in tatters. I would even be accused of attempting to blackmail my employer. This slur would be the result of an astounding breach of confidence by that same employer.

The days that followed this breach of confidence were undoubtedly the darkest of my life. I did not know at that time (and how could anyone predict what would transpire?) that there were even lower ebbs to come. There would be many more bleak moments when events almost overwhelmed me, but I did not want to let my umpiring career end in that way.

Later in this book I will go into detail about the events that followed that tumultuous day at the cricket and their long-lasting effect on my life and the lives of those around me. One of my good umpiring friends has since said to me that those events were just a test of my faith in human nature. I say 'friend' because he has subsequently proven to be a true friend, and sadly there are not many other international umpires I count in that category. I was soon to be shunned by other umpires, who feared that any association with me might endanger their own contracts on international panels.

Unfortunately, at a time that cricket umpires at the elite level needed to be strong and band together in the best interests of the game, instead they were intimidated by the ICC into stepping back, keeping their noses clean and not speaking out. At various stages in the near future these umpires would come to understand that had they taken that opportunity to stand up for themselves, they might not have been treated even more shabbily by Mr Speed's style of management.

There can be no more vivid account of an event than that told by someone who was actually there. I can describe what happened that day, but I cannot explain some of the events that occurred in the ensuing two years. I have sought to set the record straight about the facts behind the now notorious incident in August 2006 during the fourth Test match at The Oval between England and Pakistan. Malcolm Speed recently brought the issue back into public focus in his own book, *Sticky Wicket*, published earlier this year, in a chapter which he named 'Darrell Hair'. This book also responds to a number of allegations and comments made by him in that book.

To put this story into perspective, I will also take you back to the beginning of my life in cricket and to the people who helped shape my beliefs and values not just about cricket, but about life in general. Many of these individuals are true role models for society and sport and the unsung heroes of our game. International cricket cannot survive without the game's solid grassroots platform, from which players and umpires rise to first-class and Test matches. I will introduce you to people I believe to be truly courageous, and to a courage that has nothing to do with calling a no ball or giving a batsman out, however difficult such a decision might seem. I will also tell you something of my life before I stepped out onto the international cricket grounds of the world and how that background made the pain of the past four years endurable — but the injustice and culpability of certain people impossible to ignore.

Cricket is an intoxicating sport, with an international flavour and the new Twenty20 format, but sometimes, beneath the surface, it stinks to high heaven. My story, I believe, reveals an organisation that trumpets vision and mission statements, yet turns its back on the very values that bind the sport — its tradition and the spirit of the game.

In its present state, cricket does not bear close scrutiny. It is suffering falling attendances and a lack of general direction, with three diverging formats of the game. Quite obviously some fans have stopped believing. But I am convinced of one thing: it is the greatest team game in the history of sport. It will always survive because most followers believe in the game for the right reasons: they have the spirit that honours the game's traditional values, the exchange of cultures and playing styles, and the lifelong friendships made.

This is the story of one true believer in cricket.

PART 1

WHY BE AN UMPIRE?

CHAPTER 1

UNDER THE SUN AND OVER THE MOON

A question I am often asked is, 'Why do you do it?', closely followed by, 'It must be so hard. You wouldn't get me out there in a million years!' The 'it' in question, of course, is umpiring cricket matches. The 'why' is evidently beyond the comprehension of many ardent sports fans and cricket lovers.

People take up umpiring for many reasons. For some it begins during their early years at school or when looking after their own children's matches. 'Someone has to do it!' The era of fully professional umpires, paid a salary to officiate in matches at first-class international cricket, has lured a few recently retired high-grade players into umpiring. That can only be good for cricket, as many former players can absorb the pressure with a touch more resolve than most, and this can equip them with better player management skills.

Others find that, after playing at whatever level, a clean break from cricket is not an option, so they take up umpiring 'to keep in touch with the game'. Some of us find the game far too contagious to walk away from! So when I am asked that question, my simple answer is, 'Why would I *not* do it?' Show me another game that can take five days to play, during which you get to build your life skills, make friends, meet others with mutual interests, sample different cultures and exchange interpretations of the finer points of the laws over a cool refreshment.

I have acknowledged many times how fortunate I have been and how much I have learned in more than 25 years of umpiring. How lucky I was, for example, to spend time in the Caribbean, where the fanaticism of cricket watchers has to be seen to be believed! Grounds like the Kensington Oval, Barbados; Queen's Park, Trinidad; the Antigua Recreation Ground; or Sabina Park, Jamaica — unless you've been there your cricket cannot have the same soul. Or what about the tradition of Lord's; the friendliness of historic Trent Bridge; the daunting prospect of a full house at Eden Gardens, Kolkata; the magnificence of Newlands in Cape Town; or the intimidation of the 'Bull Ring' at Wanderers, Johannesburg? And how about the full grounds during one-day internationals at the SCG Sydney; the MCG Melbourne; Adelaide Oval; the WACA in Perth; or the Gabba in Brisbane? The tranquility of Hobart; the beauty of Queenstown; the eerie feeling of a Test match being played to a virtually empty house in Lahore; the history surrounding Faisalabad; the delights of Chandigarh; or the steamy Wankhede Stadium in Mumbai? Yes indeed, why wouldn't I enjoy being an umpire? It may have (quite obvious) downsides, but looking back on my career as a whole, I wouldn't have had it any other way. Now I will give you some more specific reasons why I enjoyed my international umpiring career so much.

I umpired in 78 Test matches until my retirement in September 2008, and I cherish the memory of every one of them – including the fourth Test at The Oval. I completed 139 one-day internationals and 68 first-class games, including 8 Sheffield Shield finals. Those finals were often tougher than Test matches, and when you review the participants it is easy to understand why. Umpiring bowlers like Geoff Lawson, Greg Matthews, Carl Rackemann and Merv Hughes, and watching batsmen like Stuart Law, Michael Slater, the Waugh brothers and Mark Taylor score centuries was what the Sheffield Shield competition was all about. Tough, uncompromising and no doubt the reason why Australian cricket had such a golden era through the 1990s and into the new century.

My first Sheffield Shield final, in 1993 at the Sydney Cricket Ground, was especially memorable. Wayne Holdsworth and Glenn McGrath bowled Queensland out for just 75 in their second innings to turn the game on its head, resulting in an unlikely win for New South Wales. In a great display of very fast swing bowling, Holdsworth took 7 for 43, becoming the leading wicket taker for the season. McGrath, who was only just coming onto the scene, his immaculate line and length already evident to most of the Australian selectors, bagged 3 for 28. Still, it was hard to imagine that McGrath, completing his first season of domestic first-class cricket, would be such a great player in the future. Holdsworth's superb bowling won him a spot in the Ashes tour of England, but it was not to be a successful trip for him: he never played another Test match and was never selected for Australia again. When McGrath played for Australia the following year, it was still hard to envisage the bloke they called 'Millard' (because he lived in a caravan) would become one of the all-time greats of Australian cricket. His later nickname of 'Pigeon' (this one because there was no meat on his legs) belied the talent he was to unleash on the world's opening batsmen over the next decade and a half.

If I were to include one-day, domestic and second eleven matches, I have officiated at more than 1000 days of cricket of the highest quality. Many matches stand out. Here is a sample.

Fun and Games in the West Indies

My first appointment as an ICC Independent Panel umpire in a Test match was in Barbados on 8 April 1994. Richie Richardson won the toss and sent England in to bat. Richardson obviously began with the thought that England's spirit had been well and truly broken following a humiliating defeat in the 3rd Test, at Trinidad, where they were set the reasonable target of 194 to win, batting last. England found the rampaging duo of Curtly Ambrose and Courtney Walsh at their absolute best and capitulated — all out for 46 off just 19.1 overs. The West Indies had wrapped up the series in Trinidad and were clearly looking for another quick win in Barbados.

England, however, did not follow the script. Alec Stewart hit a century in each innings, becoming the first English player to achieve that feat against the West Indies, and Angus Fraser took 8 for 75 in the first innings, also the best figures by an England player against the West Indies. Phil Tufnell even took a catch running backwards at mid-wicket to dismiss Brian Lara in the second innings. Wonders never cease! Another interesting feature of the match was that in the West Indies first innings all batsmen were out to catches, eight in the slips/gully cordon. It proved that the bowlers, particularly Fraser, were putting the ball in the right areas and reaping their rewards. The match ended with Ambrose bowled by Chris Lewis when he tried to swing a good-length ball over mid-wicket. Both middle and leg stumps were uprooted. Ambrose then angrily swatted down the remaining stump, an act that would cost him a $1,500 fine from referee John Reid. This matter passed unnoticed by most of the England supporters, who were already on the field celebrating.

As an interesting aside to the way the game ended, Alec Stewart approached me when the ninth wicket fell and asked if I would do him a small favour. He was fielding at fine leg on the boundary and would not be able to collect a stump as a memento of his achievement of a century in each innings. Alec asked if I could grab one for him. I looked around at the crowd that was already congregating along the boundary rope and said to Alec, 'I'll do my best!' The thought then left my mind as Walsh and Ambrose put on 21 for the last wicket, and when the stumps went flying so did I — straight towards the pavilion, surrounded by ecstatic England fans with beery breath and Barbadians who were happy to salvage anything as a souvenir, from my hat to my tie. I think even my shoes would have been fair game if they hadn't been securely laced.

When Ambrose did the demolition job on the remaining stump, most people failed to notice that Alec in fact did get his souvenir. At the code of conduct hearing held two days later in

Antigua, Curtly Ambrose initially pleaded not guilty, so John Reid produced the video evidence, which clearly showed what we all knew anyway — that after being bowled by Lewis he had swung his bat and collected the only stump left standing. Just as the camera started panning to a wider angle, there in the top right-hand corner ran Alec Stewart, who caught the cartwheeling stump in one hand and sped off to the pavilion. I couldn't suppress a laugh and Richie Richardson and a now poorer Curtly Ambrose looked at me strangely. If only I had been composed enough to explain Stewart's request, maybe John Reid would have let Ambrose off with a warning. Unlikely, but possible!

Cricket's facility for producing surprise results has seldom been so convincingly demonstrated. England arrived in Barbados, the bastion of West Indian cricket, with their form and confidence at rock bottom. Team manager Keith Fletcher admitted before the match that a draw would be considered a triumph after the debacle on days four and five in Trinidad. The West Indies had won their last 12 Tests on the Kensington Oval. England became the first visiting Test team to win at Bridgetown since R.E.S. Wyatt's team 59 years earlier, and only the second ever — a truly remarkable effort.

But having viewed the match from such a prime position I can say categorically that it was no fluke. England dictated the game and won on merit. Each of the five days had attracted capacity crowds, including about 6,000 holidaying England supporters, producing an unusual ambience for a Caribbean Test. I had been told that Caribbean cricket supporters were among the fairest of them all and always acknowledged good play and sportsmanship from both teams, unlike many other crowds. To hear so many England supporters cheering on their team created a unique atmosphere that I will cherish for the rest of my life. This was my first Test as a 'neutral' umpire, as we on the ICC Independent Panel were to become known under the sponsorship of the National Grid Company from England. All the reading about the Caribbean I had done before the trip and the wonderful stories I had heard about the knowledgeable, responsive and noisy calypso style of the West Indian crowds hadn't really prepared me for the experience. Now the yearning for more matches had been firmly implanted in my plans for the future as an umpire.

The Brian Lara Experience

Brian Lara has always been my pick as the best batsman I have seen. His batting average of 52.88 from 131 Tests does not do his sheer class and ability full justice; neither does the fact that he scored 34 centuries, with a highest score of 400 not out, and has twice held the world record score in Test cricket. It is what he was able to achieve at various stages of his career and how he played in a side that was continually outclassed that set him apart. I stood in the match when he scored his first Test century — a double, in fact — when he made 277 against Australia at the Sydney Cricket Ground in January 1993. It was a fine innings, hailed by everyone as the beginning of a remarkable career. It would be another 14 months before his second Test hundred, which came against England in Georgetown, Guyana, in March 1994, helping the West Indies to a 3–0 lead in the series. However, something really special, even for Lara, was just around the corner, and as luck would have it I was one of the appointed umpires on that occasion too.

The Recreation Ground at St John's, Antigua, had just been refurbished and the pitch was declared to be 'suitable for batting', as one West Indian newspaper reported. The final Test of the series began on 16 April 1994. Lara, at number 3, came in with the West Indies at 1 for 8 and soon 2 for 12 when Phil Simmons was out lbw to Andy Caddick. There was work to be done, and Lara set about consolidating the innings.

Lara engineered partnerships of 179 with Jimmy Adams and another 183 with Keith Arthurton to put the home team firmly in the driver's seat. One of the most remarkable aspects of Lara's innings was that he came to the crease with West Indies' makeshift opening pair of Phil Simmons and Stuart Williams having lasted barely half an hour that first morning. Another was that by the time Lara had made 50, such was his obvious determination and absolute mastery of England's bowlers on an utterly inoffensive pitch that people were already talking of his bettering the previous highest Test score of 365, held by Garfield Sobers.

The biggest partnership, though, was 219 with Shivnarine Chanderpaul. It was also the longest, extending through four rain interruptions, none of which looked likely to disturb Lara, on the second afternoon and into the momentous third morning, which Lara began on 320.

Until this point Lara had never looked likely to get out, but there was one occasion when Andy Caddick found Lara's bat playing away from his body and the ball ballooned through a now-vacant slips cordon down towards third man. Caddick asked at the end of the over if I thought he had encouraged a 'genuine edge' from Lara. I find these questions best left unanswered, especially when a batsman is on 320 and had not yet offered the slightest of chances. I also find it strange that bowlers even ask the question; it can only be painful for them in the long run.

As the remaining milestones on the way to the record were ticked off run by run, the enormity of it, probably combined with understandable weariness, found Lara not dispatching bad balls to the boundary as he had done so easily earlier in his innings. He needed supporting through the final stages by the impressively mature Chanderpaul, who at times seemed to be on strike far too much for the liking of an eager crowd.

Lara reached 365, equalling Sobers' score, with a cover-driven 4 off Caddick that had the capacity crowd on its feet. Another over passed and then, with a fully composed Lara rocking onto the back foot for the historic pull through mid-wicket off Lewis, the inevitable pitch invasion was unleashed. There was absolute mayhem for the next 10 minutes. Apparently Sobers had marched onto the field surrounded by cameras and half the crowd to officially congratulate Lara. I know this was the case, although I cannot honestly confirm I saw Sobers in that sea of people. When the celebrations had subsided, the emotional exhaustion probably set in, as on 375 Lara fell to a tired drive by edging to wicketkeeper Jack Russell off Caddick. This time it was a 'genuine edge', to use Caddick's term.

Brian Lara had batted for 766 minutes, faced 538 balls and hit 45 fours. Chanderpaul scored an unbeaten 75, his fourth half-century in his first four Tests, and all England could aspire to was the not inconsiderable task of batting out time.

England opener Michael Atherton batted with great authority after being dropped on 46, and after Robin Smith profited from two dismissals off no balls (one bowled and the other caught at mid off) from Walsh, to make an overdue century. And yes, you guessed it, I was the one who spotted the no balls from Walsh. I must say that it can be rather intimidating to stand there signalling a no ball when the crowd has clearly seen the player 'caught' or 'bowled'. But no harm was done and Courtney Walsh accepted the calls as correct.

Smith was at times treating the bowling with such disdain that the new record set by Lara just a few hours earlier did not look entirely safe. But he was still 200 short of Lara's record when he played across one from Kenny Benjamin and my finger had to go up (no chance of a no ball to save him this time). Smith and Atherton had shared a stand of 303, a third-wicket record for England against the West Indies, and it was the first time since 1976 at Headingley that two England batsmen had made centuries in the same Test innings against the West Indies.

Atherton's 135 in 535 minutes was a marathon performance that guaranteed only the fourth draw in the last 29 Tests between these teams. Once Russell and Lewis had added half-centuries and the scores had finished uncannily tied in the first innings, only 34 overs remained in the match. Of these, 24 were played out to end a game of total stalemate on the official scoreboard. For me, though, this Test match left glittering memories that would last a lifetime.

Watching at close quarters as records were broken in exceptional match play ensured that my appetite to become an established international umpire had become enormous. How could I not enjoy this sport? This experience once again focused my determination to improve my own performance so I could be part of this wonderful game for many years to come.

Brian Lara was never willing to be overlooked, no matter where he played, who the opposition were, or how weak or strong the team around him was. The famous Wanderers Ground in Johannesburg hosted the first Test match of the series in December 2003. South Africa capitalised on winning the toss on a hard, dry pitch that developed widening cracks in the constant, fierce heat of the high veldt. Parts of Johannesburg were nearly 2,000 metres above sea level, where the air is less humid than in coastal cities such as Sydney, Brisbane or Durban. The dry air combined with very clear days of hot sunshine draws the moisture out of cricket pitches, making them hard and sometimes unpredictable. Obviously the best time to bat on these pitches is early in the match, as by the end of day three there is quite a lot of variable bounce.

South Africa proved this by seizing control on the first day when the pitch was at its truest, and Graham Smith's 132, in his first home Test as captain, followed by a commanding partnership between Jacques Kallis and Martin van Jaarsveld, carried them to 3 for 368. In spite of more controlled West Indian bowling and Lara's sixth Test double century (his second in a losing cause), including a Test record 28 runs in an over, South Africa were able to complete their victory 20 minutes before tea on the last day.

Smith and Herschelle Gibbs set South Africa on their way with an opening stand of 149. The removal of Gibbs, after an unusually restrained innings, and Jacques Rudolph in quick succession brought only temporary relief for the West Indies bowlers. Jacques Kallis arrived, putting on 80 with Smith, who finally edged the quite slippery but erratic Fidel Edwards low to first slip after hitting 22 fours off 184 balls. Kallis went on to add another 128 by the close with van Jaarsveld, who seized the chance offered by Gary Kirsten's decision to attend the birth of his son (delivered during the second day), playing with attractive ease.

West Indies were handicapped when Chris Gayle, their only passable spinner, pulled up painfully in the outfield with a torn right hamstring muscle; his further participation was restricted to hobbling through two innings down the order with a runner. But van Jaarsveld was lbw in the first over of the second day from Merv Dillon, who later produced one that kept low to bowl Kallis for a chanceless 158 that featured one six and 17 fours. The West Indies claimed the last seven wickets for 189, the final 3 through Wavell Hinds' medium-pace swing.

They made an encouraging start to their reply, but inevitably it was left to Lara to eliminate the prospect of the follow-on. The follow-on is a law in Test match cricket that gives the option of asking the other team to bat again immediately, if the lead is more than 200 runs. He started hesitantly, as he can often do, offering a low but straightforward chance to Pollock at first slip off Makhaya Ntini when he was just 15, but he gradually found the timing and placement he had become renowned for. There was little progress at the other end, though. Darren Ganga needed more than two hours to add 11 to his overnight 49 and Shivnarine Chanderpaul spent more than two and a half hours to contribute 34 to a stand of 125. But Lara's momentum was building. Increasingly he left the wide balls and punished the loose ones while still harvesting the strike and keeping the scorecard ticking over. These are always ominous signs for opposition bowlers.

Lara's century was the West Indies' first on South African soil, so once again went his name into the record books. His ability to create for himself an impregnable bubble from which to rescue his team was never so evident. But most special was his fusillade of two straight sixes and four fours in the third day's penultimate over, from Robin Peterson, thereby breaking New Zealander Craig McMillan's record for most runs in a Test match over. It also reduced the deficit to exactly 200. That wasn't the end of the story for that particular passage of play, though.

The West Indies batting throughout the innings, although moulded around Lara, was not doing enough to make the Test match competitive. When Vasbert Drakes fell lbw to Kallis for a hard-fought 21, the score was showing 6 for 314 — still 247 behind South Africa's total of 561. Dillon strode to the crease with confidence but made heavy weather of trying to score runs, showing an uncanny knack of harvesting the strike from Lara by taking a single off the last ball of the over several times in succession. However, the partnership between Lara and Dillon had crept up to 19 off seven overs and in doing so had advanced the team score from 314 to 333 with these singles and the occasional two. There were just two overs left to be bowled in the day, which is usually about the time for the batting side to think about defending the remaining balls, thus surviving to bat again tomorrow. But not Brian Charles Lara.

In the hope of breaking Lara's concentration, South African captain Graham Smith summoned left-arm spinner Robin Peterson to bowl the 120th over of the innings. South Africa's fast bowlers had done a reasonable job of taking wickets regularly, but something special needed to be done in a last-ditch attempt to shift Lara. With only two overs left to bowl that day, spin was obviously the tempter. While Smith and Peterson were setting the field, Lara spoke quietly and reassuringly with Dillon, who was at my end as non-striker. I paid no attention to what was being said. My own plan for these last overs was simple: keep the concentrations level high. But Lara approached me after his talk with Dillon. He asked, 'Umps, how many runs do we need to avoid the follow-on?'

It was late in the day and the active focus of my concentration was somewhere else. The question took me by surprise, but I took a glance at the scoreboard and a quick calculation told me 29 runs were needed to take the total to 362 and avoid the follow-on. At the time I thought it a strange question to ask, given the imminent close of play — after just two more overs.

So with Peterson finally ready to bowl after his extended discussion with Graham Smith, Lara sauntered back to the other end, checked his leg stump guard with me and went down over his bat to take strike. There was not the slightest hint of what was to come. Peterson ran in to bowl the first ball of the over. He was coming left arm over the wicket. The ball was given plenty of air in flight and Lara used his feet to punch the ball in the air but well out of reach of the mid-off fielder and after two bounces the ball sped over the boundary rope. The South Africans seemed to like this shot and their chatter lit up the field. They could sense a false shot and the possibility of snaring Lara so late in the day was in the air — a real bonus, they thought.

The second delivery was similar to the first but probably a bit slower. Lara accepted the temptation, advanced down the wicket again, and even though he appeared to be beaten in flight he lofted the ball over mid on and cleared the rope for six. This prompted another discussion between captain and bowler, the upshot of which was to leave the field as it was. The third ball was much quicker and flatter through the air. Lara picked up the speed and length early and perfectly and without leaving his crease, he drove the ball straight back over the bowler's head for another six.

Another conference between bowler and captain ensued. This time the field changed and the mid on was sent on retreat to the boundary. Peterson indicated to me that he would change his delivery mode to left arm around the wicket. This change would more than likely result in the bowler's line, length and pace being revised somewhat. My guess was spot-on: the next ball was pushed through very flat and very fast and aimed just outside off stump. Unfortunately for Peterson, Lara's eye was true and he rocked onto the back foot and played the most exquisite square cut backward of point and past the sprawling Herschelle Gibbs for another boundary — this time only four though!

The fifth ball, like the previous one, was fast and flat, but it was directed more towards leg stump, in an obvious attempt to cramp Lara. The great batsmen, however, are just a little bit ahead of everyone else, and Lara was able to move onto the back foot and pull the ball safely over the mid-wicket fielder for yet another four. And the last ball of that over? Well, again it was all too predictable, with a fuller delivery aimed just outside off stump, but it was too full. Lara waited for the ball to pitch, then moved into it with ease and caressed it through the covers for four.

Lara had made 28 runs from the six Peterson deliveries, and while the follow-on had not yet been avoided, Lara's boundary blitz took the West Indies score to 361, which left them exactly 200 behind. It would seem a formality to score just one more run with four wickets still in hand.

Lara walked up the side of the pitch to talk to Merv Dillon, then he gave me a glance and nodded with a sly wink. He knew how good he was today, and if his sole target was to avoid the follow-on before the end of the day's play, then he certainly achieved it. But did he have to prove he was *that* good? Why not wait until tomorrow? Yet he had played without risk, with all six shots coming off the middle of the bat. Each shot was controlled and calculated to obtain maximum benefit and value in scoring runs. The man was a superstar, and how lucky was I to be in the midst of all this? Why do I do it? I would say the reasons are quite obvious!

Next morning, Lara reached his double-hundred with his 32nd four and then drove the next ball, the 274th that he faced, to extra cover, where van Jaarsveld took a simple catch, the ninth wicket to fall. Lara's latest masterpiece of an innings occupied seven hours and 19 minutes. He may be remembered for getting out on 202 rather than for the mastery with which he constructed such a valuable Test innings. But it was the six balls resulting in six consecutive boundaries from Robin Peterson's over that will remain forever etched in my memory.

South Africa's lead was 151 and, although Herschelle Gibbs retired with a broken nose when an edged hook off a short ball from Vasbert Drakes burst through his grille, South Africa progressed to a second-innings declaration at a more than brisk scoring rate of three and a half runs an over. Smith challenged West Indies to score 378 off the remaining 100 overs.

If they found hope in their record 418 to beat Australia in

Antigua seven months earlier, it was quickly quashed. Ntini removed both openers and nightwatchman Drakes before the close of play on day four, and Pollock followed up next morning by removing Ramnaresh Sarwan and Lara within the first seven overs. No second-innings saviour this time, but that's how much of a leveller Test cricket can be. Despite not repeating his first-innings heroics, Lara gave me one of the most enduring memories of what Test cricket is all about.

Responding to the crisis of 5 for 43, Chanderpaul abandoned his usual role as a steady accumulator and went into attack mode, stroking 13 fours in all directions to score 74 from 91 balls before he hooked Pollock and was caught at long leg. The injured Chris Gayle thumped six fours in eight balls from Andre Nel before the ninth had him taken at slip. Yes, there are plenty of batsmen who can play shots, but none matches the brilliance and beauty of Lara.

The pitch had become very difficult to bat on and the variable bounce produced a 'shooter' from Shaun Pollock that caught Cory Collymore right in front for lbw. I was standing at the bowler's end to call 'play' at the start of this Test match and I gave the final decision to end it. I had spent 1,775 minutes on the field and saw 1,285 runs scored for the loss of 36 wickets. Spending 30 hours out in the hot sun, knowing every decision you make will be scrutinised, is a challenge for umpires in Test matches. I always looked forward to the challenge, and the euphoria I felt after each and every Test was the reason I was always eager to put myself out there.

The final chapter of my Brian Lara trilogy began in Antigua almost exactly ten years after his world-record score of 375 in

April 1994, and it was to feature the same two teams, England and West Indies.

On 12 April 2004, 185 days after losing his position as record-holder of Test cricket's highest innings, Brian Lara reclaimed the record from Australia's Matthew Hayden, becoming the first batsman to score 400 runs in a Test. Hayden had accumulated 380 against Zimbabwe in October 2003, beating Lara's 375, after which Lara commented that Hayden's record should not be recognised as it was made against a second-rate bowling attack. Without getting into a discussion about the quality of England's attack on this tour, it required no genius to predict who would be the most likely player to overtake Hayden, and it took Lara only 19 Test match innings to do so. Twenty-five minutes before lunch on the third day, he danced down the pitch to hoist Gareth Batty's invitingly flighted off break into the stand at long on for the six that took him past his own 375 to level with Hayden at 380. He swept the next ball, flatter and ill-directed, to fine leg for four, to reclaim the record he had first taken from another celebrated West Indian left-hander, Garry Sobers, on the same ground against the same opposition as ten years earlier. It was the tenth time the record had changed hands; no one else had ever recovered it, though.

The reception was joyful enough, but less frenetic than first time around. There was no spectator invasion, as in 1994, except for an inappropriate appearance by a government entourage headed by the new prime minister of Antigua and Barbuda, Baldwin Spencer. As in Bridgetown, travelling England supporters formed the majority of the estimated 10,000 in the stands. They politely applauded the making of history. Over in the popular open section adjoining Independence Avenue, where hardly a pale face was to be seen, the celebrations were understandably more boisterous. The national flags of the independent Caribbean nations that somehow manage to find unity through their cricket team waved ecstatically. For the first time in the series, West Indian voices were not drowned out by the deafening, triumphal chants of the Barmy Army.

After handshakes between weary opponents, Lara again stooped to kiss the pitch — prepared under the supervision of Andy Roberts, a formidable fast bowler of an earlier era — that had favoured him once more.

Nor was he finished. He remarked at the start of the third day that his aim was a total of 750, the highest ever conceded by England in their 820 Tests. Before that, he swept Batty to fine leg again for the single that raised the first 400 in Test cricket, the tenth in all first-class cricket. Jacobs hit the next ball for four to take West Indies to 751, and Lara declared at the end of the over. He had batted two minutes short of 13 hours and faced 582 balls, scoring four sixes (in 1994 he had none) and 43 fours. He was so composed, so concentrated, so invincible that he surely could have carried on to 500 or 600 if he had been so inclined. Geraint Jones, who had replaced Chris Read as England wicketkeeper and thus had the closest vantage point, observed how fresh Lara looked throughout, hardly raising a sweat. Although he scored freely in all directions with his full range of strokes, he was, as in 1994, more calculated than extravagant.

Two other men were on the field during both record innings — England batsman Graham Thorpe and me! I had also officiated when Lara scored the first of his 25 Test centuries and the first of his seven doubles, with 277 in Sydney in 1992–93. Yet had I been persuaded by a concerted appeal for a catch at the wicket, Lara would not have scored a run. On just the fourth ball from Steve Harmison, who had dismissed Lara several times earlier in the series, Lara played an indecisive shot off a ball that was far too short to drive. The ball sailed through to wicketkeeper Jones, who gathered it and appealed in unison with Harmison and the slips cordon. In their certainty that there had been a thin edge, the obligatory celebrations were beginning to break out. Much to the amazement of the England players, however, I shook my head. Yes, there had been a faint noise as the ball passed Lara's bat, but it all boiled down to whether I believed the sound was in fact Lara's bat clicking against his pad. I declined the appeal, and television replays later indicated I was correct.

There was nothing more that seriously tested the judgement of the umpires, apart from a no ball delivered by Michael Vaughan in the 185th over of the innings that 'bowled' Ridley Jacobs when he was on 87. How or why a spin bowler would overstep the crease has always intrigued me, and Vaughan paid the price when I spotted the front foot well over the popping crease. Jacobs went on to finish on 107 not out, and when Lara declared on reaching his 400 the partnership had added 282 in 80 overs. Under normal circumstances Ridley Jacobs' century would be a memorable one, but he was overshadowed by Lara's world record achievement.

Lara offered one chance, a stinging, low, straight drive off Batty that burst through the bowler's hands on its way to the boundary when he was on 293. Only Harmison caused him the occasional bother until his third warning for running on the pitch meant I had to remove him from bowling. By then he had sent down 37 overs and Lara stood on 359. I think Harmison was the most relieved man on the field knowing he did not have to bowl again. Normally when you have to take action against a bowler for running in the protected area, it is tough for the bowler to accept. I'm certain, though, that Harmison took his cap and thanked me under his breath!

Lara's best score in the series to date had been 36. He had been jumping around uncertainly at the crease in a vain effort to counter England's fast, bouncing bowling on fast, bouncing pitches. For the first time in his Test career, he had been dismissed without scoring in two successive innings — on his home ground, the Queen's Park Oval, where he had drifted down the batting order to number 6. As it had been in his first term as captain, which had ended in resignation four years earlier, his captaincy was under critical scrutiny. 'The next five days are very important in terms of my future as captain,' he said before the match. 'No captain, no team, wants to go down for the first time in their history as losing all their Test matches at home.' He was clearly mentally ready for the challenge even if he was still troubled by a finger that had been dislocated in the first Test.

Lara was not the only one to appreciate a return to a benign pitch. Gayle and Sarwan also compensated for poor scores earlier in the series. Gayle thumped 12 fours in his 69, Sarwan shared a third-wicket partnership of 232 with Lara, contributing a polished 90. After the fall of Wavell Hinds, the experienced Jacobs entered, with Lara on 234, and followed in his slipstream for more than five hours to gather his third Test century. Their stand was worth 282 runs — a sixth-wicket record for West Indies when Lara finally declared half an hour into the third afternoon.

A minimum of 240 overs remained in the match, and had Lara not dropped a juggled catch at slip off Sarwan when Andrew Flintoff was 27 late on the third afternoon, West Indies might well have been able to work themselves closer to a satisfying win. Dropped again at 56 and 67, Flintoff made the most of his luck and spent nearly five and a half hours over his unbeaten century.

With England following on, Michael Vaughan and Marcus Trescothick put together an opening partnership of real substance for the first time in the series, steadying England nerves. At 182, it was their highest to date. Vaughan compiled a fluent and composed 140, his 11th Test century. This match was a draw, of course, but having spent a touch over 30 hours on the field I knew I had again witnessed something unforgettable. The experience reinforced how privileged I was to umpire Test cricket.

Great World Cups

The one-day international may be cricket's poor relation in the modern era of Twenty20 saturation, but during my career it played an important part in ensuring a steady revenue flow for the sport. I was lucky enough to umpire at two World Cups — England in 1999 and South Africa in 2003. A few of my 138 matches in the one-day international format remain memorable experiences for me. I will take you through several of them.

On 31 May 1999, Pakistan faced Bangladesh in the final match in Group B at the Northampton County Ground. At the last possible moment in World Cup '99, a non-Test team felled a giant. Bangladesh had never even come close to beating a major power, while Pakistan was unbeaten in the competition so far. Since this was a completely 'dead' match, accusations that Pakistan was involved in match fixing grew loud again. English bookmakers had rated Pakistan at 33 to 1 to win. There were no reports of unusual betting, but inevitably there were rumours about the subcontinent's illegal bookmakers. Nothing could diminish the euphoria of the Bangladeshi cricketers, though. It became the greatest day in their short cricketing history.

Both captains later spoke of Bangladesh soon earning Test match status. Wasim Akram told a media conference that if Pakistan was to lose a match, he was glad that it was to his 'brothers'. The only person with reason not to enjoy the result was former West Indian great Gordon Greenidge, who was sacked as Bangladesh coach just before the game and who quietly left at the end of Bangladesh's innings, in which they compiled a moderate 223 from their allotted 50 overs. Had Greenidge remained, he would have witnessed something special, if not bizarre, in a game that would be talked about for many years whenever match fixing in international cricket was discussed.

Sent in to bat by Akram, the Bangladeshi openers advanced confidently to 69 in 16 overs before losing their first wicket, and the rest of their batsmen played sensibly all through the innings. Captain Aminul Islam remarked to me when the 100 was posted in the 24th over, 'If we can just get to about 220, we *will* win the match.' I thought nothing of the comment, but you wouldn't when you're in the middle of umpiring a World Cup match. Your mind is elsewhere, on doing the things you need to do rather than on worrying about how many runs a team might get. But a target of 224 hardly looked a problem for the star-studded Pakistan batting line-up. That was until Pakistan's top order folded dramatically, or, as some might say, sensationally or even suspiciously.

When Salim Malik wafted across an innocuous delivery from medium-pace trundler Khaled Mahmud and was out lbw, the Pakistan batting hardly looked ready to fall into disarray, such was the depth of their line-up. Then Inzamam-ul-Haq suffered the same fate, lbw playing the same shot to the same type of delivery from the same bowler, and while I didn't think much about it at the time, events over the next few years suggested something might well have been amiss with the integrity of this and certain other matches.

Five of Pakistan's top-order batsmen were very quickly out by the 13th over, three to Khaled Mahmud's rather innocuous medium-paced deliveries. Azhar Mahmood and Wasim Akram, who surprisingly elevated himself to bat at number 7 ahead of Moin Khan, settled the innings down by pushing the score past the 100 mark, but it was to be too little too late. Or was it? Azhar Mahmood was going well when he seemed to misjudge a run with his skipper and, after being stranded mid-pitch, was run out easily as Wasim Akram stood safely and resolutely in his crease at the other end, the score now at 6 for 97.

Not long after Azhar Mahmood's departure, Wasim Akram played an amazingly indiscreet 'up and under' shot from the gentle off spin of Minhajul Abedin, lofting the ball successfully into the hands of the fielder at deep square leg. An easier catch you could not imagine! Wicketkeeper Moin Khan batted sensibly for a while, but then he too committed suicide by lofting Naimur Rahman's slow off spinner to deep mid-wicket. The score was 8 for 124 with 15 overs remaining.

I remember both Wasim Akram and Moin Khan carefully studying where the fielders were located before going down over their bats and then hitting the ball very high and very straight towards the fielders for an easy catch. They couldn't have picked the fielders out more accurately if they had practised it in the pre-game warm-up.

With nine wickets down, Doug Cowie called for a TV verdict on whether Mushtaq Saqlain had been run out. He was eventually ruled out by third umpire David Shepherd, but the jubilant Bangladeshi fans were already pouring onto the field. The stumps disappeared from my end and chaos ensued. I managed to make it off the ground well before David Shepherd hit the red light to signify the end of the match, with Pakistan dismissed for just 161 in the 45th over. According to the locals, the Northampton County Ground had never seen anything like it — at least in a cricket match. Not since the old footballing heyday there, when Northampton Town knocked Arsenal out of the FA Cup in 1958, had there been such jubilation among fans.

Putting aside any of my suspicions, it was fantastic to be one of the umpires on the historic occasion when the minnows of international cricket upstaged one of the strongest sides.

My appointment to the semifinal of the 1999 World Cup between Pakistan and New Zealand, to be played on 16 June, was at that stage one of the highlights of my career. The whole tournament so far had been played to packed grounds and the atmosphere befitted the 'carnival of cricket' slogan that advertised the matches. As I joined my partner Peter Willey in the umpires' room before the match, it was evident to us that this match would follow the trend. Old Trafford was absolutely packed. The official count of 22,002 seemed to underestimate the crowd numbers when the sea of faces and waving Pakistan flags greeted us as we took the field to start the match.

Before the match New Zealand captain Stephen Fleming had asked for stricter security, raising the controversial topic of fencing in (or fencing out?) the spectators. His team did not like being mobbed at the end of matches, and to be honest he had a point. I firmly believe that crowds should never be encouraged to run onto the field at the end of any sporting event. Whether they win or lose, the players should have the opportunity to savour the completion of a World Cup match, to shake each other's hand and to take in the atmosphere. But previous matches, like the recent Bangladesh/Pakistan clash in Northampton, had ended in bedlam, and this one would be no different.

Fleming's New Zealand team was well coached and well drilled by Australian Steve Rixon. This team had been the quiet achievers of the whole World Cup. They were always a danger to whatever opponents they came up against, and they relished the underdog tag that followed them into the tournament. Now they were no longer the soft target of old and were definitely a force to be reckoned with. Batting first, New Zealand built a decent total of 241, though 47 of those were extras recklessly scattered by Pakistan, including 17 wides and 12 no balls. Not a lot of teams can give away so many free runs and still win but, as I have long recognised, when Pakistan play well they are nigh on unbeatable.

The best stand came from Fleming and Roger Twose, who added 94 before Shoaib Akhtar bowled Fleming with a breathtaking yorker, uprooting his leg stump with a delivery timed on the electronic speed gun at 92 mph. Shoaib took one wicket in each of his three spells, and all three were bowled by his exceptionally fast thunderbolts. Nathan Astle was the first to go, when he was late getting the bat down before his stumps were scattered. But it was Akhtar's second wicket that was the turning point of the match.

As Roger Twose and Stephen Fleming worked along in a tradesmanlike partnership, a score of 260 runs or more looked possible. Fleming's downfall could not have been predicted by Akhtar's first balls of his new spell. Twose picked up a couple of twos then was beaten twice outside off stump but survived. Next over Fleming drove Shoaib off the back foot through the covers with panache then slashed him to third man for four. Shoaib merely shook his head, trudged back to the end of his run-up and served up the ball of the match, if not the entire tournament. It was a yorker, 92 mph and moving in through the air. Fleming jammed his bat down on it but was a moment too late. Fleming's leg stump was sent cartwheeling. It was a magnificent delivery as Fleming was well set at the crease, having faced 57 balls in his 90-minute stay, during which he had scored 41 runs in a partnership of 94 with Roger Twose. The crowd erupted, the bowler celebrated. Shoaib Akhtar showed that pace really does matter in any cricket format.

Shoaib Akhtar had only recently shot to prominence with a fiery spell in a pre-World Cup series in India. He chose the flattest pitch and the hottest day of the tournament, amid a 22,000-strong sea of green and white, with blaring horns and pounding percussion instruments, to stake his claim as the fastest and most exciting bowler in the game. Shoaib was at his blistering best and consistently topped the 90 mph mark. Best of all, he reminded everyone that fast bowling was supposed to be just that — fast and dangerous.

Following Fleming's dismissal, Twose, Chris Cairns and Chris Harris batted sensibly in the latter part of New Zealand's innings to set Pakistan a target of 242 to win, but an opening stand of 194 between Saeed Anwar and Wajahatullah Wasti, a World Cup first-wicket record, saw the contest become a little one-sided as New Zealand's bowlers struggled to make headway. The wickets just would not come and the scoring by Pakistan was far too regular. New Zealand's ability to squeeze teams into making mistakes appeared to have deserted them. Pakistan's two opening batsmen seemed quite capable of finishing the job, until Wasti skied a bouncer from Cairns, and was out in the 41st over. Anwar pushed on to a second successive century, his 17th in one-day internationals, equalling Desmond Haynes and behind only Sachin Tendulkar. With Ijaz Ahmed smashing 28 off 21 balls, victory was delayed only by a small pitch invasion with Pakistan still needing six runs to win — someone in the crowd apparently miscounted! Peter Willey and I had no option but to call a halt to play for ten minutes until the crowd finally dispersed, although they retreated only as far as the boundary rope.

Then in the 48th over, when Saeed Anwar lofted the third ball of Nathan Astle's seventh over towards long off, the crowd once again could not be contained and surged over the outfield like a tidal wave, converging on the 22 yards of pitch. Roger Twose, who was fielding at mid off in the circle, began running back in an attempt to take the catch. Spotting the onrushing crowd, however, he abandoned any attempt at a brilliant running catch and joined the rest of his teammates as they raced towards the safety of the pavilion. Twose was quickly pursued by me!

As the stumps disappeared and the predominantly Pakistani crowd celebrated on the pitch, an interesting situation arose. A small technical issue: the two runs required to win were never actually completed, as Anwar and Ijaz hugged each other mid pitch during the first run then promptly scarpered towards the sanctity of the dressing room. As we arrived back in the umpires' room, the scorers were on the phone wanting to know the result of the match. It didn't take much deciding. Common sense told me that the two runs required to win should be allowed anyway. The alternative was asking the ground authority to find new stumps, clear the ground of its invading revellers and ask both teams to resume play. No, I think the two runs are okay to count in the official scorebooks, thanks!

By then ecstatic Pakistani fans were letting off fireworks and parading flags, banners and a cardboard cut-out of Nelson Mandela (who had retired from the South African presidency earlier in the day). Officials, who had expected trouble in the India match eight days earlier, lost control when their guard was down. They weren't fully prepared to cope with fanatical cricket supporters, but they should have been. New Zealand captain Fleming called on the ICC for stricter security at cricket matches, but it was too late for this particular World Cup.

Old Trafford witnessed a very lopsided World Cup semifinal in June 1999, thanks mainly to an all-out, devil-may-care, floppy-haired speedster called Shoaib Akhtar.

The Amazing Ashes

With Sydney's reputation as a spin haven, both England and Australia prepared accordingly for the fifth Test of the Ashes series of 1998/99 at the famous Sydney Cricket Ground. Australia recalled the versatile Colin Miller, who could bowl both medium-pace swing and off spin, and Shane Warne returned for his first Test since Bangalore in March 1998 and a subsequent operation on his shoulder. England's squad included John Crawley, their best player of spin, off spinner Peter Such and left-arm spinner Ashley Giles, who had been flown out ostensibly to take part in the upcoming one-day series. Giles, however, was omitted on the morning of the match in favour of all-rounder Alex Tudor. Robert Croft, England's other spinner, was also left out. Angus Fraser and Alan Mullally were dropped following disappointing efforts during the early matches in the series and Michael Atherton, finally capitulating to his aching back, was also a last-minute scratching.

Tickets for the first day were sold out: the 42,124 who got in represented the biggest SCG Test crowd for 23 years. The crowd was rewarded by a game that sustained the tempo established in the Boxing Day Test in Melbourne, where England had won an exciting encounter by just 12 runs.

England started and finished the day memorably. Australia lost 3 for 52 in 68 minutes, including Mark Taylor for just two runs, before the Waugh brothers put on a stand of 190 to add respectability to the total. Australia then lost an astounding five wickets for three runs in the day's last 15 deliveries, which included a hat-trick by Darren Gough, showing again that Test cricket quite often throws up unpredictable twists and turns.

This was the first hat-trick I had witnessed in my 28-Test umpiring career. After getting Ian Healy caught behind by Warren Hegg, and bowling Stuart MacGill with one that left him a touch off the seam, Gough completed the hat-trick with an out-swinging torpedo that clipped Miller's off stump. Steve Dunne was the umpire in the thick of things and I was standing at square leg when all the action was taking place, as I had been when Anthony Stuart removed three Pakistan batsmen in succession in a one-day international. My hat-trick days were to come much later in my career.

The steadying partnership by Steve and Mark Waugh also saw batting of the highest quality. Faced with tight and miserly bowling, smart fielding and the adroit captaincy of Alec Stewart, they interspersed long periods of defence with brash and dangerous strokes, but could squeeze out only 41 singles to go with the rare boundary in 80 overs. However, it was to be the partnership that placed Australia in a position to unleash Shane Warne and Stuart MacGill as the match winners.

On day two, in front of another full house, Warne trapped Mark Butcher lbw with his fourth delivery, but Warne was generally outshone by the brooding but flamboyant MacGill, who improved on his Test best figures with 5 for 57. Further personal milestones included Glenn McGrath's 200th Test wicket when Alec Stewart was snared at slip by Warne's safe hands. Mark Waugh's 100th Test catch went into the book when Nasser Hussain popped up an inside edge off his pad at silly point from Miller's off spin.

England fought manfully on the third day but, according to media reports, 'the tourists were checked by a contentious and crucial umpiring decision'. Michael Slater was 35 and Australia 2 for 60 in their second innings when Slater decided to squeeze a second run from a drive towards long on. A direct hit from Dean Headley's throw to the non-striker's stumps was referred by Steve Dunne to the third umpire, Simon Taufel. Slater didn't look confident as he ripped off his gloves while awaiting the third umpire's decision but, after a long delay, he received the benefit of video doubt. It transpired that the cameras on which Simon Taufel relied were not perpendicular to the crease, and that bowler Peter Such had taken up a position beside the stumps that had inadvertently obscured the precise instant of the ball crashing into the stumps.

To call this decision 'contentious' was beyond reason. Steve Dunne did the right thing by referring a very close call for a run out, and Simon Taufel did everything in his power to find the clearest evidence on which to base his decision. There is no room for guesswork when operating as a third umpire. He must be able to see exactly what happened. Unfortunately, Peter Such got in the way of the camera's line of vision, so without evidence to prove otherwise Slater was correctly ruled to be not out.

After this close call, Slater watched every ball carefully right onto the bat and abstained from his natural instincts and extravagance until his score had doubled and the last recognised batsman, Steve Waugh (batting at number 7 because of a hamstring strain), had departed. Australia was in a precarious position with a lead of only 212. Slater then cut loose with a flurry of boundaries, including a booming drive past mid off from the tiring Darren Gough, to register his 11th Test hundred, his seventh against England. When he finally departed by edging one from Dean Headley to wicketkeeper Warren Hegg, Slater had been responsible for 66.8 per cent of Australia's 184, almost eclipsing the oldest Test record remaining, Charles Bannerman's 67.34 per cent of Australia's total, made in the inaugural Test match of March 1877.

By the beginning of England's second innings it was becoming difficult to keep pace with the profusion of landmarks. But there was much more to come! While relaxing in the umpires' room on the evening of day four I found it amazing to review all the records and milestones that had already occurred in this match. The completion of McGrath's pair equalled a 20-year-old Ashes record at the opposite end of the spectrum from Slater's — the 37th duck of the series (22 to Englishmen, 15 to Australians). When both England's openers were stumped that evening after a promising start to their pursuit of 287 to secure a miraculous victory, it was only the fourth time in Test cricket that both openers had been dismissed in this manner. To keep the statisticians on their toes, when Mark Ramprakash edged in a catch to Mark Taylor in the fifth over of the final day, it gave Taylor his 157th catch, ahead of Allan Border's 156, to reach the top of the Test fielding honour roll. Four weeks later, at the end of January, Taylor announced his retirement from international cricket after captaining Australia in 50 tests. He had won 11 series out of 14. Not a record in itself, but his captaincy was a pleasure to watch from close quarters.

Ramprakash's dismissal also undermined England's quest, as at 3 for 131, it appeared that England could work themselves into a position to successfully chase down the target of 287, but their remaining seven wickets could muster only 78 runs. It was Stuart

MacGill who put the icing on the cake. MacGill took the last five wickets to fall in the match, and it was fitting that as he took a return catch from Peter Such to end the match, he also pocketed the ball as a souvenir of his overwhelming performance. MacGill's third-day figures of 6 for 23 from 73 deliveries were just reward for his intelligent exploitation of the conditions. MacGill's match total of 12 for 107 was the second-best by an Australian bowler at the SCG, behind the 122-year-old record of 12 for 87 set by C.T. B. Turner in 1888, moving Shane Warne's 12 for 128 against South Africa in 1994 down to third position.

Even more interesting, MacGill out-bowled Shane Warne, who could only manage 2 for 110 over both innings. He bowled 40 overs in the match compared with Warne's 39. To put MacGill's overall Test career in perspective, he averaged 4.7 wickets per Test, with Warne slightly edging him on that front with 4.8 wickets per Test. MacGill was also the third-fastest Australian to reach 200 Test wickets (in just 41 matches), standing behind Clarrie Grimmett and Denis Lillee, who took 36 and 38 matches respectively to reach that milestone. Shane Warne is only one match behind MacGill, on 42 Tests. For England, Dean Headley finished with match figures of 8 for 102 and Peter Such took 5 for 81 in Australia's second innings. On most occasions each of these figures would make headlines and would probably be good enough to ensure they played in a winning side, but somehow Michael Slater and Stuart MacGill completely overshadowed them. It shows how special Test matches really are to the players.

The reason I am highlighting these amazing statistics? They again indicate how much satisfaction is to be found in being a cricket umpire. Not everyone gets the chance to see as many records fall, and such emphatic control of leg spin, as I was lucky enough to witness in just one of my 78 Test matches. Sometimes I pinch myself to check it wasn't all a dream, and I know I would never have had it any other way. Ashes Test matches like this one are few and far between. In fact, because of the ICC's strict policy of appointing independent or neutral umpires to all Test matches, these matches will never again see an Australian or English umpire officiating. While I fully agree that the integrity of the game benefits from the removal of any perceived home-town bias, it is a real shame that other umpires will never experience what I have — the pleasure of being right in the middle of the Ashes. Why wouldn't you want to become an umpire?

Memorable Hat-tricks

Besides watching the best batsmen go about their trade, umpiring also provides the opportunity to monitor the great bowlers of the world. Not just to call no balls or wides, but to witness some great moments surrounding the special feats and achievements of bowlers. Being on the field when a hat-trick is taken is a special moment for an umpire too. So few hat-tricks have been achieved in international cricket. The skill required to take three wickets off successive balls against high-quality batsmen should not be underestimated.

The Test match in which England stormed the West Indies' once-impregnable fortress of the Kensington Oval, Barbados, on 1 April 2004, just as they had done almost exactly ten years earlier, was an experience Matthew Hoggard and I would remember for the rest of our lives. In 1994 an overwhelmed England team that was low on confidence, being already down 3–0 in the series, staged an improbable one-off smash-and-grab raid to win the Test, with Alec Stewart and Angus Fraser contributing extraordinary performances with both bat and ball. Against the well-marshalled invading force of Michael Vaughan's England team of 2004, the West Indies could muster little or no defence. For much of this brief but compelling Test match, the two teams looked very evenly matched, but England had the inner strength and resolve to play through their crises. Their bowling was effective, disciplined and, at moments, touched by magic. The West Indies bowlers, in contrast, gave the England batsmen far too many scoring opportunities and their batsmen fell all too regularly.

In the past, a result like the one produced in this Test match, in which the West Indies capitulated inside three days, would have been unthinkable. England not only clinched the series but also ensured their most successful Caribbean tour ever, with a 'whitewash' still a possibility. As the sun set over the Kensington Oval on that Saturday night, exultant English supporters stood on the field for hours after the match had ended, yelling their support for each of the players in turn.

Like many of England's games in the Caribbean, the match felt like a home Test to many English visitors. This was despite the West Indies Cricket Board's differential pricing system, which squeezes a higher ticket price out of the visitors than out of the locals. This handicap failed to prevent the ground from being entirely dominated by English holidaymaking fans. Many of them may have suffered more than a little heatstroke and have already overindulged on cold Banks or Carib beer, but for the most part they applauded politely when the need arose. A core minority, known around the world as the Barmy Army, maintained a cacophony of weird patriotic chants and likeable song variations throughout the match.

Yet the game did not start well for England, with Vaughan surprisingly opting to bowl first on a pitch with some bounce that most observers thought would play easily most of the game. Vaughan was obviously not thinking of how Richie Richardson had unwisely asked England to bat ten years earlier — a decision that ended in disaster for the West Indies. England put down three rather simple slip catches on the opening day. Although Andrew Flintoff got Brian Lara caught in the gully for 36, Ramnaresh Sarwan and Shivnarine Chanderpaul put together a fourth-wicket stand that took West Indies past the tea interval with some comfort. However, their batting line-up had become so fragile that it was now prone to crumple at the slightest threat. Once Steve Harmison found his length in the session after tea and had Sarwan caught at second slip, it was Flintoff's turn to collect some wickets — his first bag of five in a Test innings, as the last seven wickets fell for a paltry 57 runs.

If England fancied this might set them up for a big lead, they were soon disillusioned. The return of Fidel Edwards to lead the West Indies attack gave their bowling the old-fashioned feel of a four-man pace attack, all Barbadian, with three of the four coming from the same small village, Boscobel, and two of them, Edwards and Pedro Collins, being half-brothers. The pitch refused to calm down into a featherbed as expected, and Edwards' 90 mph pace with a slinging action removed England's top three batsmen with only 33 runs on the board. Steadily, the rest of England's batting succumbed too, with one remarkable exception.

Graham Thorpe, so often the linchpin of the England middle order, produced an innings of outstanding determination and quality. He held firm in defence and, when the bowlers dropped short, unleashed a series of high-class shots square and on both sides of the wicket, receiving just enough help from the tail to reach his own century moments after the new ball was taken at 9 for 189. The last man, Harmison, stayed with him to add 39, which inched England into a psychologically vital two-run lead. Thorpe also had help from a most unexpected quarter, when captain Brian Lara insisted on bowling Chris Gayle's innocuous off spin for 11 overs, even though he had four young and fit fast bowlers champing at the bit. It gave England important breathing space, though the batsmen may have been distracted by speculation on what on earth Lara was playing at.

In theory, the game was now evenly poised, but as we know theory can quickly be overwhelmed by the dynamics of a Test match. The third morning was cloudy, with rain showers lurking in the distance. In almost English conditions, roared on by the English crowd, the most English bowler on display, Matthew Hoggard, emerged from his relative obscurity to seal the game. Sarwan flicked wide outside off stump to a shortish delivery and handed a simple catch to Ashley Giles standing in the gully. Next ball Hoggard produced a perfect inswinger to trap Chanderpaul lbw dead in line with middle and off stump. Then the third ball moved away off the seam to take the thickish outside edge and Ryan Hinds was safely caught at second slip by Flintoff. Hoggard had become the tenth England bowler to take a Test hat-trick, the third to achieve the feat against the West Indies, after Peter Loader and Dominic Cork. It was not quite his first though; he had taken one as a 14-year-old in the Yorkshire Dales Council third division.

It was my first Test match hat-trick as an umpire standing at the bowler's end. Again, I could hardly believe my luck as the match was turned on its head, and there I was watching every ball. Once the crowd had calmed down, and I can tell you the celebrations went on for quite a while, the rest was reasonably straightforward. When Lara fell it was 9 for 85, and without his fighting qualities the West Indies were soon all out for 94, the fourth time in seven Tests that England had bowled them out for a two-figure total.

It was an eerie feeling going onto the field to begin the fourth innings just after lunch on the third day. When I arrived at the ground in the morning I had foreseen a long day ahead, with the West Indies accumulating a large score while the pitch was at its absolute best. But here we were with Marcus Trescothick and Michael Vaughan setting about adding 57 of the required 93 to win in just 11 overs before Vaughan departed. The rest was a formality, and when Mark Butcher took a single behind square leg England had wrapped up the series 3–0.

Graham Thorpe's 119 not out and Matthew Hoggard's hat-trick were the extraordinary performances that swung the game in England's favour. Test cricket really is unique. Don't listen to those who have decided it no longer has a role to play in developing strength of character in international cricket.

With Australia already out of the finals, the match between Australia and Pakistan at the MCG on 16 January 1997 was meaningless in terms of finishing positions on the table. But it came to life when lively New South Wales pace bowler Anthony

Stuart became only the second Australian to take a hat-trick at this level. (Bruce Reid had taken the other one against New Zealand in 1985/86.) Stuart was playing his third one-day international at the mature age of 27. As a teenager he had been a wicketkeeper, but he found his niche in history as a bowler.

The first batsman dismissed was Ijaz Ahmed off the third ball of Stuart's sixth over, when Ijaz sparred with a good-length ball outside off stump and Ian Healy took the catch. Mohammad Wasim strode out, took guard and edged an identical delivery to the previous one straight to Healy for the second catch. Moin Khan, normally reliable in a crisis, was unable to prevent history from being made when he edged a perfectly pitched leg cutter into the very safe hands of Mark Taylor at first slip. This was the 12th hat-trick in the history of one-day internationals.

Pakistan rallied from 5 for 29 to reach a total of 181, with Wasim Akram, Shahid Afridi and Saqlain Mushtaq batting out the full 50 overs in sensible fashion. Australia looked no certainty at 4 for 110, but Michael Bevan's cool 79 saw them home with three wickets and three balls to spare.

As for Darren Gough's hat-trick in the Ashes of 1999 in Sydney, I was standing at square leg and Peter Parker was the lucky one at the bowler's end. A crowd of 48,218 revelled in the Australian players' celebrations by loudly acknowledging another very special feat by a cricketer.

The last of my hat-trick appearances was in the one-day international between the West Indies and South Africa at Bridgetown, Barbados, on 11 May 2005. I had been in the Caribbean for the whole of this series, and after two routine

South African wins, the international burst outrageously into life. With just seven balls remaining, the West Indies were chasing 285 and seemingly easing towards victory at 6 for 281. When Makhaya Ntini found the leading edge of wicketkeeper Courtney Browne's bat, losing a seventh wicket seemed no more than a slight hiccup. Singles off the first two balls of the last over by Ian Bradshaw and Dwayne Bravo from South African swing bowler Charl Langeveldt appeared to confirm it, with just two runs now required from the remaining four balls.

But for some strange reason Bradshaw swung wildly, and not only did he miss — he was bowled. Bravo and Bradshaw had had a long mid-pitch discussion, so I'm sure the plan must have been to take a single. It seemed logical that Bravo, who had scored 21 off 19 balls faced, should be back on strike. On the next ball Daren Powell inexplicably did the same, with the identical result — out bowled! I thought, 'What on earth is happening here?' as Cory Collymore, not the most accomplished of batsmen, arrived at the crease. With two balls remaining and two runs to win, Bravo must have been desperate to get back on strike for the last ball and scramble through to win the game. Langeveldt's fifth ball of that final over, however, produced a wicked inswinger that rapped Collymore on the pads bang in front of middle and off stumps. Collymore had shuffled across and tried desperately to make some contact with his bat. But it was an easy decision for me to make and my finger went up.

Somehow, incredibly, South Africa had won the game by one run, courtesy of an 'unassisted' hat-trick, with the West Indies lower order batsmen unable to make one strike of the ball with their bats. Langeveldt's work meant that a measured 123 from

South African opening batsman Boeta Dippenaar was consigned to the forgotten basket. More amazingly, a surprisingly restrained 132 from Chris Gayle, who hit seven fours and two sixes, was also bounced from the headlines. Maybe Gayle should have been the responsible one to bat out the innings, but he skied a short ball from Andre Nel for Pollock to take the catch. Even so, at 6 for 258 the West Indies needed only 29 off the last 26 deliveries, a task that would normally be achieved without too much fuss.

Witnessing Langeveldt's heroic effort was just one more standout example of the pleasures afforded me as an umpire of international cricket.

PART 2

THE CONTROVERSY

CHAPTER 2

THE OVAL

Statement issued on behalf of the International Cricket Council, the England and Wales Cricket Board and the Pakistan Cricket Board, 20 August 2006

After lengthy negotiations which resulted in agreement between the teams, the ICC match referee and both England and Wales Cricket Board (ECB) and Pakistan Cricket Board (PCB) to seek to resume the fourth npower Test on Monday, it was concluded with regret that there will be no play on the fifth day.

The fourth Test match between England and Pakistan has therefore been forfeited, with the match being awarded to England.

In accordance with the Laws of Cricket it was noted that the umpires had correctly deemed that Pakistan had forfeited the match, and awarded the Test to England.

At a meeting between the captains, ECB, PCB and ICC match referee, the players, ICC match referee and boards indicated that they would offer to resume play if at all possible on day five. The umpires, having awarded the match to England and having consulted with the Pakistan captain, reconfirmed their decision to award the match to England.

The Pakistan team was aggrieved by the award of five penalty runs to England. The award of those penalty runs for alleged interference with the ball is under review by the ICC match referee Mike Procter, whose report will be considered in due course.

ICC will be issuing a separate report concerning action which may be taken in relation to the forfeiture of the match by Pakistan.

Footnote to scorecard: Pakistan refused to come out after the tea interval, leading to the umpires awarding the match to England 20 minutes later. Despite Pakistan later being willing to play, the umpires insisted the result must stand. This was confirmed by the respective boards later that night at 10.00 p.m.

So what went wrong? Why did the major players in this saga issue this statement, only to then burn it as quickly as those effigies of me were simultaneously being lit halfway across the world in Pakistan?

There comes a day in everyone's life that changes things forever. Some look forward to that day while others fear it. Many people struggle in their chosen careers in the hope of advancement, a better lifestyle and maybe just a feeling that it has all been worthwhile — that the struggle has paid off and their life has moved forward. There were times in the weeks following the forfeiture of the Test match when I felt depressed, deserted and vilified by those within the game whose major responsibility was to preserve the integrity of cricket.

People who should have stepped back and measured their input became involved. Comments were made with a great deal of passion but little understanding. Darrell Hair was a cheat, a racist who hated Asian teams. The train left the station with no driver and no destination other than to get rid of the 'problem' — Darrell Hair. Frighteningly, the ICC was to lead the charge.

The news came via a phone call from Doug Cowie, ICC umpires' manager, in late June 2006. I had been appointed by the ICC to umpire the fourth Test between England and Pakistan at The Oval from 17 to 21 August. Included in this batch of appointments was the third Test at Headingley. My colleague for both matches was to be Billy Doctrove from the West Indies. Billy had umpired eight Test matches and 52 one-day internationals. He was appointed to the Elite Panel in April 2006 as a result of excellent performances throughout his career. I had umpired with him in his second Test match, the West Indies against South Africa, on 17 March 2001 in Port of Spain, Trinidad, and he had performed admirably in the face of pressure from the South African team.

It is quite normal practice for teams to exert pressure on umpires they have not seen before, and this match was no exception. I remember one particular instance when Shaun

Pollock complained about a few no balls that Billy called. Pollock, like just about every other international cricketer, believed he never bowled no balls, but Billy stuck to his guns. The pressure ended when Pollock attempted to put his foot into the marks left on the popping crease. 'I've been around long enough to know a no ball when I see one,' said Billy. Pollock gave the obligatory shrug of the shoulders and nothing further was said.

It therefore came as a surprise to me when Doug Cowie asked me to 'look after Billy as he is a bit green'. Billy Doctrove was no rookie by any stretch, and if the ICC had doubts about his ability to withstand pressure, then why appoint him in the first place? Also, why was Cowie asking someone else to do his job for him?

The training, preparation, assessment and feedback coming from the ICC for umpiring at international level was virtually non-existent before Chris Kelly took over as the ICC umpires' manager. Chris succeeded Keith Medlycott, who was, in my view, less satisfactory in the role, having come into it with no umpiring experience to speak of.

Chris Kelly had a comprehensive background in grassroots cricket, having umpired at minor counties and ECB second eleven fixtures. He was also a very good educator, with a teaching career behind him. Chris was an excellent choice to move umpiring forward at the international level and, more importantly, came without the baggage of friendships with international umpires. He would be able to start afresh with his own ideas.

Kelly implemented and managed a detailed assessment program that, while not perfect, was a huge improvement on what had previously been in place. No doubt some of Billy Doctrove's earlier Test match performances would have been assessed by Chris Kelly's processes.

Later ICC comments that Doctrove was led by me, agreed with everything I said and acted in accordance with everything I did reflected poorly on the ICC, were demeaning towards Doctrove and suggested a total lack of trust in their own umpiring system.

The Test match at Headlingley resulted in an easy win for England. I got a decision wrong in giving Kevin Pietersen not out caught when he did actually get an inside edge onto his thigh pad before the ball carried through to Kamran Akmal. Those decisions are never easy but I put my hand up at the time and admitted the mistake. The captains' reports on my performances did mention the decision but indicated 'there was no malice intended'. More about that report and the timing of its submission later.

After an eight-day break I made the drive to London to prepare for the fourth Test at The Oval. The first three days were relatively uneventful from my perspective. England had played poorly in the first innings on a very good pitch, scoring just 173 in 53 overs. Pakistan batted extremely well to post 504, with a century to Mohammad Yousuf, 95 to Mohammad Hafeez and 91 to Imran Farhat. Faisal Iqbal batted well in lower-order partnerships to post an extra 123 after Inzamam was dismissed with the score at 5 for 381. Faced with a deficit of 331, England had to bat for two more days just to save the match. Andrew Strauss and Alistair Cook survived until the end of day three and had put together 77 for the loss of Trescothick.

Strauss, Cook and Pietersen all played well on day four. When Cook was dismissed lbw to an inswinging yorker from Umar Gul,

England were 3 for 218 off 51.5 overs. At the end of the over, I asked Mohammad Yousuf for the ball to make an inspection of its condition. I found nothing untoward, with only the normal wear and tear you would expect at that stage of the innings.

Many uninformed reports about the match would later imply that the Alistair Cook dismissal was the result of 'reverse swing'. Nothing could be further from the truth! The delivery by Umar Gul was a standard inswinger to the left-handed Cook. This was one of Gul's stock deliveries. When I inspected the ball it was still hard and one side was well shined, which would account for the late swing obtained by Gul and contribute to his dismissing Cook. The ball was then returned to the fielders and play continued.

The next four overs produced just 11 runs. Pietersen struck a boundary through the covers off Danish Kaneria, the ball just reaching the boundary rope at deep cover. Paul Collingwood got off the mark with a three through mid-wicket and then a single off Gul. Pietersen took a single and a two off one of Kaneria's overs.

At the end of over 55, I inspected the ball again and was immediately horrified by what I saw. Deep, crescent-shaped scratches had appeared along one quarter section of the ball. In addition, several crescent-shaped indentations were clearly evident on another section of the ball. Both of these areas of scratching and indentations had appeared on the same side of the ball.

It looked as though the ball had been attacked with a blunt knife or similar object. Although I don't believe for a moment that any of the Pakistan team were carrying such an implement, the condition of the ball had definitely changed considerably in a short period of time, and such deterioration was not consistent with the way the game had progressed since Alistair Cook's dismissal. There was quite a lot of dead bat defensive play and use of the pads by Collingwood and Pietersen in what had become quite a tense 20-minute period of play.

An understanding of this passage of play was vital in determining the final outcome. There were only five scoring shots played and of these only one was a forceful stroke — the boundary by Pietersen. Despite this issue being raised in the subsequent ICC code of conduct hearing, no one at the ICC could either believe (or comprehend) the manner in which the condition of the ball had deteriorated in such a short space of time.

Someone must have interfered with the surface of the ball — of that I was certain. It could not have been caused by the ball hitting boundary boards, as was later claimed by members of the Pakistan camp. This left only two options: the ball could have been 'worked over' by fielders as it was being relayed back to the bowlers; or the bowlers themselves could have dug their fingernails into the surface of one side while appearing to be polishing the ball as they walked back to their bowling marks. It doesn't take long for considerable damage to occur once a deliberate attempt has been made to accelerate the normal deterioration of the ball.

I consulted Billy Doctrove and showed him the ball, expressing my concern, and he too was horrified. That left the umpires with two options: either ignore the incident and hope that no further deterioration would become evident, or change the ball as required under the Laws of Cricket.

For me, there was only one decision to make. The ball had quite evidently been tampered with. It could only have been an attempt to gain an unfair advantage. I could not knowingly allow one team an advantage to which they were not entitled. Still, one umpire may have an opinion on any matter concerning the running of a Test match, but nothing happens to change the status quo unless the umpires agree. Billy Doctrove agreed that the ball's condition had been changed and the correct procedures were then implemented in the correct order:

1. Change the ball forthwith.
2. Inform the batsmen that the ball has been changed.
3. Award five penalty runs to the batting side.
4. Inform the captain of the fielding side of the reason.

I was often criticised later for that award of five penalty runs to England. Did I enjoy doing it? No, I certainly did not, but when there is a required procedure under the Laws of Cricket, you must follow it. The five-run penalty itself is a ridiculous one and serves no real purpose other than to tell everyone that an illegal or unfair act has occurred, just as when a no ball is declared. Although it was a joint decision, as the umpire at the bowler's end, I was required to signal it.

Pakistan captain Inzamam-ul-Haq asked why the England batsmen had been allowed to pick a replacement ball. It was clear from Inzamam's tone that he was not happy with the ball change or with the umpires' conclusion that the ball had been tampered with. This conversation is important because it torpedoes Inzamam's later defence that we didn't keep him fully informed.

We explained that the ICC rules are clear: when the condition of the ball has been changed unfairly, the umpires shall offer the batting side a choice of replacement balls. ICC Standard Test Match Playing Conditions Clause 42.1.2(b) confirms this to be the correct course of action. Inzamam then demanded to see the ball and Trevor Jesty, the fourth umpire, took it from his pocket and allowed him to view it. Before the resumption of play I signalled five penalty runs to the scorers.

Inzamam was later to repeat on many occasions that he was not told why the ball had been changed. He was. During that prolonged discussion on the field we certainly were not talking about what was on the menu for dinner or who had won the 2.50 at Ascot! Inzamam's repeated protestations reminded me of a child caught with his fingers in the cookie jar. Embarrassed at being caught, the child resorts to all sorts of excuses, even telling lies, to get off the hook. Inzamam failed to take responsibility for the actions of his players and chose to shift the attack onto me personally.

After a delay of approximately four minutes, play did resume and continued without further incident for another 15 overs, until 3.45 p.m. when, with the cloud cover increasing, a light-meter reading was taken. The reading indicated that the light conditions had fallen below the benchmark for this match (there had been some poor light issues earlier in the match) so we offered the batsmen, Kevin Pietersen and Ian Bell, the option of deciding whether they wished to play on in the current conditions. They decided not to continue batting, as was their right. As the stoppage was within 30 minutes of the scheduled tea break, the break was taken immediately, with play scheduled to restart at 4.05 p.m.

A very important aspect of this whole affair is to understand that the Pakistan cricket team agreed to continue playing after the ball had been changed and the five-run penalty awarded. There was no protest other than Inzamam-ul-Haq's expressing his disagreement with our judgement that the ball had been tampered with. By continuing to play, the Pakistan team implicitly accepted the penalty and showed they were prepared to get on with the game.

It was apparently when the Pakistan team arrived in their dressing room during the tea break that the dismantling of the umpires' role began. Shaharyar Khan, the Pakistan Cricket Board chairman, was to say later in the day, during an interview at 5.42 p.m. on BBC Radio (the timing of which is important in light of a statement made by ECB chairman David Morgan in evidence at the ball-tampering hearing): 'We feel that there is no evidence whatsoever of deliberate scuffing of the ball. Once you accuse a team of deliberately tampering with the ball, it becomes a very big deal. We felt we should make a protest, but we simply said that we would stay inside for a few minutes, and go out when the protest had been registered.' Khan added, 'We are still hopeful that the match can start again.'

These comments may have influenced the ICC to take the actions they did. 'The game must go on at all costs' was to become a mantra from high-ranking ICC officials. But at what cost should the game go on? Are the public expected to pay to watch teams cheat, refuse to accept umpires' decisions, play on regardless? If the ICC believe the public wish to part with their money to watch this type of conduct, then I feel they are misguided.

★

Bob Woolmer, the Pakistan team coach, arrived in the umpires' room during the tea break to ask for an explanation, which he was duly given. He was accompanied by Waqar Younis, who, ironically, had been banned for ball tampering during the one-day international between Sri Lanka and Pakistan held in Colombo on 8 July 2000. More on him and other members of the Pakistan team later!

Woolmer addressed ICC referee Mike Procter. Much of the conversation took place with the clear intention of excluding the umpires. I was not asked any questions by Woolmer. As Woolmer was leaving the room Procter reminded him that play was to resume in a few minutes. 'Don't count on it' was Woolmer's response.

With play due to resume at 4.05 p.m., Billy Doctrove and I made an inspection of the ground. Despite persistent cloud cover an improvement in the light conditions was evident. At 4.30 p.m. we considered the conditions had improved sufficiently to ask fourth umpire Trevor Jesty to advise both teams that play would resume at 4.40 p.m.

At 4.36 p.m. we walked out onto the ground and made our way to the middle, replaced the bails and prepared for play to restart. Under normal circumstances, the fielding side will follow the umpires onto the field and the two not-out batsmen will follow the fielders. It quickly became apparent that one of these components was missing. The Pakistan side were not to be seen and the door to their dressing room was firmly closed. We waited for what seemed an eternity but was in fact only four minutes. At 4.41 p.m., with still no sign of the Pakistan team, action was required by the umpires. Following a brief discussion, Billy and I agreed that while it was evident that Pakistan was refusing to play, we were required under the Laws of Cricket to follow a certain procedure.

It is important to note here that it is only necessary for one umpire to consider that any action by any player or players may constitute a refusal to play, but it requires both umpires to ascertain the cause of the action. The MCC Laws of Cricket 21.3(b) states: 'If the umpires do consider it a refusal to play, they must inform the Captain of that side. If the Captain persists, the umpires shall award the match to the other team.'

A visit to the Pakistan dressing room was now necessary.

It is no easy task to get from the umpires' room to the players' dressing rooms at The Oval. It requires a ride in an elevator and a long walk along corridors, all in the company of security guards. Trevor Jesty accompanied Billy and me on this journey. We arrived at the Pakistan dressing room at 4.46 p.m. and were met at the door by a stony-faced Pakistan team manager, Zaheer Abbas. We asked to see Inzamam, who quickly appeared with Bob Woolmer by his side. Waqar Younis hovered in the background but did not participate in the conversation.

Waqar is an interesting, extraordinarily adaptable person. In 2009 I attended a fundraising event for the Parramatta District Cricket Club in Sydney, where Waqar joined me on a celebrity panel. When asked about umpiring decisions, Waqar replied, 'The man beside me was one of the best and we always had confidence in his decisions.' I almost fell out of my chair! Had I known his views of me as an umpire, I might have asked that he be called as a witness before the Employment Tribunal in London. But as a fundraising event for grassroots cricket, this luncheon was not the place for controversial comments from me, so I let it pass.

While both umpires are required to satisfy themselves about the cause of any possible refusal to play, most of the questions will usually be asked by one umpire, with the other free to contribute at any time. No particular agreement was made between Billy Doctrove and me as to who would ask the questions. In the event, I appeared to be the one at the forefront, as has often, although not always, been the case during my umpiring career.

It is strange how things pan out over time. Our recollections and memories of important events are constructed within our own minds. Thinking back on the discussions that followed, I recall that at no time did Doctrove say anything, but I know he was always standing beside me. On the few occasions I looked to him for comment or confirmation, he was always there on my right. There were no signs of weakness. During all the later events and at the ball-tampering/forfeiture code of conduct hearing, Billy Doctrove consistently reiterated that he agreed with all of the procedures followed.

We were not invited into the Pakistan dressing room and the hostility in Woolmer's eyes in particular was palpable. The following conversation took place at the door.

> **DH:** Inzamam, we are here to find out why you didn't take the field after the tea interval.
> **Inzamam:** Why did you change the ball? There was nothing wrong with it.
> **DH:** That is a matter for another time and place. At the moment we need to know if you intend to resume play.
> **Inzamam:** Why are you doing this thing?

To which I reiterated that we needed to know if he would be leading his team back onto the field. There was silence for quite a few moments, after which I said, 'Can you please tell us now if you intend to take the field, because if you do not, the match will be forfeited and awarded to England.'

Zaheer Abbas, who had said nothing up to this stage, then stated, 'You umpires go and do what you have to do.'

I again looked at Inzamam for a response, and when none was forthcoming I said, 'We are about to go back onto the field and if you do not follow us, the match will be considered forfeited by Pakistan and will be awarded to England.'

We then went straight to the England dressing room, where we found Paul Collingwood and Ian Bell padded up and apparently ready to resume play. I informed them that we were about to make our way onto the field to resume play and the batsmen should take the field as soon as we did. Then we made our way back to the umpires' room, collected our hats and counters, and walked straight onto the field. The time was 4.54 p.m. The two England batsmen came onto the ground almost immediately. The Pakistan team did not.

Kamran Akmal, the Pakistan wicketkeeper, came out of the dressing room and sat on a seat in front of the Pakistan dressing room, in full view of the public, reading a copy of the *News of the World*. He had no pads, gloves or other equipment with him. He obviously had no intention of taking the field of play. How ironic it would be for Pakistan cricket that a little more than four years later *News of the World* journalists would blow apart the protestations that the Pakistan cricket team does not and has never cheated!

A couple more minutes ticked by with no sign of Inzamam or his team. I walked down the side of the pitch to consult Billy Doctrove. He said, 'They are not coming out, that much is clear.'

In a later statement he tendered at the code of conduct hearing to finalise penalties against the Pakistan captain and team for refusing to play, Inzamam said, 'A few minutes after the umpires left our dressing room, the bell rang in the dressing room, which normally signals the return of the umpires to the field. We did not follow them out.' Pakistan were now actively refusing to play. There could have been no misunderstanding of what was said to him by the umpires. He knew what he was doing.

I suggested to Billy Doctrove that Pakistan had now been given three opportunities to resume play and by not doing so had clearly forfeited the match, a view that Doctrove shared. I asked him what he wanted to do. He was adamant that the match should be awarded to England, and I agreed. Billy then walked back to his end and removed the bails. I told Paul Collingwood and Ian Bell that the match had ended and I then removed the bails from my end and left the field.

This passage of events is important because I have long stood accused as the umpire with sole responsibility for removing the bails and declaring the match forfeited. These accusations continued long after video footage and still photographs showed that in fact I removed the bails well *after* Doctrove. Talk about give a dog a bad name!

It was now 4.58 p.m., 18 minutes after play should have resumed. The Pakistan team had refused to restart play on three occasions — first at 4.40 p.m. when play was due to resume, again outside the Pakistan dressing room when no verbal agreement was reached, and for the third time at 4.58 p.m., with a very clear no show.

Back in the umpires' room, Mike Procter asked, 'What happens now?' I replied that Pakistan had forfeited and the match must be awarded to England. Procter looked at Doctrove, who agreed. Procter immediately stood up and said, 'I had better go and tell Pakistan then,' and left the room.

It is quite clear that Procter did nothing of the sort. According to the statement Bob Woolmer tendered at the code of conduct hearing, 'At no stage did Mr Procter mention that the match had been forfeited. In fact, Procter asked me to delay the Pakistan team's return to the field while he placated the umpires.'

Procter was an enigma in international cricket. Obviously a great player in his heyday, he later took on a raft of jobs in cricket, including coach and selector and team manager of South Africa from time to time, but he was less than a success in any of those roles. The communication that the match had ended had quite obviously not been conveyed to either the England or the Pakistan team.

Procter arrived back in the umpires' room some time later in company with ECB chairman David Morgan and CEO David Collier. Collier asked if he could speak to the umpires. I had known David for some time as former CEO of Nottinghamshire County Cricket Club. He was a former hockey referee and we had shared some stories about the difficulties of officiating in sport. I found him to be a competent administrator and a friendly face at most of the matches I umpired in England.

Collier first declared his belief that umpires' decisions must be final; however, he wondered if any concessions could be made in this particular case to ensure the Test match continued into the last day. Billy Doctrove pointed out that the match was already over and Pakistan had forfeited. I told David that in my view the match had been properly concluded and a result obtained under the Laws of Cricket, and that as umpires we had made our final decision.

Morgan then informed us that the Pakistan team were now willing to take the field and asked whether I was prepared to return to the field to allow play to continue. Billy and I patiently reiterated that play could not continue because the match was *over*. Morgan then asked third umpire Peter Hartley and fourth umpire Trevor Jesty whether they would be prepared to umpire the match if it were to be restarted. Trevor and Peter were aghast and replied that they were not and that they agreed with us that the match was at an end.

What did David Morgan think he was doing, and did he even pause to think what damage would ensue for the game itself if this type of pressure was allowed to continue? Morgan may have had in mind the commercial aspects of the event at the time rather than upholding the spirit of the game itself.

I said any decision to restart the match would be severely flawed and not in the best interests of the game. By then the respect I had had for Procter had dissolved. Looking rather embarrassed, Collier and Morgan exited the room.

Then Mike Procter, out of the blue, said that a meeting had been arranged in an attempt to 'resolve things'. He gave no indication of how this meeting had been arranged or who would be chairing it. I agreed to attend but reiterated that I would not be reconsidering the result or umpiring the 'match' if it were to continue tomorrow. Billy Doctrove also said that he would not umpire such a game.

Apparently Doug Cowie and Mike Procter reached an agreement that before the match could be declared forfeited, they would make representations to the Pakistan team and try to negotiate a settlement. Whatever 'settlement' they had in mind was not mentioned to the match umpires, but I could only suspect that it would involve convincing the umpires to reverse their decision.

The four umpires and the referee at an international match are known as the Playing Control Team and they work together as a team. The duty of the Playing Control Team is to 'ensure a level playing field' for both teams, and to guarantee that the game is played according to the contract the teams have entered into when agreeing to play, which includes their adhering to the playing conditions, the Laws of Cricket and ultimately the spirit of the game. Doug Cowie and Mike Procter were representatives of the ICC, but I question how much leadership they showed on this occasion.

I duly attended the meeting, along with Procter, Billy Doctrove and Doug Cowie. Along with Morgan and Collier, Andrew Strauss and Duncan Fletcher were also present at the meeting. The PCB chairman, Shaharyar Khan, led off by saying that the reason the Pakistan team did not take the field was because they were conducting a 'short protest'. I suggested briefly that there is no room for 'protest' at an umpires' decision, as to do so strikes at the very heart of the spirit of cricket. Questioned by Inzamam about our decision to penalise Pakistan, I was in the middle of explaining the protocol when Inzamam waved me aside with what felt like a belittling gesture.

The meeting itself lacked any leadership from Mike Procter. As the umpires' decision had been well and truly conveyed first to the ICC referee and later to Morgan and Collier, I could see nothing to be gained by allowing others to attempt to influence it. In view of the impending code of conduct report to be lodged by the umpires and the consequent, yet to be scheduled hearing, I was not required to discuss matters to be addressed in the report.

David Morgan later provided a statement to the ICC code of conduct hearing that contained the following:

> At around 5.10 p.m. I was in the Committee Room with David Collier. We had seen the umpires take the field twice, the second time with the England batsmen, but each time the Pakistan team had not emerged. We were both deeply concerned. David Collier said that he thought we should go to the England dressing room to see what was happening. I accompanied David Collier to the dressing room and left him there. I saw Shaharyar Khan on the balcony of the Pakistan dressing room. I felt that I should know what Chairman Khan's position was on the ball tampering allegation and the Pakistan team's protest. My worst fear was that Shaharyar might have been encouraging his team to boycott the match. However, when I spoke to Shaharyar this was clearly not the case. His problem was that the team would still not take the field. I asked if it would help if I spoke to the Captain. Shaharyar replied that it would be a great help.

★

A couple of points to note here: David Morgan was obviously concerned that the Pakistan management (through their chairman) might be influencing the team's decisions, and Morgan, in talking with Shaharyar Khan, introduced the term 'ball tampering'. That may well have inflamed the situation, moving it from a delicate situation that the umpires could deal with into a passionate denial that Pakistan had done anything wrong. He is surely not showing much faith in one of his fellow ICC board members if he believes Khan might have been interfering in team decisions.

If Morgan's account was correct then Shaharyar Khan must have lied to David Morgan about his involvement. At 5.42 p.m., some 30 minutes after his denial to Morgan, Khan was recorded in a BBC Radio interview as saying: 'We felt we should make a protest, but we simply said that we would stay inside for a few minutes and go out when the protest had been registered.'

Well, so much for that! If the protest was to be short, why then did the Pakistan team continue to refuse to play after three requests had been made? And why does Morgan refer to the Pakistan team's refusal to play as a 'protest'? It was not described as such until Shaharyar Khan used the term during his interview with the BBC.

I remember Doug Cowie saying to me at the time, 'That Khan fellow from the Pakistan Cricket Board, he seems a bit of a smart cookie — getting himself on television and saying plenty.' He was indeed a smart cookie, when it came to the media. I certainly saw no effort by Mike Procter, or Doug Cowie for that matter, to get in front of a camera or microphone and tell everyone that the match was over because of the Pakistan cricket team's refusal to play. That sort of strength and leadership was sometimes missing when it was most needed.

Much later, in October 2010, Cowie would tell me that he made the trip to England because it was his first Test match in his new role as umpires' manager. He also suggested he was there to support Billy Doctrove, who was in his first Test series since his Elite Panel appointment. Cowie went on to tell me that although he saw me as Doctrove's main support, that was never to mean there should be a senior umpire/junior umpire approach as far as ICC cricket operations went. He did, however, confirm that he recognised my role on the MCC Laws Committee and as a key umpire in setting interpretations.

Cowie also told me in October 2010 that he was certain the umpires followed the procedures as set down in the playing conditions and Laws of Cricket and that he concurred — as did all officials, including Mike Procter — that the ball showed signs of having been tampered with. Cowie added that the ICC relied on the official reports from the umpires of when this scratching must have happened, which was between the 52nd and 55th overs.

The photos taken next day confirm the 'scratching', but that ball was never in the same condition again, as subsequent handling, even through the plastic bag, could only smooth down any markings. I believed that proof of tampering and scratching was not the real issue for the hearing, as the umpires are the sole judges of those things, yet the ball itself seemed to be a main focus during the code of conduct proceedings.

★

That night I tried to relax over dinner at our hotel, but my mind was locked on the events of the afternoon. I still felt confident that matters would be properly dealt with over the next few days and life would soon return to normal. During the meal, shared with my wife, Amanda, Doug Cowie and Mike Procter, my phone rang again. It was approximately 9.45 p.m. and David Collier wanted to ask me some more questions.

After reiterating that he would never question the umpires' decisions, he asked me one more time if I would be prepared to umpire the Test match if it were to continue tomorrow. I answered that I would not, unless Malcolm Speed instructed me to do so. Even then I would have to consider whether such an instruction was in the best interests of the game — although I felt sure, myself, that it would not be. Collier said he doubted that Speed would issue such an instruction.

Collier now seemed to be speaking solely from an ECB commercial perspective — sell more tickets, fill more seats! He said Pakistan were prepared to express regret in a public statement and that 12,000 ticket holders and other supporters, as well as television viewers and radio listeners, would be disappointed if play did not continue the next day. There is big difference between the Pakistan team's 'expressing regret' and actually apologising to the umpires for their behaviour. I noted that Collier did not mention anything about an apology. In any case, the match had ended. The Pakistan team had had their choices clearly laid out for them and they had chosen their course.

But why was there such a persistent determination by the

administrators that play should 'resume' on day five? How would the ECB and ICC have marketed the fifth day's play? It would have been a farcical exhibition match to provide entertainment for a misinformed public, rather than the culmination of an authentic Test match.

I asked Collier if he had spoken to Billy Doctrove and he said he had not. I suggested he might wish to do so, as I could not answer on his behalf.

I then referred Collier to my conversation with Malcolm Speed earlier that evening, in which I had given him a run-down of the day's events. I told him that in the absence of a direction from Speed that the match be continued or restarted, the match had officially ended in one of the ways provided for under the Laws of Cricket. He accepted my answer, thanked me for listening to him and wished me well for my trip back home to Lincoln.

I asked Billy Doctrove, who was sitting with friends in the hotel lounge, if he had fielded any calls from anyone at the ICC or the ECB. He said he had not. This conversation with Collier only confirmed my belief that umpires should never be swayed by external issues in their application of the laws concerning fair play. Umpires make decisions almost every day (for instance, on adverse weather, the condition of the pitch and light issues) that may deprive the paying public of seeing more cricket, but those decisions that relate to unfair play are clear and concise: the game must be played fairly 'in the sole opinion of the umpires, who are the sole judges of fair and unfair play'.

I had never been instructed by an ICC official to change an umpiring decision on the continuation or suspension of play. It seemed that plenty of pressure was being exerted in this instance, though, to resume a match that had been suspended because one team showed their displeasure at a decision by the umpires.

The omission of Billy Doctrove from conversations and telephone calls with David Collier and Malcolm Speed was later used by my detractors, who was accused me of being the sole instigator, the driver of the whole ball-tampering and forfeiture incident.

The afternoon phone call from Malcolm Speed had been unnerving. I had the strong impression that he was gathering facts, not to ensure the ICC code of conduct was implemented, but perhaps to get rid, once and for all, of a 'difficult' umpire.

At 10.35 p.m. on the evening of 20 August 2006, the International Cricket Council, the England and Wales Cricket Board and the Pakistan Cricket Board released a joint statement acknowledging that the fourth Test had been forfeited by Pakistan and there would be no play on the fifth day. That should have been the end of the matter, apart from the upcoming code of conduct hearing. But unknowingly, with assistance from one of the ICC's own staff, I would soon provide Speed with something that I believe was then used to tarnish my reputation and bury my umpiring career forever.

CHAPTER 3

THE AFTERMATH

Lincoln was for me a great place to live. I loved the history of the area and was amazed during my morning strolls by the towering structure of the 11th-century Lincoln Cathedral with the Norman-built castle across the old town's cobbled square. The place became a part of my life and remains unforgettable for its beauty and history. But if I had any thought of being able to come home to relax, I was sadly mistaken. A media circus had camped outside my house awaiting my return. One newspaper, *The Guardian*, even printed a photograph of the house along with the street name, making it not at all hard to find if some idiot wanted to cause me real grief. Although they didn't actually publish our address, it was the next best thing.

Our next-door neighbour managed to contact Amanda through her office to warn her of the invasion. Journalists and photographers were knocking on neighbours' doors, trying to find out what sort of person I was. They even visited the local newsagent, where I was known to purchase a copy of the *Racing Post* every now and then, waving my photo and harassing staff. They made quite an impact on the small community around Burton Road, Lincoln.

The final straw was when journalists camped at my local watering hole, The Strugglers Inn, where I had been known to spend a quiet evening with friends sipping pints of Black Sheep Bitter. The landlord protected my privacy as best he could, and as they were not buying much ale he asked them to find somewhere else to camp. I was told later that everyone at The Strugglers denied ever having seen me and the journalists responded with frustration: 'He's a 6 foot 4 inch Aussie — how can you have missed him?'

Originally we had invited Doug Cowie and his wife, Gilly, to spend a few days with us following the Test match. While we were never what you could call close friends, I had umpired with Doug on several occasions in international matches, including the 1999 World Cup held in England. He was also my manager, having been appointed to the position some months earlier. I had strongly supported his application with a reference imploring the ICC to stick with proven umpires from the international scene when appointing managers and coaches.

Given the likely media circus, however, Cowie decided not to make the trip, opting to remain in London to wait for a date to be set for the hearing into the forfeiture and ball tampering. This was something I regretted later, when he failed to back me over the emails affair. If he had been seen a little more in my company he may not have been able to wash his hands of the matter so easily.

Of course the media will do whatever they feel necessary to get a story but many of the headlines in the print media and the stories carried on the internet went far beyond fair comment or truth. 'Darrell Hair: the Racist Cheater' wrote Kashish Aziz on 21 August on a site called Cricketviewer.com. Simon Barnes, writing in *The Times*, was particularly scathing, although I wondered at his understanding of the fairness of a sporting contest when he wrote the following diatribe on 20 August:

> So now we know it. Officials are more important than players, laws are more important than people, one man's vanity is more important than the pleasure of millions, principles are more important than common sense, intransigence is better than decency, vindictiveness is better than compromise, trouble is much more fun than peaceful co-operation and an umpire's dignity is more important than mutual understanding between nations.
>
> These are all conclusions we can draw from umpire Darrell Hair's disruption and destruction of the fourth Test between England and Pakistan at the Brit Oval.
>
> The question of whether or not Pakistan was guilty of tampering with the ball is no longer relevant. The point at issue is how a single man's pigheadedness was allowed to disrupt the fun of millions, to give cricket a terrible, gaping wound and to add to the tensions between Muslims and white Westerners at this, of all moments in history.

Comparing a decision in a sporting contest with political tensions 'between Muslims and white Westerners' is ridiculous and misses the point. In fact, all it does is provide excuses for people who act badly. Pakistan is not the only nation in world cricket that has attempted to cheat and it will not be the last. Getting caught was their fault and no one else's. A sporting contest is based around every player in the teams involved demonstrating the spirit of the game and adhering to the laws as they are structured at the time, and may the best team win. Any other way of playing cricket will not work, and if umpires stand by and knowingly permit breaches of the regulations, then those umpires should admit to the public that they are presiding over fraudulent contests.

Simon Barnes also writes a column on wildlife in the Saturday edition of *The Times*. Maybe his views on the animal world are a little better researched than his views on cricket.

As no date had yet been set for the code of conduct hearing, I decided to take a few days away to relax. In a way, I suppose, I went into hiding. I had no desire to confront the media circus on my doorstep. In any case, there was nothing I could tell them until after the hearing, and even then very little could be said as all umpires are bound by the code of conduct, which prohibits public comment on any disciplinary matter. So Amanda and I took a trip to South Yorkshire and stayed in a hotel near Barnsley. I have long been accused of craving the limelight, but nothing could be further from the truth. Had I gone home, there would have been further articles about me and the unresolved matters. I certainly did not want to fuel speculation, so keeping away from the media seemed the best option.

We spent Tuesday and Wednesday driving around, enjoying the scenic countryside. On Tuesday evening I received an email from Malcolm Speed. He stated that he'd been given copies of the emails that I had sent to Doug Cowie concerning my future employment, and the matters I'd raised were 'entirely inappropriate' and that there 'is a clear process that is to be followed ... I will call you tomorrow to advise as to progress.'

I responded immediately with the following:

From: Darrell Hair
Sent: Tuesday, August 22, 2006
To: Malcolm Speed
Subject: Re: Letters
Thanks Malcolm, I have revoked the email. As you say it is inappropriate and we will see how things unfold over the next few days. It would appear that life will go on regardless. I have just sent Doug another message with you and David copied in about events under my control and some others that are not! Cheers, Darrell.

Speed's email indicated that he was not happy. As was his right, he suggested that my original email to Cowie was inappropriate. I agreed and revoked the offer. I was, however, relieved that Speed was at least moving forward with the hearing and had indicated he would call to advise me on progress. That call never came. Not even an email to say he was unable, for whatever reason, to pick up the phone.

I thought little of this until Wednesday evening, when I received a call from Cowie to tell me that Speed and David

Richardson would be in London on Friday for a meeting to discuss the arrangements for the code of conduct hearing. I was to travel down on Friday morning for the briefing. I asked him if Speed had mentioned that he was going to call me about the hearing, but Cowie said nothing had been mentioned to him.

At last something seemed to be happening, and as far as I was concerned the sooner the better. Disciplinary hearings are supposed to take place at the close of play or as soon as possible thereafter. Had Procter 'excused' himself from handling the hearing? Or was he considered incapable? I had been kept in the dark.

Meanwhile, a barrage of abusive and unsavoury comment was unleashed by the Pakistan captain and his officials and administrators. In an article on Cricinfo on 21 August 2006, Shaharyar Khan was at the forefront:

> Shaharyar Khan, Chairman of the Pakistan Cricket Board, has launched a scathing attack on the Australian umpire Darrell Hair, accusing him of intransigence and insensitivity, and has requested to the International Cricket Council that he never officiates in a Test involving Pakistan again.
>
> Speaking to the media at the Marriott Hotel in North West London, Khan described the incidents that led to the forfeiture of yesterday's fourth Test at The Oval as 'a grievous blow to the spirit of cricket', adding that the team was 'deeply indignant' at the manner in which the ball-tampering issue arose.
>
> 'Darrell Hair has trained his guns on the team,' said Khan. 'It is a slur on the players and a slur to Pakistan itself.

The team has had problems with him before, and has lost confidence in him as an umpire. They are deeply offended by his attitude. Ask the Sri Lankans, ask the Indians about the same man.'

There are many things to challenge in Khan's statement. His assumption that the forfeiture of a Test match is a 'grievous blow to the spirit of cricket' is laughable. Who tampered with the cricket ball? Who refused to play on three occasions in 'protest', as Khan himself admitted? It was not Darrell Hair or Billy Doctrove but Inzamam who, as captain of the team, had full responsibility for ensuring play resumed. It is legitimate to question a decision made by an umpire, but it is not acceptable to trash the spirit of the game by refusing to play in protest. Khan's last sentence, 'Ask the Sri Lankans, ask the Indians about the same man', amounts to an accusation of racism. He calls on others to back his claim. Khan's whole statement is itself in breach of the ICC code of conduct, which prohibits comment on matters yet to be heard.

That day (Wednesday) I had noticed the following article of support from Malcolm Speed on the Cricinfo site:

Speed supports Hair and Doctrove
Cricinfo staff

August 23, 2006

Two days after The Oval fiasco Malcolm Speed, the ICC chief executive, has said the conclusion to the fourth Test was 'hugely regrettable', but he insisted it was not the organisation's role to overrule any umpiring decision.

As expected, Speed has supported the umpires Darrell Hair and Billy Doctrove in their 'correct' move to award the game to England when Pakistan did not return to the field after tea following a five-run punishment for ball tampering.

'It is not the role of the ICC to overturn the decisions of on-field umpires, the ultimate arbiters of the game,' Speed said in a statement. 'In this instance the decision to award the match to England was the correct one under the Laws.'

Speed also confirmed the ICC had received a letter from the Pakistan Cricket Board expressing its concerns over the appointment of Hair to matches involving the country. 'This is the first time they have put them in writing, even though they have previously been invited to do so,' Speed said. 'However, it remains the role of the ICC and not our members to appoint umpires to Tests and one-day internationals.'

So although Malcolm Speed had not called me as he had promised, at least he was active in supporting the role of his umpires. I felt heartened by this.

The media barrage continued unabated, however. On Thursday the following appeared on Cricinfo and other websites around the world:

Pakistan's Sports Minister has warned that the ball-tampering row which blew up here last week could split the cricket world's Governing Body. Mian Shiman Haider said there was a 'real possibility' Asia's four Test playing nations would form a faction within the International Cricket Council over the row, which has prompted racism claims against umpire Darrell Hair.

Browsing through Cricinfo on Friday morning I noticed the following item:

Code of Conduct hearing date set today
Speed flies in for emergency talks
Martin Williamson
August 25, 2006

Malcolm Speed, the ICC's chief executive, landed in London late on Thursday night with Pakistan's one-day series against England starting next week still not certain to go ahead.

Speed is scheduled to hold a series of meetings on Friday with relevant parties, including a media conference at 3.30 p.m., although at this stage that is not expected to include any of the Pakistan team.

Series of meetings? Relevant parties? Still the alarm bells did not ring, as I had already been informed of the 11.00 a.m. meeting and the need for my attendance. I had no interest in the brinkmanship of the Pakistan Cricket Board regarding whether they would honour their obligations and play the one-day series. I assumed that the series was going ahead, and to have the ICC chief executive involved in those negotiations was probably essential.

Amanda and I drove to Doncaster to catch the train to London. This pleasant trip passes through the magnificent countryside of Yorkshire and Lincolnshire, taking less than two hours to reach King's Cross, London. I was in high spirits and looking forward to getting the code of conduct hearing out of the way so life could return to normal. Or as normal as an umpire's life could be, anyway! I had no idea that by midday events would have spiralled out of control. It seemed to me that to ensure that Pakistan would continue with the one-day series, Speed and ICC president, Percy Sonn, were about to hang me out to dry. They, along with David Richardson, would release to the world what I regarded as part of a confidential exchange of emails with my manager.

All this was to be delivered at a specially prearranged press conference. Of course I didn't know what was around the corner and so had no opportunity to be fully prepared. I would be given about 90 minutes to seek legal advice. Unsurprisingly, that advice was that the ICC had no right to disclose this confidential information. I was advised to contact Speed immediately to tell him that under no circumstances did I give my permission for him or any other person to do what he was so obviously determined to do.

This is the confidential email I sent to Doug Cowie that the ICC released to the public.

> From: Darrell Hair
> Sent: Tuesday 22nd August 2006
> To: Doug Cowie
> Subject: The way forward
>
> Doug, just to firm up what we discussed earlier this evening. I appreciate the ICC may be put in an untenable position with

regards to future appointments and having taken considerable time and advice, I make this one-off, non-negotiable offer.

I am prepared to retire/stand down/relinquish my position on the elite panel to take effect from 31st August 2006 on the following terms:

1. A one-off payment to compensate the loss of future earnings and retainer payment over the next four years which I believe would have been the best years I have to offer ICC and world umpiring. This payment is to be the sum of US dollars 500,000 — details of which must be kept confidential by both parties. This sum to be paid directly into my account by 31st August 2006.

2. ICC may announce the retirement in any way they wish, but I would prefer a simple 'lifestyle choice' as this was the very reason I moved from Australia to settle in the UK three years ago.

3. No public comment to be made by me as to possible reasons for the decision.

4. This offer in no way precludes me taking legal action and/or instigating libel suits against various sections of the electronic and print media for comments made either previously or in the future.

5. This in no way precludes me taking civil action (and exercising my rights as a resident of the UK in any court of law and by any other avenue open to me) against any organisation or persons currently part of ICC and in particular, members of the Pakistan cricket team and the Pakistan Cricket Board.

I reiterate this is a once only offer and if I fail to obtain your agreement I shall continue to be available under the terms of my current contract till March 31 2008 to fulfil umpiring appointments as and when ICC sees fit in any country at any time in any series or matches involving any affiliated teams.

I would also insist that my ongoing contracted employment continue in its current form until such time as an ICC performance assessment deems me to be no longer able to perform the duties to the high class expected of an international umpire.

Would you please let me know at your earliest convenience of your acceptance or otherwise of this offer.

Sincerely, Darrell Hair.

Doug Cowie's reply to my email was also released to the public.

From: Doug Cowie
To: Darrell Hair
CC: David Richardson
Sent: Tuesday 22nd August 2006
Subject: Re: The way forward.

Darrell, Your offer may have merit and is acknowledged and under discussions with ICC management. Your timeframes seemed impractical at first glance even if agreement were achieved on the suggestion. Will discuss this further tomorrow.
Doug

CHAPTER 4

THE AMBUSH

Press Release: Statement of Mr Darrell Hair
Release of Confidential Correspondence by ICC
Date: 27 August 2006

We act for Mr Darrell Hair;

The purpose of this press release is to address certain misconceptions that appear to have arisen as a consequence of the release of certain confidential correspondence between Mr Hair and ICC.

Mr Hair makes the following statement:

'I refer to the disclosure of email correspondence dispatched by me in confidence to ICC on Tuesday, 22 August 2006 and disclosed to the media on Friday, 25 August 2006. I did not consent to the disclosure of that correspondence. However, since it is now in the public domain I wish to correct certain misapprehensions that have arisen as a result of the partial disclosure of the relevant exchanges.

'The context within which the emails were dispatched is important: I was encouraged to make the offer that was disclosed by ICC on 25 August 2006. During an extended conversation on 21 August 2006 with Mr Doug Cowie, the Umpires' Manager for ICC, I was invited to make a written offer.

'The opening words of my first email to Mr Cowie confirm this: "Just [to] firm up what we discussed earlier this evening." I note that Mr Cowie replied on the same date: "Your offer may have merit and is acknowledged and under discussions with ICC management".

'I would have thought that it was quite apparent from the text of correspondence that I had been in discussions with ICC about the issue prior to sending the email. I was encouraged to make a written offer by ICC. The figure in the email correspondence was in line with those canvassed with the ICC.

'I do not intend at this point to make any further statement until after the conclusion of the scheduled ICC Code of Conduct hearing next month as I do not wish to do anything that would interfere with the integrity of those proceedings. I will make a further statement after that time to correct misconceptions in respect to my conduct currently being aired in the media.

Furthermore, I reserve all my rights.

Darrell Hair

ICC Umpire

Gillhams Solicitors

Leigh Ellis, Partner

The ICC quickly followed up on my statement:

> Following a statement issued today by Darrell Hair, the ICC re-confirmed that Mr Hair did discuss the future of his umpiring career with ICC Umpires and Referees Manager Doug Cowie, before sending an email to Mr Cowie on Tuesday 22 August but at no stage was there any discussion of a pay-off, nor secrecy, nor deadlines, nor misleading the public regarding reasons for retirement.

I have always had a basic belief in human decency. I know that cricket is generally played by people of good nature and principles. The game operates under a set of laws that form the contract between all participants, embodying the spirit in which the game is played and defining the role of the umpires and captains in upholding that spirit. Decisions on the field come and go, and the vast majority of players accept them with good grace and move on. The thought never crossed my mind that because of a decision made in good faith, and in conjunction with and with the full agreement of my umpiring partner, I would be embroiled in what some would report as the greatest controversy that cricket had ever encountered.

Never at any stage in my life had I believed I would need the assistance of lawyers. I had certainly never needed a legal opinion on the conduct of a game of cricket. It was after all, in essence, just a game to be enjoyed, and for the lucky few a means to derive a full-time living. I would very soon come to meet several outstanding people in the legal profession, with all of whom I shared certain beliefs, values and ideas about integrity.

On the evening of Monday, 21 August (what would have been day five of the ill-fated fourth Test), I had had dinner with my wife, Doug Cowie and his wife, Gilly, along with Doug's daughter and her boyfriend, at a local pub not far from where we had been staying in South London. During the meal I sat next to Cowie and we continued a conversation we had begun earlier that day.

I had spent most of the morning writing out the code of conduct report. ICC regulations at the time stipulated that if the person(s) responsible for tampering with the ball could not be identified, the captain was held responsible. Therefore the charges would be laid against Inzamam. Billy Doctrove had told me earlier that he was happy to let me complete the reports and would sign them later, which he did.

In my informal discussion with Doug I had noted that it would be very difficult for him (that is, the ICC) to appoint me to future matches involving Pakistan. Effigies of me were already being burnt publicly in Pakistan. It was a country I had visited five times as an international cricket umpire. I had always been made to feel welcome during these visits and always looked forward to the challenge of umpiring well in match conditions that were outside my comfort zone. However, it was highly unlikely I would now be welcomed back. So I had put forward the idea (with no monetary conditions) that it might be easier for all concerned if I decided to retire from international umpiring and take up a training or development role within the game. The massive overreaction to what had happened made me feel as if the ceiling had fallen in on me, and having been through a similar media and public overreaction in 1995 concerning the throwing call on Sri Lankan bowler Muttiah Muralitharan, I felt it might be time to look at other options. Cowie's response was that if I were to make that decision, I should be well compensated.

I need to try to convey how it feels when the world seems lined up against you. I know the Sky Sports commentators started to blame me from the moment the five penalty runs were awarded. One Sky commentator, David Gower, presented a balanced view, but I understand that as a result he was promptly removed from the microphone. Much later, following the Employment Tribunal case in London in October 2007, Michael Atherton, who witnessed the behaviour of the ICC at the hearing, publicly apologised for the comments he had made about me the previous year.

Others, such as Rameez Raja, Nasser Hussein and Ian Botham, continually dwelt on the fact that Sky Sports cameras had captured no evidence of ball tampering and that I must produce real proof. I can't help but feel that Botham had his own reasons to worry about what he could say about the Pakistani team, given the court case he was involved in with Alan Lamb. That case turned rather sour when it was won by Imran Khan, who described Lamb as a racist. Did all this mean that if Sky Sports, or any other broadcaster for that matter, does not capture any evidence of ball tampering, then it did not happen? The people running television sports coverage seem often to believe, mistakenly, that nothing gets past them.

Bob Woolmer was later to give evidence that the Pakistan team had 'sat in stunned silence' in the dressing room watching Rameez Raja, Nasser Hussein and Ian Botham discussing Darrell Hair's actions on television. This was the starting point of the public perception that I was the only umpire involved, which was to become part of media discussion and other comment for some time to come. The umpires at the time were the only ones, apart from the Pakistani players responsible, who were aware of the accelerated deterioration of the ball. Commentators should have let the normal procedures for dealing with these matters take their course. But they did not. Instead they embarked on wild speculation.

Taking all this initial negative comment from Sky Sports into account, I believe the rest of the world jumped on the bandwagon and fed off their misinterpretation of both what happened initially and what was required to happen during the ensuing hours. I had no appetite for becoming the scapegoat again!

Returning to that fateful Monday night, my discussion with Cowie then moved on to a general review of my career — how much I had enjoyed it so far, how I had met the challenges head on and done my job to the best of my ability under various, often difficult, circumstances. We both agreed that I was fully capable of umpiring at international level for at least five more years, but I remarked that I preferred the idea of finishing my career before I was told to go.

Little did I know that over the following 48 hours Malcolm Speed and David Richardson would be planning to execute a course of events which would publicly cut me adrift. Meanwhile, Cowie would be ducking for cover and then deny that he supported the career change idea I had put to him. 'You should be well compensated' were words that would ring in my ears for years to come.

At the end of our talk, Cowie had suggested I go off and put together 'a proposal for your structured exit'. So that is what I did. I prepared an offer, although with hindsight I am the first to admit it was a poorly constructed offer. I would have been much better off seeking legal advice first but, again, I had not imagined the need for such caution over what seemed to be a simple, private exchange that was fully supported by my manager. When Cowie responded by saying, 'Your offer has merit and has been passed on to management', I felt that a decent outcome would ensue.

Evidently Speed and Richardson decided to secure legal advice on whether the offer should be communicated to the Pakistan team management and released publicly at a media conference on Friday afternoon. But were other events unfolding behind the scenes? Apparently so, according to the sequence of events recorded on the Pakistan Cricket Board website:

> August 22
> Inzamam warns cricket chiefs: Clear me of ball tampering or the tour of England is finished.
>
> August 23
> Speed on his way to London to help broker a deal that could keep Pakistan's tour of England on track.

The warning signs were there but I still had some faith in the system.

On Friday, 25 August 2006, at 11.00 a.m. I walked into the Royal Gardens Hotel for what I had been led to believe was a simple meeting to discuss the upcoming code of conduct hearing. Present were ICC chief executive Malcolm Speed, cricket manager David Richardson, and umpires' manager Doug Cowie. A lawyer by the name of Richard Verow was also in attendance. Verow had previously done work for the ICC on legal matters.

This particular meeting would propel me back into the media storm, but this time I was burned at the stake by my own employers. The results of actions taken by Speed on that day have always been a contentious issue with me, as I will now explain.

Greeted by Speed, Richardson and Cowie, I noted the fact that none of them made eye contact with me. I sensed their mood to be unfriendly. I felt uncomfortable. Cowie in particular looked flushed and edgy. He had obviously been briefed by Speed on what was about to happen. Speed asked me how I was feeling and I recall making a couple of remarks: 'It hasn't been the greatest week of my life' and 'I am rather tired but nothing that a good night's sleep wouldn't fix!' Speed said, 'Your week is not about to get any better.'

I was stunned by his remark. I was expecting management to show me some support, given the litany of insults that had been printed in the media, insults that had gone completely unanswered by the ICC. I sensed I was about to be ambushed and I felt helpless to prevent it.

Speed immediately raised the matter of the email, which Cowie had passed on to him and Richardson, and detailed how he intended to deal with it. He said that he had obtained legal advice and that he intended to release the emails to the management of the Pakistan Cricket Board. He further advised that he had arranged a media conference for 3.30 p.m. at which he intended to release the emails publicly, also on legal advice.

I felt completely numb. I had not been given any agenda for this meeting and had no idea what it was to be about. I had not brought legal representation because I had not even remotely anticipated needing it. To be called to this meeting in order to have a damning legal opinion thrust at me, having had no opportunity to seek advice myself, seemed to me to be very unfair. I felt abandoned.

The meeting concluded at around midday when Speed said, 'I have to go now as I am meeting the PCB lawyers to give them this information.' He then warned me, unnecessarily, that this would be a difficult time for me and expressed the hope that I would be able to continue umpiring, but he was unable to give me an assurance that this would happen. Speed would later say at the media conference that he hadn't ruled out laying charges against me under the ICC Umpires Code of Conduct.

I asked him once again why he was set on destroying my credibility and career and he responded by saying that he intended to act on the legal advice he had received. What about my right to legal advice? Speed said that Richard Verow would be able to provide legal advice if I wished to speak with him in private. Yes, well, I would be only too happy to accept legal advice from a person I knew was providing legal advice to the ICC, wouldn't I?

Leaving the meeting extremely upset, I tried to call a solicitor I had spoken to earlier about the public comments being made about me in the media. I finally reached him just after 3.00 p.m. His advice was that the ICC had no right to treat me in this manner, and that to release confidential information to the media against my wishes was a clear breach of the duty of trust and confidence that exists between employee and employer.

At 3.22 p.m. I emailed Cowie:

> Dear Doug, I have left a message on your voicemail at 3.18 pm today relaying the following information. Having just taken advice, I am required to tell you that ALL correspondence sent to you regarding the matter is confidential information and cannot be disclosed without my permission. It is not for you or any other person to disclose the information.
>
> I do not understand the basis on which you say you are either entitled or duty bound to disclose this information to the public or any other person, if in fact you are entitled to do so at all.
>
> Please explain to me in writing the reason and basis for doing so.

I asked Cowie to convey this email directly to Speed and Richardson. He rang me to say he would do so. I left a message on Speed's message bank explaining the advice I had received. I then left a similar message for Richardson. Futile efforts I know, but what else could I do? Neither Speed nor Richardson ever responded, either in writing or by any other means. I had hoped to be able to convince Speed to cancel the release of the documents until such time as I could speak with him again, this time accompanied by my own lawyer.

I was conducting all this business in the GNER lounge at Kings Cross Station. Although Amanda and I had tickets for the 4 o'clock train, I was willing to remain in London if it meant I could work through the matter with my employer. Shortly before the media conference began, Doug Cowie sent me a text saying

'Catch the train'. The 3.45 p.m. media conference was broadcast live by BBC News 24, which was the channel showing in the lounge at Kings Cross. I watched the first few minutes, then we boarded the train for Doncaster.

The release of the confidential emails was obviously set in stone. An email was sent out by the Dubai-based ICC in-house lawyer Ms Urvasi Naidoo at 3.30 p.m., before the press conference had begun, to all Elite Umpires and Referees, with advice on what had transpired. I received a copy of this email on my laptop while I was still at Kings Cross. The timing of this email further proved that Speed had set this up in advance.

Naidoo's email began by suggesting the press conference was called to discuss 'issues surrounding the Test match at The Oval'. This was not accurate – it had actually been advertised as providing information on the one-day internationals between England and Pakistan, but Speed appeared to be using the occasion purely to confirm his decision to take action against me. The email went on to say that the 'reason for the meeting with the media is that Malcolm and I have been provided with correspondence between Darrell Hair and Doug Cowie which has placed us and the ICC in a difficult position in relation to the impending Code of Conduct hearings filed against the Pakistan captain, Inzamam-ul-Haq.'

The email also stated that, after consulting three senior lawyers, 'the advice that we have received is that as a matter of proper legal process and fairness to the Pakistan team, ICC has no alternative other than to make the documents available to the PCB ... both Malcolm and I [Naidoo] agree with this advice.'

I had been given no opportunity to obtain any legal advice. I recently asked Speed to explain why he had never considered my rights to legal representation or advised me in advance that I might need it. He did not respond.

I have often wondered whether Speed and Percy Sonn, the then ICC president, would have been quite so confident of themselves if I had been present. If I had been legally represented, the media and public in general might have heard a conflicting legal opinion and been better informed about what was taking place. Instead, what occurred felt like a public execution. I had met Sonn once or twice and he appeared to be a fair and reasonable man, but listening to him at that press conference and again on the tapes of an ICC board meeting that discussed my banishment due to their 'loss of confidence' in me, I can only conclude I was wrong about him.

I was not alone in petitioning my ICC employers to make some public response to the constant attacks on me in the media during the weeks leading up to the much-delayed code of conduct hearing. Fellow umpire Simon Taufel also wrote to David Richardson to ask what action the ICC was taking. Finally, on 4 September, Speed released a public statement in which he issued a warning to the PCB. It read in part:

> Over the course of the last two weeks there has been a stream of unnecessary and inappropriate public comment from the PCB, much of which could be seen as prejudicial to the pending Code of Conduct hearing. The acute international diplomatic and political sensitivity of this issue has persuaded me not to lay a charge.

I was disappointed by this weak response. It appeared to me that the ICC was afraid to take action for fear of criticism, even though Speed had noted that the comments could be seen as 'prejudicial to the pending Code of Conduct hearing'.

Following the release of the confidential emails I began to seek out legal opinions. I received several views that conflicted with those given to the ICC. Many months later, when I asked Speed to reveal the names of the three legal experts from whom he obtained his advice, it became apparent to me that none of these lawyers were truly independent of the ICC and therefore not completely objective. The first advice was from David Stewart, a lawyer from Olswang, the company acting for the ICC in the ball-tampering case. The second was from David Pannick QC, a lawyer who would later work as the ICC's advisor in the code of conduct hearing and ball-tampering case.

Last but not least was Brian Ward, an Australian lawyer. Ward had conducted hearings about player behaviour involving Glenn McGrath and another famous walk-off threat in world cricket, the Sri Lankan team in Adelaide in 1999. That case involved umpire Ross Emerson, yet Ward told Speed that I was the umpire concerned and that I had a habit of being a bit of a troublemaker.

Memory can be unreliable, but Brian Ward got it wrong on this occasion. I was at Randwick racecourse in Sydney on the day that Ross Emerson called Muralitharan for throwing in Adelaide, prompting a threat to boycott the one-day international between England and Sri Lanka. I have never met Ward and have never been in a code of conduct hearing in which he adjudicated.

★

After the press conference the abuse from the Pakistan captain ceased for a short period. All focus was now on the one-day series, which Pakistan said they were happy to compete in.

After a brief lull in hostilities the Pakistan Cricket Board resumed the release of improper statements. These followed the familiar path, with some amazingly racist comments made about the block voting of the four Asian Test-playing countries on the ICC board. The following is an excerpt from an article by Mihir Bose in *The Daily Telegraph* on 26 August:

> An hour and a half before Malcolm Speed, chief executive of the International Cricket Council, released the letter Darrell Hair had written asking for a payment of £392,000 in exchange for resigning as an umpire, Speed, Richard Verow, the ICC in-house lawyer, and David Richardson, head of the cricket department, met the lawyers for the Pakistan Cricket Board at the Royal Garden Hotel in Kensington.
>
> The Pakistani lawyers, headed by Mark Gay and Wasim Khohkar, thought they had come to be told the one-day series was going ahead. Instead, Speed handed them a copy of Hair's letter and told them that the advice they [the ICC] had received from David Pannick, the QC, was that if they had kept the letter secret and it had later emerged that it had existed then this would have jeopardised the hearings against Inzamam-ul-Haq.
>
> The Pakistani legal team then withdrew to consider the letter. The Pakistan Cricket Board were consulted and it was agreed that the letter should be made public, resulting

in unprecedented transparency on the part of an organisation not known for always revealing their dirty linen. But while legal considerations played a part, releasing the letter was also part of a careful ICC strategy to assert their authority and prove to the world that they are in charge of running world cricket.

That 'strategy' seemed to include providing my head on a plate to the Pakistan Cricket Board. It also compromised the integrity of the upcoming code of conduct hearing. The events of Friday, 25 August appeared to be a concerted effort by Speed to stamp his authority on the game. In doing so, he provided the ICC board with ammunition to further damage my integrity and career.

The article went on:

> The past week has seen the prestige of ICC as the game's governing body take a terrible knock, with commentators freely talking of the powerless ICC. This was demonstrated last Sunday afternoon when, with Pakistan and England ready to resume the fourth Test at the Oval and provide spectators with a final day's play, Speed, despite several telephone conversations, was unable to persuade Hair to rescind his decision that the Test was over. Pakistan's failure to take the field after tea meant they had forfeited the Test.

This paragraph raises two issues. First, Speed made only one phone call to me (and importantly none to my fellow umpire,

Billy Doctrove). Whether Speed actually spoke to Mihir Bose I do not know. Second, the article talks about the prestige of the ICC as the game's governing body taking a knock. Would not the integrity of the game be better preserved if they took strong and swift action to ensure that a match conformed to the Laws of Cricket, as judged by the umpires? The article continues:

> Since then [the forfeiture of the Test] the ICC have wrestled with how they can reassert their authority and Hair's letter — despite the fact that he withdrew it two days later — provided them with a splendid opportunity. Speed could not have been more dismissive of Hair, calling him 'silly' and 'misguided', unprecedented behaviour by the chief executive of an organisation towards one of their own most high-profile employees.
>
> I am told by well-placed ICC sources that though Speed has let Hair hang out to dry in a quite remarkable fashion, this does not mean that the ICC are backing away from holding Inzamam accountable for his actions. If anything they want the hearing to be held but only after the one-day series is over, probably late in September when time has taken some of the heat out of last Sunday's fiasco.

The article went on to describe legal preparations and the use of Urdu interpreters to ensure the views of the Pakistan team were properly recorded. As it turned out, the hearing arrived at a perfect outcome for Inzamam by finding him guilty of refusing to play but clearing his team of ball tampering.

THE AMBUSH | 107

★

I had plenty of time to think about the hearing, which had now been postponed to 27 September, more than five weeks after the event. The daily newspapers maintained their barrage of negative comment. Despite my own determination to ignore uninformed or unsubstantiated comments, it eventually took its toll.

Many within the Pakistan Cricket Board had plenty to say. Shaharyar Khan was at work very early, chipping away in this *Guardian* story on 22 August, just two days after the forfeiture:

> Khan refused to categorically rule out an early abandonment of the tour of England, scheduled to finish on September 10, when he said Pakistan had asked the game's ruling body, the International Cricket Council, to remove Hair from any matches involving his side. He also confirmed one of the game's worst-kept secrets: that the Pakistan team and the Australian umpire cannot stand the sight of each other.

Here was another bit of misinformation planted by Khan and the PCB. The 'worst-kept secret' was actually that the Pakistan team did not like strong umpires who made their decisions without feeling a need to placate or favour either side. It would, of course, be racist to treat a team differently because of their race, and that seems to be what was being demanded by the article. I did not at any time say or imply that I couldn't stand the sight of the Pakistan team. In fact, I had said on many occasions to my fellow umpires and in interviews with the media that I enjoyed umpiring Pakistan teams, especially in Pakistan, because I found it tested my skills as an international cricket umpire. This was just another attempt to undermine my integrity, yet I was powerless to respond. I had had a reasonable expectation that Speed would jump on the Pakistan Cricket Board, and Khan in particular, but he chose not to.

'We have had problems with Mr. Hair before,' Khan said in the same interview. 'The team has lost confidence in him and they feel deeply offended by his attitude towards the Pakistani team. Therefore we feel that his presence officiating in any match in which Pakistan is playing is not desirable.' This from the highest ranking cricket official in Pakistan in defiance of the ICC's Code of Conduct for Players and Officials, which prohibits any comment either prior to, during or following any code of conduct hearing.

Speed and his team in Dubai ignored these attacks on one of their own umpires. Given free rein, Khan blustered that he was incensed that the reputation of his team had been sullied, especially as no evidence had been presented. Quite correctly, actually, as no evidence or comment should be put into the public domain before an official hearing. The crucial factor was the decision by both umpires that the ball had been tampered with. This was not an 'allegation', as has so often been suggested, but a decision made by the relevant officials on the field.

Khan referred to having read an 'article somewhere' earlier in the tour that applauded the staging of a cricket match between Muslim and Christian countries in these times of political tension. Cricket could create a bridge of peace between nations, declaimed Khan. 'Why destroy this over a technicality?'

Flouting the rules is not a 'technicality', nor is refusing to play a cricket match because you don't like an umpires' decision. The fabric of the game is worthless if Khan's views are acceptable to fair-minded cricket lovers. This was stirring but absolutely ridiculous stuff from Khan, who had once been a diplomat and Pakistan's foreign secretary. He was clearly more upset by the charge of cheating than that of bringing the game into disrepute. He demanded that an independent inquiry be held by the ICC into the whole issue.

At least Khan and I agree on that — boy, I would have really liked any type of independent inquiry! An inquiry without Speed's involvement would have been great. An inquiry that allowed me and Billy Doctrove to defend the Laws of Cricket and their correct implementation without pressure being exerted by the likes of David Morgan of the ECB, and one that didn't allow commercial interests to outweigh the correct conduct of an international cricket match. Yes, that would have been an inquiry I would have welcomed with open arms. Had I known fully what was going on within the ICC board of directors and how they would affect my future, I might have settled for any independent inquiry.

CHAPTER 5

THE CODE OF CONDUCT HEARING

ICC MEDIA RELEASE
FOR IMMEDIATE RELEASE
London, 28 September 2006
Decision on ICC Code of Conduct hearing involving Inzamam-ul-Haq
Below are details of the verdict and the reasons for the penalty imposed, as announced by the adjudicator, ICC Chief Match Referee Ranjan Madugalle to the ICC Code of Conduct hearing at The Brit Oval, London, on Thursday 28 September.

ICC DISCIPLINARY PROCEEDINGS
THE OVAL

THE CODE OF CONDUCT HEARING | 111

BETWEEN:

ICC

v

Inzamam-ul-Haq

I will give my decision now and summarise my reasons. More detailed reasons will be given in writing later.

Ball-tampering

On the first charge of ball-tampering under paragraph 2.9 of the Code, I find Mr ul-Haq not guilty.

Having regard to the seriousness of the allegation of ball-tampering (it is an allegation of cheating), I am not satisfied on the balance of probabilities that there is sufficiently cogent evidence that the fielding team had taken action likely to interfere with the condition of the ball.

In my judgment, the marks are as consistent with normal wear and tear of a match ball after 56 overs as they are with deliberate human intervention.

Mr Saini (acting on behalf of the ICC) submitted that I should not reject the consistent views of the experienced ICC witnesses. I have considered their evidence, honestly and fairly given, very carefully. But my duty is to form and give my own judgment.

Bringing the game into disrepute

On the second charge of bringing the game into disrepute by refusing to play, I find Mr ul-Haq guilty in that on two occasions he led a protest against the Umpires by failing to come onto the field of play at the relevant time.

I take the view, subject of course to any further submissions Mr Gay may wish to make, that this is a Level 3 charge, leading to a penalty of a ban of between 2 and 4 Test Matches or between 4 and 8 one-day international Matches.

I will now hear Mr Gay (acting on behalf of the Pakistan Cricket Board) on any submissions you wish to make on the appropriate penalty.

Ranjan Madugalle (The Adjudicator, and Chief ICC Referee)
assisted by
David Pannick QC
(Counsel to the Adjudicator)
28 September 2006

What happened to ICC referee Mike Procter? When and why did he relinquish his duties in this matter? Who issued the orders and why? On the notification sheet, Procter indicated the hearing would be held 30 minutes after the close of play, which I admit might have been a little difficult for him given that he more than likely had not told the Pakistan team that they had forfeited the match. However, the hearing was delayed for a considerable time. Why weren't the umpires privy to the reasons for the delay?

Madugalle's judgement used the term 'allegation of cheating'. This term had already been used by David Morgan, chairman of the ECB, in one of his statements. Madugalle, of all people, should have known better: it is not an allegation, it is a judgement made by the umpires under unfair play — and there is a difference.

A former Sri Lankan captain, Madugalle had become an ICC referee in the late 1990s and was later appointed ICC chief referee by Speed. In my previous dealings with Madugalle, he generally appeared committed to upholding the role of umpires and ensuring the code of conduct was implemented whenever necessary. There were a couple of times when I disagreed with his urge to press charges against players, most notably during the Test between Australia and South Africa in Melbourne in 2002. After being given 'run-out' by me, Steve Waugh asked if I was sure without referring the decision to the third umpire. I responded by saying I was certain and that the referral was not necessary. This type of conversation takes place regularly between umpires and players and I saw nothing untoward in Waugh's comment.

Not so Ranjan Madugalle. He had heard the exchange via the stump microphone and considered it a clear case of dissent. I disagreed, explaining that Waugh had been diving to make his crease and was probably unsure how close he came. Also, Waugh had 90 runs at the time and could see a century not far off. Any player worth his salt would first be disappointed and second look for a way to save himself in those circumstances.

When I arrived back in the dressing room at the close of play, Madugalle said the incident was definitely reportable but it would look better if the umpires reported it; otherwise he would have to do so, and that might not reflect well on the perceived strength of the umpires. The report form was placed strategically in front of me. He obviously wanted me to fill it out without delay so he could get into the action. Reluctantly, I completed the form and a hearing followed, with Waugh being reprimanded and fined for showing dissent at an umpire's decision.

I believe the code of conduct report against Waugh was not correct because even if there had been any hint of dissent, it was not broadcast to the public. The conversation was heard only by the referee and third umpire through the stump microphones. It seemed to me that Madugalle was merely trying to flex his muscles.

It now seems absolutely absurd to me that the report, made at the insistence of Madugalle, was also heard and judged by Madugalle. I say absurd because in his judgement on the whole issue of ball tampering and refusal to play by Pakistan, Madugalle would insist that player management and effective communication by umpires is an important aspect of umpiring at international level. Yet on that earlier occasion Madugalle had barged into an issue between player and umpire that had been discussed and settled on the field.

I was weak to have bowed to Madugalle's wishes in 2002. It was the last time I ever took advice from ICC referees, who conservatively cost the ICC $2,000,000 a year but who contribute little to the running of the game other than dishing out a few fines and very rare suspensions. Their major purpose seems to be to monitor the captains at the toss before each match and to maintain minimum over rates.

The almost insufferable delay in scheduling the code of conduct hearing was difficult for me to accept in the first place and then to prepare for in the face of my own employer's scapegoating of me. This five-week interval allowed many people to attack my character and my standing and reputation as an umpire. It also meant that the ICC effectively lost control of their own hearing.

Where was the ball, and who had seen it or handled it since it was handed over to Mike Procter? Then I received a letter from John Beveridge, a retired QC from London who had been following the events through the media. He asked if I would like some help. Would I like some help? Yes please! Certainly none was forthcoming from the ICC. On the phone Mr Beveridge asked if I would be prepared to visit him in London to formulate some responses to the attacks.

First, a letter to David Richardson was drafted in which I asked for his agreement that I be separately legally represented. This was justified, Mr Beveridge advised, in light of the extraordinary manner in which Speed had made public my private emails. I was also vulnerable to personal attacks during the hearing owing to the uninformed and irresponsible comments made by the Pakistan Cricket Board's staff and officials. This reason alone indicated the need for the presence of an experienced legal adviser to ensure that my interests were protected. In addition, I asked Richardson to advise me specifically why the ICC had acted outside its own parameters in removing from the case the ICC referee at the match in question, Mike Procter, and appointing Madugalle in his stead.

Richardson responded that Mike Procter was considered a witness at the hearing so it was deemed inappropriate that he should also adjudicate. This decision seemed ridiculous in light of the Steve Waugh hearing in Melbourne in 2002 in which Ranjan Madugalle was not only the referee and the instigator and driving force behind the report that I very reluctantly signed, but was also a key 'witness' (via the stump microphone) as well as judge, jury and executioner. Richardson insisted that in the current case procedural fairness was foremost in their minds.

Richardson concluded by saying that the ICC lawyers would be looking after my interests during the hearing. That they failed to do so was proved when a crucial piece of evidence was not presented at the hearing: the television coverage of the period between Alistair Cook's dismissal and the intervention by the umpires when the ball was deemed to have been tampered with. If I had expected the ICC to look after my interests or those of the game in general, I would be disappointed, but my opinion of the organisation's management was already at a particularly low ebb. I had completely lost confidence in them.

I next saw the tampered ball two days before the hearing. It was sealed in a plastic bag and did not look like the same ball that Billy Doctrove and I inspected on the afternoon of 20 August. The ball had taken on a darker colour and the scratch marks, which had been quite clear on 20 August, were, on 25 September, a full five weeks after the event, marginally less obvious. Whatever journey that ball had taken had evidently affected the marks.

When an umpire makes a decision on the field, his standard of proof for the decision is based on what he sees and hears (contributing perhaps 99 per cent of the proof needed) and his intuition or gut feeling (perhaps 1 per cent). The Laws of Cricket list certain actions the fielding side may take in the way they deal with the condition of the ball. In essence, they may polish, dry or remove mud from the ball, the last being done under the supervision of the umpire. The laws then clearly describe what is prohibited — rubbing the ball on the ground, interfering with any of the seams or the surface, using any implement or taking any other action whatsoever that is likely to alter the condition of the ball. If the umpires, during their regular inspections of the ball, decide that a fielder has changed the condition of the ball, they must take action as set out in Law 42.3(d). It is not necessary that they actually see the ball tampering taking place. The umpires, therefore, are never 'alleging' anything — they are basing their decision on what they see before them, which in this case was a severe deterioration in the condition of the cricket ball that could not have happened during the normal course and conduct of the match. No opinions from people outside the game in question are even remotely relevant.

Madugalle placed much weight on his own judgement of the tampered ball. Of course he had the right to form his own opinion, but he had no authority to overrule the judgement of the umpires. By handing down a not guilty verdict for ball tampering, he firmly established the ICC's power to overrule any umpires' decision in the future.

To compare the decisions made by Doctrove and myself with procedures in criminal law where the standard of proof is 'beyond reasonable doubt' is laughable. Umpires are not foolproof, but they make their decisions in good faith.

There is no burden on the umpires to suspect unfair play, but the laws direct that frequent and irregular inspections of the ball be made. On this occasion, within a very short time (15 minutes) the condition of the ball had changed markedly, indicating that it had been tampered with.

The Pakistan players, to a man, provided sworn statements that they did not alter the condition of the ball. This was to be expected. After the intervention of Shaharyar Khan in support of a 'protest', I don't think any Pakistan player would have been willing to stand up and admit his involvement. However, if the evidence (the ball itself) shows that its condition has indeed been altered, the case must be upheld even though no individual can be identified as the culprit.

In his judgement, Madugalle wrote:

> I am not satisfied on the balance of probabilities that there is sufficiently cogent evidence that the fielding team had taken action likely to interfere with the condition of the ball.

But Madugalle was incorrect for the following reasons:

He was not one of the umpires making frequent but irregular inspections of the ball during the match.

He was not present when the umpires consulted and decided that the condition of the ball had changed significantly between the 52nd and 55th overs.

The one and only thing Madugalle had to determine was what action to take against the captain and team concerned.

As ICC representative, Madugalle had misinterpreted his duties. Neither the ICC code of conduct nor the Laws of Cricket permitted him to arrive at his own determination of events. In my view, his sole duty was to decide whether action should be taken by the ICC and, if so, what penalty should be imposed. Perhaps he was also swayed by the 'evidence' of expert witnesses Geoff Boycott, John Hampshire and Simon Hughes, despite an argument put forward during the hearing to disregard it.

Whatever Madugalle's motives were, one clear conclusion can be drawn: in making the judgement he did, he broke the long-held principle that the umpires' decisions on the field should be final.

THE CODE OF CONDUCT HEARING | 119

★

Among the expert witnesses enlisted by the Pakistan Cricket Board was John Hampshire, a former Test cricketer and Test umpire, a coach of Zimbabwe with a lifetime in cricket. What could his motives have been in offering an opinion on a ball he had not seen prior to the hearing? Perhaps he was approached by Boycott, a fellow Yorkshireman. Hampshire played eight Tests and three one-day internationals, and went on to umpire 21 Tests and 20 one-day internationals, and to pursue a career as a very well-respected umpire in English county cricket. I first met Hampshire in 1994 when the first ICC Panel of Umpires was formed. I had spent time with him in 1996 at an ICC training course in Malaysia and met him socially on many subsequent occasions. I felt we had a good working relationship and I took the time to talk to him about recent ICC playing conditions when he was coaching Zimbabwe on a tour of Australia in the late 1990s.

Whatever his motives for participating in the hearing, he did the game no favours. All he could manage to say in summary was that the ball in his opinion 'could have' been tampered with but in any case he would have done things differently. Hampshire told the hearing he had been asked to act as an independent expert by Inzamam-ul-Haq and the Pakistan Cricket Board and that he had been specifically instructed:

1. to review the television footage of play and examine whether he could find any evidence of ball tampering taking place between overs 52 and 56 of the England inning; and

2. to examine the ball used and to give his views as to whether the condition had been changed unfairly and whether the decision reached by the umpires was reasonable and in accordance with the spirit of cricket.

I have to comment on a few things about Hampshire's evidence. It was quite clear initially that no supporting television evidence was available, a point made by the umpires on the report form, which stated 'Video evidence *will not* be used'. We could have saved Hampshire the trouble of trying to locate something that the broadcaster's cameras had not picked up. Should broadcasters assign a dedicated camera to follow all fielders who come into contact with the ball over the full course of each Test match? I think not, and just because a camera does not capture a particular event, that does not prove it didn't happen, does it?

Hampshire's next task was to examine the ball and decide whether its condition had been changed unfairly such that Law 42.3 could or should be invoked. One minor detail: he could not make that judgement because he hadn't seen the ball at other stages during the match. How would he know how little or how much the condition of the ball had deteriorated in the space of such a short time? The truth is, he couldn't.

Hampshire was then to assess whether the decisions the umpires reached were reasonable and in accordance with the spirit of cricket. Well at least he did acknowledge that there were two of us, something that most others completely ignored. But hang on a minute! Hampshire talked about the spirit of cricket but not the laws. Yet surely it is incumbent on all players to contribute to the spirit of the game in the first instance by playing according to the laws? Hampshire admitted that the Pakistan team 'protested', but he failed to point out that by making such a protest they put themselves in danger of forfeiting the match. Later in his evidence, Hampshire argued that the Laws of Cricket tell the umpire *when* he should act but the spirit of the game informs an umpire *whether* he should act. What gobbledygook is that! As an expert witness Hampshire completely torpedoed his own credibility: initially he claimed to be flabbergasted that the ball, as he had seen it, could be the subject of such controversy, but then he concluded by saying that he noticed a number of scratch marks on one side and that 'it is more than possible that the marks were man-made'.

Hampshire then offered his own solution, had he been confronted with a similar situation. 'I would have issued a caution to the fielding captain and hopefully the attempt to change the condition of the ball would cease.' If he had noticed any further ball tampering, his approach to the fielding captain would have become 'more urgent', whatever that means. An interesting contribution from someone with a rich cricketing background! Hampshire is actually saying that yes, it looks very much like one team is cheating but we will ignore it and hope it goes away. In the meantime, wickets may fall because of the unfair play that had already taken place, putting the batting side at a distinct disadvantage, but all is well because he has avoided a confrontation.

An umpire cannot pick and choose which of the laws he enforces on any given day. Hampshire's credibility as an umpire vanished at that point.

Next came Simon Hughes, summoned as an expert witness in a ball-tampering hearing! Hughes' record in English county cricket playing for Middlesex and Durham between 1980 and 1993 netted him 466 wickets, which over 14 seasons amounted to an average of approximately 30 wickets per season. He took five wickets in an innings ten times in a career of 205 matches. So Hughes shone in his performance with the ball in less than 2 per cent of the matches he played; he never threatened to tear a batting line-up apart but he was a hardworking toiler.

Hughes trotted out much the same lines as Hampshire had before him. His remit, too, was to review the footage of that critical section of play and to examine the ball to determine if it had been tampered with. He went on at length with his analysis of where each ball pitched and what shot was played by the batsmen, all of which were actually available on video.

Hughes stated in his evidence that three balls bowled by Kaneria, the Pakistan leg spinner, had pitched in 'the rough' and that any damage to the ball had been caused by those three deliveries. Did Hughes actually know what part of the ball had made contact with the pitch from each of the said deliveries? Of course not! He was, it seems, trying to show what a great analyst of the game he was. But he saved the best for last, when he reported on his inspection of the ball:

> … there are small striations on the rough side of the ball. These appear in the form of superficial lines which are slightly curved. These marks could have been caused by human interference and I find the concentration of such marks to be suspicious. However, in my opinion, the damage could have been caused by the ball repeatedly pitching in the rough.

Hughes said in closing that if he had been umpiring the match and saw a ball that had been tampered with, he would simply have a quiet word to the captain of the Pakistan team to the effect that 'he would not expect the marks to get any worse'. The ICC lawyers could have silenced Hughes and his diatribe in a flash. Instead, he was given free rein.

The day after the match was forfeited by Pakistan, Hughes wrote a double-page article with colour photos in one of the broadsheets, demonstrating how to tamper with the ball and how it could give the bowlers an advantage after the ball stops swinging normally.

Next up was Geoffrey Boycott. He began his evidence by declaring that the ball was a 'good' ball and he would be happy to play with it. He laughed off suggestions that the umpires should not permit one team to cheat and intimated that because Doctrove and Hair had never played first-class cricket, they would not understand how to make these judgements.

Again, the ICC's lawyers failed to ask meaningful questions of Boycott under cross-examination — for example, on how much umpiring experience he had and whether he had seen the ball on the day of the match. Boycott simply refused to answer the questions he was asked by the ICC lawyers, despite his duty to do so. For this he should have been discredited and dismissed, but Madugalle seemed to be enjoying the performance. He continually smiled and chuckled during Boycott's evidence. David Pannick QC, assisting Madugalle, sat on his hands and made no effort to advise Madugalle to instruct Boycott to answer the questions as put to him. Madugalle showed amusement as Boycott spoke about umpires having a responsibility to warn players about ball tampering before taking any action.

How Madugalle could take the evidence presented by Hughes and Boycott without a giant bucket of salt is beyond my comprehension, yet he obviously preferred these performances, plus the strange and mischievous contribution from John Hampshire, to the evidence of the two on-field umpires, third umpire Peter Hartley, fourth umpire Trevor Jesty, ICC referee Mike Procter and umpires' manager Doug Cowie.

Bob Woolmer's statement and evidence were also interesting. He talked for some time about the unpredictable habits of reverse swing, which in fact had no bearing on whether a ball is deemed by the umpires to have been tampered with. There is nothing in the Laws of Cricket that instructs umpires to wait until the ball starts to swing around prodigiously. Woolmer said he saw 'Hair and Doctrove examining the ball together'. He also provided further information to prove Inzamam knew why the ball had been changed and the ramifications of the matter. In his written statement Woolmer recorded that he learned from Inzamam during the tea break that 'Mr Hair had told him [Inzamam] the condition of the ball had been changed, contrary to the Laws of Cricket.'

Woolmer also stated that he later saw Inzamam approach Billy Doctrove to 'ask him if what was happening was correct'. Well, how about that? Finally, there was another umpire involved, and both Woolmer and Inzamam confirmed that both umpires had made the decision *jointly*. Inzamam was later to vehemently deny this version of events in his own statement, and somehow the lawyers employed by the ICC failed to focus on this small but important part of the evidence. That and the fact that the ICC team appeared powerless to glean anything of value from Boycott, or to discredit Hampshire and Hughes, indicated to me that they were not trying very hard.

Woolmer's statement verged on comedy when he said that as he knew trouble was brewing, he asked the Pakistan team liaison officer to take him back to his hotel to get a copy of *Wisden*, which has the Laws of Cricket in the back. He also wanted his copy of the relevant ICC regulations. However, whatever information Woolmer gleaned from the books did not appear to be referred to in his evidence.

Woolmer said he agreed with the Pakistan team that they had to make a protest. This, it was suggested, could take one of three forms: walk away from The Oval and forfeit the match; register a small protest by delaying their return to the field for a few minutes, announcing their reason for doing so to the media; or return to the field and sit down when the umpires called play. The short delay in returning to the field was the preferred option, but as we all know, it backfired. Even so, this conversation between coach and captain again proves that the Pakistan team knew all along that they were in danger of forfeiting the match. These facts, once again, were never really rammed home by counsel acting for the ICC.

Inzamam's statement was inconsistent with what occurred on the field and was nowhere near factual. He said that when he asked me why the ball was being changed, I replied, 'I will tell you in a minute.' He also said that I first refused to let him see the ball in question and then held it up in one hand for a moment. This is untrue, as the ball had already been handed to fourth umpire Trevor Jesty, who took it from his pocket to allow Inzamam to hold and view it. Inzamam also claimed in his statement that I had told him he could view the ball in the match referee's room afterwards and that the umpires could change a ball whenever they wished to, which was untrue. He conveniently omitted to mention in his statement that his team had discussed taking to the field of play to stage a sit-down protest when the umpires called play.

Near the end of his written statement, Woolmer finally gave an insight into the real reason Pakistan forfeited the match. He recorded that following the visit by me and Doctrove to their dressing room door, during which Inzamam failed to give any assurance that they would be returning to the field to resume the match, Inzamam asked the team to vote on the question. 'The team voted unanimously that the protest should continue,' reported Woolmer, nonetheless adding, 'There was no intention not to play the fixture to its conclusion, particularly as Pakistan had a good chance of winning.'

Well, you can't have it both ways! Either you agree to play or you don't. What are umpires expected to do? Ask any discontented team to take their time and maybe come out to play when they have made their point through delay? Maybe what should have happened was that the heavy hitters of Pakistan cricket, Shaharyar Khan, Zaheer Abbas, Waqar Younis, Inzamam-ul-Haq and Bob Woolmer, all unequivocally said to their team, 'Let's go out and play cricket!'

In the face of all this conflicting and questionable evidence, Madugalle reached his incorrect verdict, for whatever motives drove him at the time. In suspending Inzamam for bringing the game into disrepute Madugalle had the chance to redeem himself by handing out a hefty penalty. Instead, he gave Inzamam a ban of four one-day internationals. Test matches are scheduled over five days, and I believe the minimum ban that should have been handed out was two Test matches, or three or four if Madugalle wanted to be tough.

I will leave the last word on the hearing to Richie Benaud, who remarked in a BBC Radio interview on 2 October that he had no doubt I had been let down by ICC. In sum:

- He believed I had been stabbed in the back.
- He found PCB chairman Shaharyar Khan's complaint that Pakistan's reputation as a nation had been insulted 'ludicrous'.
- He questioned whether any umpire would now have the courage to call a player for ball tampering.
- He was not surprised at the outcome, which saw Inzamam-ul-Haq receive the minimum penalty.

Benaud argued that ball tampering could be stopped immediately if a law were introduced that allowed only the bowler to shine the ball. He felt that the umpires' power had been eroded, and that it would undoubtedly be further eroded if countries tried to pick and choose which umpires were allowed to officiate in their matches.

Benaud was particularly incensed at the relatively light sentence imposed on the Pakistan captain after he was found guilty of bringing the game into disrepute. 'Why didn't he get a Test ban?' he asked. 'His proven offence of "bringing the game into disrepute" was committed in a Test.' Benaud stopped short of calling the hearing a whitewash but said, 'The outcome is close to what I expected.' He was unsure about my future. 'If fairness is part of the criteria, he and Billy Doctrove will umpire again in international matches,' he said. 'But it depends on the degree of "if".'

'There are two men [Darrell Hair and Zaheer Abbas] with stilettos between their shoulder blades,' Benaud said.

CHAPTER 6

HUMBLE PIE IN DUBAI

I was at home in Lincoln on the afternoon of 3 November 2006 when I noted the following story on Cricinfo:

> It was widely rumoured yesterday that Hair's future was in doubt, when a reliable source at the ICC leaked the news to a TV station in India. The Asian bloc, comprising India, Pakistan, Sri Lanka and Bangladesh, tabled a motion at the meeting that Hair be taken off the panel. The motion was put to vote and was passed by a 7–3 majority. The four Asian nations plus South Africa, Zimbabwe and the West Indies voted against Hair. England, Australia and New Zealand wanted him to continue.

I was naturally alarmed by this report, as I knew that the ICC board meeting was still taking place. However, I had come to believe that the ICC was not an organisation I could trust, and no decisions they came up with would surprise me. I had effectively been cast aside on the flimsy grounds that the board had 'lost confidence in me'. Nothing to do with my abilities or my record as someone who had given his time freely to the ICC to assist with training, developing and mentoring umpires as they rose through the ranks. Pressure from the four-nation Asian bloc had apparently forced the ICC's hand.

I soon received a telephone call from Speed. He began by admitting that he did not have any good news for me, adding wryly that he never seemed to have any good news for me. Speed explained that the PCB had presented a paper listing a range of charges against me under the ICC code of conduct. He told me the paper was discussed at length by the board but was later withdrawn, shortly after which the vote on my future was taken. He said the board had indeed voted against me that day and confirmed that I had not actually been sacked but was not in future to be appointed to any match involving a full-member country. The board also directed, said Speed, that I be utilised to train and develop umpires from the ICC Associate countries, which I had already been doing. I asked Speed if he thought it was logical for an employee who had lost the confidence of his employer to be used to train some of the most promising upcoming umpires. He agreed that it was not, but 'that is the way it is.'

At the conclusion of the ICC board meeting, the usual media release explained their position, as appeared in this Cricinfo report on 4 November 2006.

Speed said that he'd spoken to Hair last night, after the decision was taken and added that they will make an effort to protect Hair's interests. 'I've said a number of times that I hope we can find a way for Darrell to umpire,' he said. 'The board has resolved that they don't wish Darrell Hair to be appointed to umpire international matches. I spoke to Darrell yesterday after the decision was made. I told him about it and he was very disappointed. David Richardson, who is the ICC General Manager of Cricket, and myself will speak to Darrell over the next few days and talk about what it means to him.

'ICC has a number of lawyers on staff, who are well aware of our legal position,' he continued when asked if the ICC had considered the legal recourse that Hair might consider. 'It's correct that Hair is contracted till March 2008. But we need a little time to discuss the matter with him, to protect whatever interests he has.'

Speed also made it clear that this wasn't a decision taken at the spur of the moment, confirming that the board had considered the issue in detail.

'The ICC board — which consists of 13 representatives from the member countries — was presented with a very detailed paper that ran into 15–20 pages. The board certainly had a lot of information before it started its procedure yesterday. They had two hours of discussion on the issue.

'As it was reported, the Pakistan Cricket Board (PCB) had lodged a formal charge under the ICC code of conduct. That was also considered by the board. This was no knee-jerk reaction. The board had a good deal of information in front of it as is the case of any decision on the board.'

I was later to find out, at the Employment Tribunal, that far from taking two hours, the decision took about five minutes and was agreed to over lunch by John Anderson (New Zealand), Peter Chingoka (Zimbabwe) and Nasim Ashraf (Pakistan). What a wonderfully fair and unbiased subcommittee they formed, including Nasim Ashraf, one of my biggest critics in Pakistan. Given that the Pakistan Cricket Board had lodged a formal charge against me under the ICC Umpires Code of Conduct, this line-up hardly seemed conducive to justice or a fair hearing.

On 6 November, David Richardson called to invite me to a meeting with ICC management in Dubai. He said he was very concerned about the recent turn of events and wanted to discuss things with me face to face. I travelled to Dubai on 8 November accompanied by Amanda, who would be sitting in on the meetings I was due to have with Richardson, Speed and Cowie. I had vowed that never again would I speak to ICC staff while unaccompanied. If legal counsel were not possible, at least I would have someone else present as a witness.

Arriving for the meeting, Amanda and I were joined by David Richardson and Malcolm Speed. I asked why Doug Cowie was not present and Speed replied that he was not part of the management team. I asked that Cowie be present anyway, as he was my line manager and there were questions I wanted to put to him. Speed summoned Cowie.

The meeting was frank. I was permitted to speak at length about how disappointed I felt in the ICC board's treatment of me, and about how they, the management team, had let me down. I spoke about how the very public release of confidential correspondence had affected members of my family, and how the relentless public and personal attacks by members of the PCB had gone without sanction by the ICC, even though such comments were in clear contravention of the ICC's own code of conduct. Speed did not agree that releasing the email was wrong.

None of the three men expressed any concern at the effect their actions had had on me or my family; nor have they since. I spoke of my view on the conflict of interest regarding Pannick's role in the matter. Speed did not agree. I pointed to the advice I had received from two senior QCs that was in direct opposition to Pannick's views. Speed did not agree with those views either.

I asked Speed why he did not read out the letter to the board I had sent him dated 30 October, even though he had agreed to do so. Visibly agitated, Speed shot back aggressively, 'Who told you I didn't read out the letter?' David Richardson, I told him. Richardson shifted uneasily in his seat during this exchange. Could this be the first sign of disquiet in the ICC management camp? I told Speed that his decision not to read out my letter to the board, a letter in which I described how much I loved the game and how I just wanted to get back to doing what I do well, went against our agreement. 'Such arbitrary or selective decisions on your part precluded me from putting my honest thoughts and feelings to the board,' I argued.

Speed said he had asked Richardson to present a paper he

[Speed] had prepared that was generally supportive and recommended no action be taken against me under the ICC Umpires Code of Conduct. 'If I had presented the paper it would not have done you any favours,' Speed said. 'Parts of the letter might have helped but I don't think some other parts would have been seen in the same light. This was because my relationship with the ICC board was so bad and India would have voted against my proposal.'

Speed explained that Nasim Ashraf took exception to the report presented by Richardson and produced a document — effectively a charge sheet — with six itemised charges against me under the ICC code of conduct. What Speed did not tell me at the time but later came to light was that Ashraf criticised Richardson for supporting me and wanted the presentation from Richardson expunged from the records.

What could Ashraf's motives have been for this? And would not expunging the records of a board meeting amount to a deceitful practice? This would not have been the first or the last time that ICC staff or board members had misled the public, in my view, something that Speed actually accused me of doing back in August when I offered to resign.

Richardson said the board understood that my decision making was very good. Their complaint against me was the manner in which I applied the laws. 'We don't want soft umpires,' he said, but he claimed that they (the ICC) had raised the issue of my manner several times and that Ranjan Madugalle had also spoken to me several times. I told them that this simply was not true. I have no record of this issue being raised with me either verbally or in writing, and neither does the ICC. I reiterated that Madugalle had quite often complimented me on the way I handled matters on the field. In the third Test at Headingley in early August, Madugalle had commented that I had handled a couple of potentially explosive situations very well. I knew Madugalle had reported that my match management skills during that particular match were excellent.

I raised the issue of the meeting on 25 August. The decision to release confidential correspondence had done considerable harm to me personally. The fact that the information was not used in any way during the code of conduct hearing, despite the advice received by Speed, confirmed to me that it would be that the decision to release the correspondence had been wrong. To consult a QC (David Pannick) and act on his advice without offering me the same courtesy was unfair. For the same man to then assist the adjudicator at the code of conduct hearing was, in my view, a conflict of interest. Speed did not agree and showed no interest in defending his decisions.

I had by then received legal advice from two sources on top of the hurried counsel I received on 25 August. Unsurprisingly, all three sources insisted that the email should not have been released. I now read out in full the advice I had received from John Beveridge QC:

> I was disappointed by the nature and standard of David Pannick's advice to publish Darrell Hair's unfortunate letter. That post hoc act can have no evidential relevance whatever to either the issue of whether a fielder had tampered with the ball, or the issue as to the conduct of the team in not taking the field on two occasions.

Its only utility at the hearing would be for cross-examination of Darrell Hair as to credit and this use would be peripheral and of very limited value, a view reinforced by the fact that it was not, in fact, so used.

It is fair to say that such use would probably have been permitted, despite the fact that the obvious explanation for Hair's letter was his concern at the public reaction to his future as an umpire, rather than self-doubt as to the quality of his umpiring decisions.

Again, I do not accept that it was the duty of the ICC to disclose this extremely peripheral material. Even if it had to be disclosed, it was a mistake to move straight to the step of making the letter public, in disregard of any obligation of confidentiality. If disclosed on a confidential basis it may, or may not, have remained confidential, but if it had not remained confidential, the consequences to Hair would have been no worse than those attendant on the ICC's open publication and, at least, the ICC would have been seen to have, and would have, attempted to keep faith with its umpire.

Next I started to read out the opinion of Robert Griffiths QC. Speed interrupted by saying, 'Oh yes, we know Robert Griffiths very well. He's very anti-ICC.' Griffiths wrote:

> I am concerned that Hair may not have been treated fairly. His confidential communications with his employers were disclosed when in my opinion they should have been treated as 'without prejudice' and disclosure regarded as being in

On the field with great umpire and mentor David Shepherd during a One-Day International, Australia v West Indies, January 2001. Shepherd had a calming influence on every game no matter what the situation.

The first match in an Ashes series is always a fantastic experience – conferring with Sri Lankan umpire K.T. Francis at the Ashes Test in Brisbane, November 1998.

Third umpire assistance. I always preferred to make the decision on the field, if possible, but sometimes things are just too close to call – that's where technology can help.

With wife Amanda outside 4-5 Gray's Inn Square, the chambers of Robert Griffiths QC and Stephen Whale QC.

At an ICC conference in London, 1995.

England's Andrew Flintoff gets the answer he was looking for at Edgbaston in July 2004, England v West Indies.

Inzamam-ul-Haq acknowledges being warned for running on the pitch during the England Test match in Faisalabad, Pakistan, November 2005.

The fourth Test at The Oval, 20 August 2006 – with umpire Billy Doctrove showing Pakistan captain Inzamam-ul-Haq the reason for the ball being changed and a five-run penalty for ball tampering.

The tampered ball. The lighter marks (a) around the quarter-seam show where the surface of the ball has been gouged. Another section (b) shows an area where the the leather has been deliberately scratched away. The criss-cross marks (c) cannot be the result of normal use during a match. None of these marks were present when the ball was inspected some 15 minutes before.

Getty Images

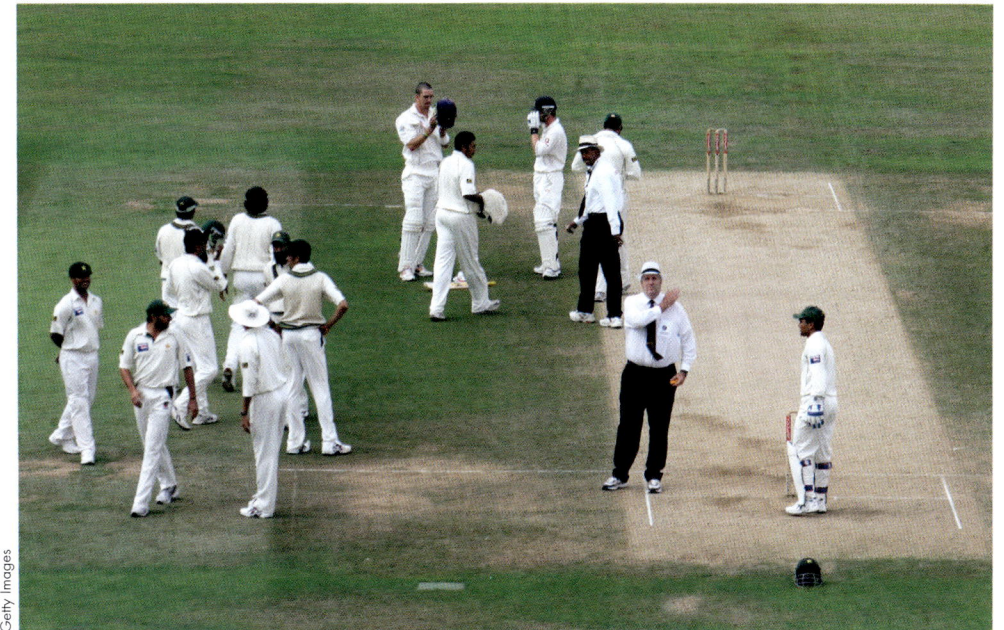

Making the official signal to the scorers for the five-run penalty in the fourth Test.

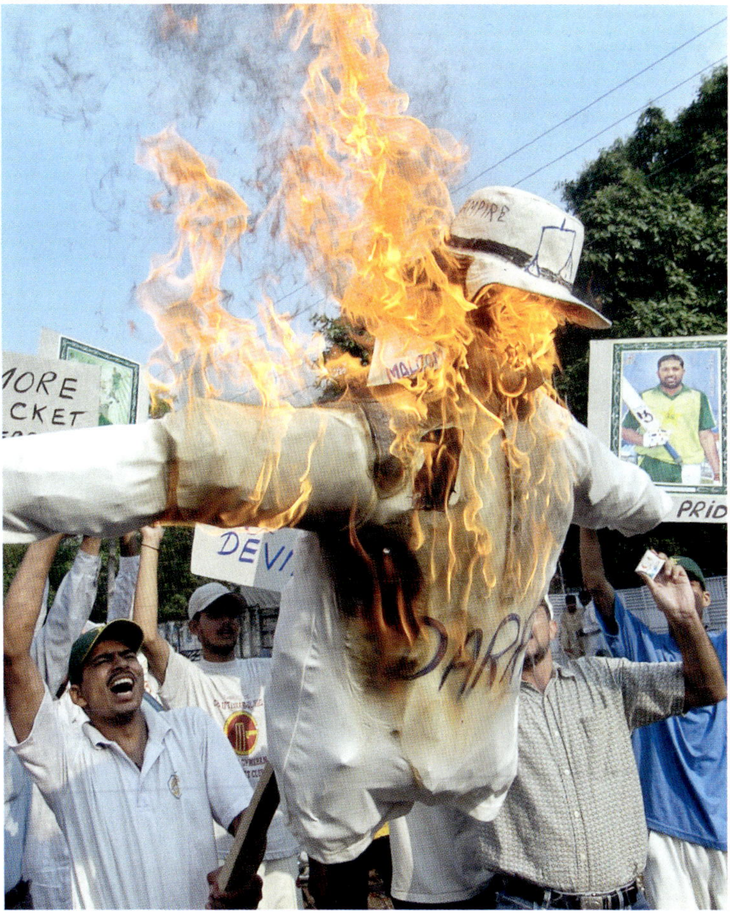

Getty Images

An effigy is burnt by Pakistan fans in Lahore after the decision in the fourth Test.

Preparation for the Employment Tribunal Case with (from left to right) Robert Griffiths QC, Paul Gilbert from Finers Stephens Innocent, and Stephen Whale QC.

Umpiring at an Associate match. Scotland's John Blain bowling against Kenya in Mombassa, January 2007.

Reading the form guide the day before my 'comeback' Test.

In the nets with left-arm spinner Monty Panesar before my return Test match at Old Trafford.

Stepping onto the field at Old Trafford, 23 May 2008.

Back at work. Ryan Sidebottom, England's opening bowler, in his delivery stride for the first ball at Old Trafford. Fielder Ian Bell waits for an edge at short leg.

Getty Images

New Zealand skipper Daniel Vettori suggests the ball might be out of shape at Old Trafford, May 2008. A good captain to communicate with, Vettori always accepted a decision as final.

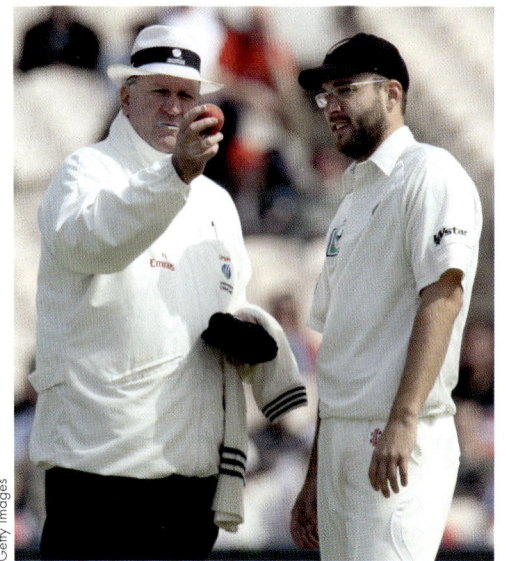

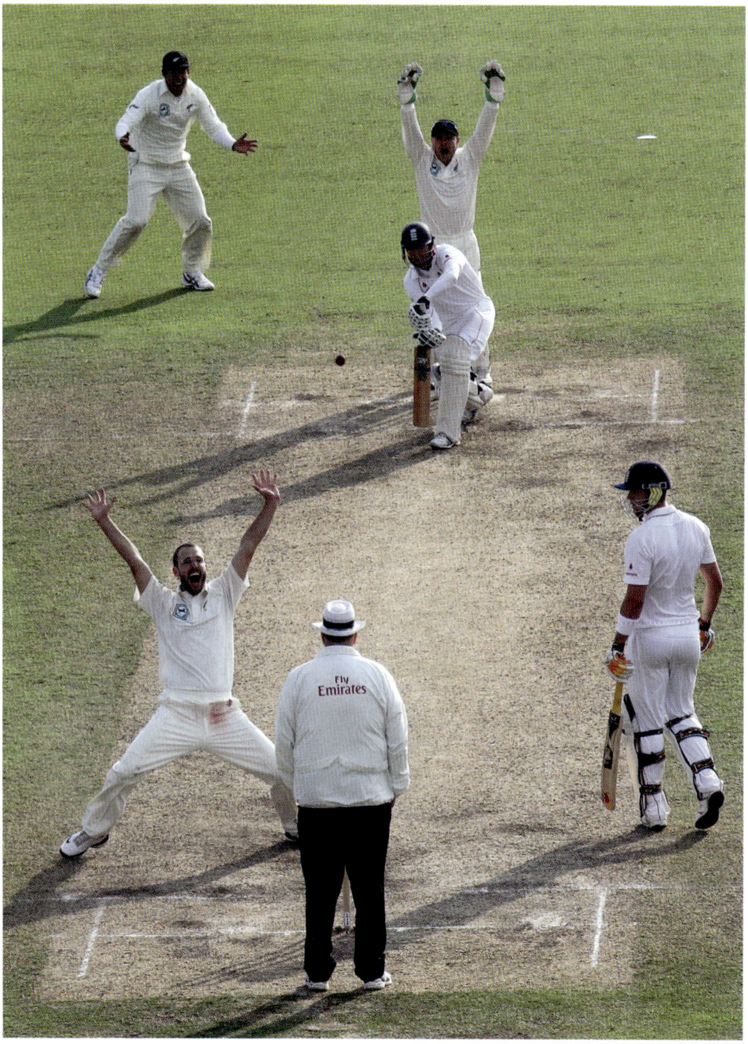

Getty Images

My last Test match at Trent Bridge, June 2008. Daniel Vettori is unsuccessful in convincing me that Tim Ambrose is out lbw.

breach of confidence. Even if they could be disclosed, where was the justification for disclosing them to the world at large? Colloquially, Hair has been hung out to dry.

Umpires' decisions are not and should not be subject to the constraints of judicial standards of proof. There should be a reassertion that the umpire's decision is final and binding, otherwise no umpire will risk taking action and this will lead to the demise of cricket.

To change a cricket Law in these circumstances is like saying that one miscarriage of justice in a murder trial should lead to the abolition of the law on murder.

I asked Speed for his view on public statements made in the media that I should be aware of cultural sensitivities, including racial ones, and deal with teams in such a way as to satisfy those sensitivities. In short, did he think I was racist or biased? This question was important for me. If the governing body of a sport believes certain countries should be treated differently, then they should be up front and say so. Just because ball tampering and other law infringements may be common practice in some countries' domestic cricket, it does not mean they can expect that if they are caught out in international cricket they can simply play the political, racial and religious sensitivities card.

Speed responded, 'I'm not here to answer questions.' Richardson, however, said, 'I don't feel you are,' and Cowie said he had seen no evidence of bias or racism. Almost reluctantly, it seemed, Speed then admitted bluntly, 'I have seen no evidence of bias or racism.' Richardson offered, 'Bob Woolmer has said he thinks you are biased. I have disagreed with him.'

Speed claimed that ICC management had supported me but had made a decision not to argue publicly on the matter. Why not argue for something if you believe it to be right or, dare I say it, in the best interests of the game? The world is full of people and organisations that are happy to sit back and allow things to happen that they disagree with morally and ethically, but I believe that the management of an international sporting body such as ICC should not stay silent on such important issues.

I then asked a question of all three present: 'Do you believe that the decision taken by the ICC board to remove me from international umpiring was one that they had the right to make?' Speed said again, 'I'm not going to answer these questions. Amanda is taking notes and that is not appropriate. I am not here to answer questions and I'm directing Doug and David not to answer them either. Board meetings are confidential. I've told you what was said at the board meeting and how we supported you. You can either accept it or not.'

I asked four more questions:

'Do you believe the decision of the board was the correct one?'

'Do you believe that I have been treated fairly?'

'Do you believe the ICC board meeting was a de facto umpires' code of conduct adjudication with a hearing held in my absence?'

'Have I been treated this way because of my race or religious beliefs?'

While refusing to answer these questions, Speed did criticise me for walking out of the meeting at The Oval. Speed said, 'Mike Procter was doing his best to get the match going again and you walked out of the meeting because Inzamam made some gesture towards you. I expect better of you than that.' Although Speed had completely missed the point on the issue of 'restarting' the match, I accept that he had the right to criticise me on this point, but I also had expectations of my employers. I expected that they would act honestly towards me, back me up when I made decisions in good faith on the field, and above all uphold their own code of conduct by taking action against those players and officials who made unfounded attacks on me.

Speed resumed the attack from the sand bunker end: 'The emails you sent were extremely stupid and I am critical of you for sending those emails. You publicly blamed Doug Cowie and I am critical of you for that. We supported you as well as we were able in a difficult environment.' By 'difficult environment' Speed confirmed for me that he considered himself and his staff unable to apply the ICC code of conduct to certain members because of the political power they held.

The meeting was not achieving much in finding a path by which I could get back into umpiring at international level. Speed then asked: 'Where to from here? We have a contract to March 2008. We would like to discuss what alternatives there are. Post 2008, I don't know what will happen. The ICC board is unlikely to renew your contract. It may be possible to change the mood of the board, but I doubt it. I don't know if there is any training role you could do.' I was disappointed that Speed was seemingly unwilling to commit to an effort to help change the minds or mood of those board members who wanted me removed.

Amanda and I then had a separate meeting with Doug Cowie, who admitted the the ICC needed to consider suitable alternative employment. On the matter of fees, Cowie had calculated that, umpiring Test matches and one-day internationals, I could have expected to earn approximately US$178,000 up to 31 March 2007 and another US$148,000 between 1 April 2007 and 31 March 2008. These figures were based on the then current match fees and retainer.

I pointed out (just in case it was not obvious to him) that if I were appointed only to Associate one-day internationals at a match fee of US$1,500, I would need to umpire some 50 one-day internationals a year to achieve similar earnings. It would not be possible to stand in so many matches, even were that number scheduled. The meeting closed with Cowie promising to get a schedule out to me to indicate how I would be employed in the coming months and to work out a plan that would convince the ICC board to renew my contract.

Suffice to say that no such plan ever eventuated. I did not receive any structured plan from the ICC about my future. Cowie asked me if I would be available to perform umpire assessments during the World Cup 2007, but I received no further word from him. It seemed the ICC really wanted to move on from any involvement with Darrell Hair.

There were times when I felt that the best course of action would be simply to hand in my resignation and move on — perhaps to somewhere where I could work with people who shared the same values and beliefs I did, and who I believed really did have the best interests of the game at heart. That would come later on in my life, but for the time being I had unfinished business. I still believed I could contribute to international cricket as an umpire, and even in the face of official rejection I retained a deep desire to do so. The next stage of my life would also prove difficult, but it was one I was determined to see through. I had decided to lodge a claim against my employer for racial discrimination.

CHAPTER 7

BACK ON THE FIELD AND BACK TO SYDNEY

'Controversial umpire is set to stand again, once he has found his suitcase'
— headline in *The Guardian*, 18 January 2007

It was five months almost to the day since the match between England and Pakistan that ended so turbulently at The Oval in South London, and I was greatly looking forward to my return to umpiring.

As luck would have it, as so often happens during international travel, my luggage disappeared somewhere between London and Mombasa, on the coast of Kenya. All I had was the clothes on my back (last night's) and a pair of sunglasses. Unable to umpire the match to which I was appointed that day without any of my gear, I wandered around the ground at the Mombasa Sports Club in my civvies. The field there must be one of the most extraordinary to host international cricket. There is a mango tree with a whitewashed trunk a few metres inside the boundary rope near the pavilion and a baobab tree so thick that the wall of the Mombasa Sports Ground had to be built around it.

The weather was warm, as I had expected, but a gentle breeze took the edge off the heat. All in all, it wasn't a bad day for a game of cricket. The match? Scotland was doing battle with Kenya in an ICC Associate one-day international. It may not have been Trent Bridge or the Sydney Cricket Ground, but this was the first day of cricket I had seen since 20 August the previous year. I greeted a group of spectators and stopped to talk to John Blain, the Scotland opening bowler, who was fielding at fine leg. 'The wicket is very flat,' said Blain rather drolly, but then bowlers always say that when the pitch is not bouncing or seaming about, which means that wickets are scarce and runs flow freely.

Kenya, in England's group in the ICC World Cup due to be held in the Caribbean in March, looked a decent side, especially when batting first, as they were today. When they had to chase a total it might be a different matter. A wicket fell and I did not mind one bit that it was my good friend from Nepal, Buddhi Pradhan, whose finger sent Maurice Ouma on his way, lbw for 12. Ian Gould, from England, was patrolling the other end. If and when my luggage arrived from Dubai, it would be my turn in the middle. I looked towards the pavilion, which looked cool and inviting. 'I need something cool to drink,' I told myself and headed for the shade of the Mombasa Sports Club.

For the first time since The Oval Test, I was almost back in the cricketing fold. The ICC had announced two days earlier that I was to officiate in the triangular series between Kenya, Scotland and Canada — a decision that caused widespread surprise in the cricketing media. Why such short media notice when I had known for several weeks that I would be standing in this tournament? My guess was that the ICC wanted to avoid further publicity about the events surrounding the forfeiture. It was only in November, several weeks after the ICC code of conduct hearing chaired by Ranjan Madugalle had found no evidence of ball tampering by the Pakistan players, that I was formally advised that until my contract finished in March 2008 I would no longer be called on to umpire full international matches. The loss of confidence in me expressed by the ICC board went both ways, of course, but I wasn't going to let anything distract me from doing a good job when I finally got the chance.

In a statement, the ICC insisted the decision to appoint me for the Kenyan series was not contradictory, as the tri-series teams were all Associate rather than full members. It also confirmed that I would umpire in the six-team ICC World Cricket League Division One series, which was to begin in Nairobi later in the month and which also included Bermuda, Ireland and the Netherlands. I wonder what sort of message they were trying to send to their own Associate members by my appointment? Was it 'You guys can have the ones we don't have any confidence in'?

Given the publicity the appointment was likely to create, the choice of Kenya as the venue for my return to umpiring was ideal, though. Far from the eyes of the British and Asian media (well, almost), I would be able to pick up umpiring again without being under too much scrutiny. 'Long way from home, aren't you?' remarked a British reporter who approached me later that evening at my hotel. A long way indeed. I had been further from home before, but never under these bizarre circumstances. Having been virtually ostracised by the ICC for several months, I was really looking forward to proving myself as an umpire at the top level again. This batch of appointments was, for me, the start of that climb back to where I belonged.

According to the ICC board, I was to be utilised in the training and development of Associate Panel umpires, many of whom I had already worked with and assisted over the years. Ian Gould was already a well-respected decision maker, but I felt he bounced quite a few ideas off me. In the not too distant future Gould would join the ICC Elite Panel, and quite rightly so.

Then there was Buddhi Pradhan. I had played a part in his development for several years. Buddhi had umpired with me in various ICC Associate tournaments, where he had learned the trade well and his progress had been outstanding. He is an excellent listener and committed and passionate about improving his umpiring standards. It was very satisfying indeed to see him making his mark as a very competent umpire at international level. I reminded myself that I should not underestimate my value to my umpiring mates, even if I did have indifferent relations with my employers.

The purpose of the Associate Umpiring Development Program was to promote and develop the umpires who were initially identified at Associate level but could well move up to full-member one-day internationals. These included the likes of Roger Dill from Bermuda, Sarika Prasad from Singapore, Shahul Hameed from Indonesia and Buddhi Pradhan from Nepal.

It seems, however, that since 2008 the ICC has made a decision to cast the program adrift, as since 2008 little development has been done. As recently as January 2011, several Associate Panel umpires have told me they feel they are no longer being given the same support and encouragement. One went so far as to write the following:

> Here in our region things are very much a balancing act between family, office and umpiring appointments. This is the mantra you had passed on to me way back in 2005 at the ICC trophy final in Belfast, Ireland. Unfortunately we are very much missing your leadership and constructive development programs as well as mentorship role in the present setup, especially for our A&A panel, which is not going further — a bit of a stalemate and we are not having enough opportunities now. However, our sincere efforts are there continuously as we have been brought up by great mentors like you and we will always be proud of it.
>
> Once again thanks for all your guidance and moral support, as always.

I have always taken great pleasure in passing on valuable information that can help other umpires improve and progress. The ICC associate umpires are among the best friends I have made during my time in the game. It really would be a shame if the ICC did not maintain a strong commitment to their progress and future in the game.

Being an Associate tournament, the hospitality in Mombasa was not quite of the standard I was accustomed to when travelling for full international cricket matches. Still, the Royal Court Hotel in the centre of Mombasa, which was hosting the players and officials, was managed by Dinish Antony, a cheery chap who, on welcoming me, admitted that he was 'surprised' when he heard I would be among his guests. I was not in the least concerned about the standard of accommodation. It was great to be back on the cricket field and with friends, among both players and umpires, many of whom I had known for more than a decade. Over breakfast there was the usual banter, with several players from Scotland and Canada urging the umpires to make certain the lbw decisions were spot-on during the upcoming matches.

At last I learned that my suitcase had been located and was waiting for me at the airport. Having filled out several declarations confirming that the suitcase was indeed mine, I retrieved my luggage, containing all of my umpiring gear, and was all set to officiate in my first match. On the morning of the game, 18 January 2007, I sat quietly in the umpires' room studying the team nominations from Scotland and Canada. It was a ritual I always followed. I found it useful to know which bowlers were playing, who the best fielders were and where they were likely to be fielding. Then I'd take a cursory look at how many left- and right-handed batsmen there were in each team. Canada had several left-handers, which would mean constant changing sides as runs were taken while I was standing at square leg.

Familiarising yourself with the nuances of each team is always good preparation. It can help you anticipate crucial situations during the course of a match: 'forewarned is forearmed'. I noticed that the Scotland team included Dougie Brown and Gavin Hamilton, who had played one-day internationals for England, while Canada had John Davison as captain. John had grown up in Australia and played first-class cricket for South Australia and Victoria. Anderson Cummins had played five Test matches and 76 one-day internationals for the West Indies between 1991 and 1995. In fact, Cummins played in my umpiring debut in international cricket — the one-day international between West Indies and India at the Adelaide Oval on 14 December 1991.

The day promised a great game of cricket and one I was determined would go well in terms of my decisions and techniques. I was confident and prepared. It felt good to be back and I couldn't wait for the first ball. It proved to be an excellent match too, with Canada posting a mammoth total of 292 and Scotland chasing down the target with eight wickets down and only one ball to spare. I enjoyed the game thoroughly and used every ball to ensure my techniques and thought processes had not suffered during my enforced layoff. It was a match that would become one of my most cherished sporting memories.

John Davison, who at one stage held the record for the fastest century in a World Cup, gave Canada a flying start with a typically flamboyant 41 off 32 balls. Ashish Bagai kept the tempo going with a run-a-ball knock but was forced to retire suffering from dehydration, although he returned to bat again late in the innings. Many of the players in both teams were already complaining of illness and dehydration, the cause of which was unknown at the time. Later the medical trail led to the possibility of food poisoning at the team hotel. Ian Gould and I would not entirely escape illness either, although our symptoms were mild compared with the descriptions we heard from some of the players!

Canada's effort was impressive on a tough day for bowlers, but, as they say, you still have to occupy the crease to make big scores. Scotland's Ryan Watson overcame the stifling conditions to guide Scotland to a memorable three-wicket win with one ball to spare, which must have been a heartbreaking loss for Canada, who had earlier posted their record one-day international total. This was another reason why umpiring international cricket matches is so memorable. Records are constantly being broken, and to see cricketers achieving and improving is a great experience for the umpire too. Scotland's run chase was given a kick-start by Navdeep Poonia, who was a Warwickshire County player. He compiled a brisk 67, but once he departed, Scotland suffered a middle-order wobble. Poonia, a talented stroke-maker, had shown his ability in a number of one-day outings for Warwickshire the previous season. Today he struck 11 fours and two sixes off 68 balls before he was bowled. The rest of the middle order made starts but no one seemed to be willing to bat out the innings with Watson, and when Majid Haq was out to John Davison's nagging off spinners Scotland were in trouble at 6 for 238, needing 55 with only six overs remaining.

Watson was to be the hero of the day, though, and he showed his class by hitting two sixes in the 45th over, bowled by left-arm spinner Sunil Dhaniram, to raise Scotland's run rate. Then skipper Craig Wright was stumped trying to hit one down the ground and it was left to John Blain to show impressive resolve in his role as a bowling all-rounder. Blain's two boundaries in the 49th over effectively sealed the result. Canada's fielding had slipped as the match progressed, and in the heat a number of crucial run-out chances were missed and balls misfielded.

Ryan Watson's 123 not out came off 120 balls. He had battled the extreme heat for just on three hours to prove himself a player of real class and the right man in a crisis. Canada's and Scotland's combined effort to put on such an exciting encounter was impressive on a day on which it was tough work being a batsman or bowler and just as tough being an umpire. It really was very satisfying to be back.

The remaining matches all went well and my enjoyment increased with every ball bowled. Unfortunately, nearly all the players and umpires suffered a bout of food poisoning and the matches had to be deferred by two days until everyone had recovered — a common pitfall of travel. It felt like everything was getting back to normal at last! There were, however, some other things on my mind — matters of utmost importance to me and to my future.

During the turmoil that followed the forfeited Test match at The Oval, genuine public support from within the cricket community was often sparse. Two umpiring associations stood out from the rest, and not surprisingly it was my own state association, the New South Wales Cricket Umpires and Scorers Association, that became the most vocal. The other was the Institute of Cricket Umpires and Scorers, based in the United Kingdom, which had invited me to become a director.

Any sports organisation that has community interests at heart will always get my support. My grassroots background taught me to put as much back into the sport as I got out if it — even more if possible. The support from New South Wales took two forms. First, letters were sent to Malcolm Speed and all the ICC directors voicing their concern over both the treatment dished out to me and, more broadly, the damage the ICC had done to the spirit of cricket.

In addition, NSWCUSA published a full-page advertisement in the *Daily Telegraph* (Sydney) in the form of an open letter to Malcolm Speed. The advertisement was paid for by the association out of its own funds, and my colleagues donated a day's umpiring fee to help offset the costs. I felt very humble and grateful that an umpiring body and its members would take such a stand, not only by funding the advertisement but also by contributing the umpiring fee from their match that day in the Sydney grade cricket competitions. It was heartwarming to know how committed my own umpiring association and its members were to having me reinstated to international umpiring. They were also determined to send a public message to Speed and the ICC directors that the traditions and spirit of the game meant far more to cricket in the longer term than commercial concerns. Here is the letter to Speed as published in the *Telegraph* on Saturday, 10 November 2006:

 Advertisement

An open letter to Malcolm Speed

Mr Malcolm Speed
Chief Executive
ICC
Dubai — United Arab Emirates
November 2006

Dear Mr. Speed

As you know the NSW Cricket Umpires and Scorers Association Inc. is an independent body established 94 years ago to recruit, train and develop umpires (and more recently scorers) for the game of cricket. It is the largest such association in Australia and possibly the second largest in the World with over 1,200 members mainly based in New South Wales with others throughout the cricket playing nations. Together with its 36 Affiliated Associations in NSW it has a degree of influence over 2,500 umpires and scorers. It is recognised for its training methods that have been taken up by such organisations as the MCC, Cricket Australia and indeed the ICC. Darrell Hair is a Life Member and a past President.

The recent decision by the ICC to ban Darrell Hair from umpiring international matches is a travesty of justice not only to our past President but to those of us who know and respect him as a man of great integrity and is, to the worldwide cricketing fraternity at large, a recognition that, as for much of the rest of society, politics has firmly taken command of our great sport.

The decision to remove Darrell from the ICC Elite Panel of umpires has clearly not been taken — and cannot be justified — on grounds related to his ability as an umpire. He is the fourth most capped Test umpire of all time with 76 Test matches and 124 one-day internationals. Nobody has suggested that umpiring decisions made by Hair and Doctrove at The Oval were incorrect or wrong in Law (they were not), or that his performances as an International and Test and one-day international umpire over the years have been incompetent (they have not). As recently as August you described Darrell as 'one of the world's best umpires'. Yet not three months later Darrell has, not via the players or by the umpires' selection panel from whom appointments to the Elite Panel are made, had his career unceremoniously terminated by you at the ICC.

At the ICC meeting held in Mumbai your Board voted to ban Darrell because, as stated by ICC President Percy Sonn, 'the ICC had lost confidence in him'. This is a very curious and dubious legal basis upon which the ICC has chosen to act. If that was indeed the charge, then it is so vague as to be a legal nonsense. As a lawyer yourself you will know that a charge can only be effective if it is specific, unambiguous and capable of being refuted. Furthermore, your own ICC website states that the Elite Panel comprises 'the top umpires in the world'. How can the ICC have lost confidence in Darrell's decision making and match management ability, having recently renewed his contract until 2008? Mr Sonn should also be challenged to explain and justify why Billy Doctrove — Darrell Hair's colleague and equal on the day of The Oval Test match — has not been similarly censured and disciplined by the ICC and why, unlike Hair, Doctrove was — with hypocritical acquiescence of the Pakistan Cricket Board — appointed to stand in two of the England v Pakistan one-day international matches immediately following that Oval Test match.

The sole reason for this pre-emptive action can only be interpreted as a need to appease the Pakistan Cricket Board (PCB) and the ACC-led majority on the ICC Board who have been noisily critical of Hair for some time, presumably because he is known as a 'no-nonsense' umpire who actually does what he is paid to do — ensure fair play by applying the Laws of the game when those on the ICC Board would prefer to have difficult matters swept under the carpet. Why else did the ICC-appointed representative who chaired the 'Inquiry Hearing', held several weeks after the Oval Test match, bow so readily to demands from the PCB's extensive legal team that the decision made by both on-field umpires on the day that the condition of the match ball had been clearly deliberately changed (scuffed up) should be overturned on the grounds that it had not? These demands to overturn the umpire's decision weeks after the match had ended were made by individuals who are unqualified in — and clearly have no understanding of — the interpretation and application of the Laws of Cricket. Overturning or reversing umpires' decisions after 'Time' has been called in the match is in direct contravention of the Laws, which quite specifically prohibit such retrospective action.

The ICC's website contains a lengthy and very legalistic statement about the rights of participants in the game to natural justice. One wonders if you took time out to reflect upon that very statement before you unceremoniously dumped the fourth most capped umpire in the history of Test cricket. While the statement refers to judicial hearings, it can equally apply to the manner in which umpires under the ICC jurisdiction should be treated. It states that a person shall have 'the right to a fair hearing ... (with) prior notice of the case against him ... (and) a fair opportunity to answer it'. What was the case against Darrell? These matters are presumably now between Darrell and his lawyers and the ICC and your in-house lawyer Urvasi Naidoo but, for all of us who dedicate enormous amounts of time to the interests of the game, demand, and are entitled to an explanation of your actions.

It is worth noting that at the same meeting that the Board dispensed with an honest and brave servant of the game it overturned the life ban imposed on the former Pakistan fast bowler Ata-ur-Rehman for perjury during an inquiry into match fixing in Pakistan. Neither prospect bodes well for the future of international cricket or, for that matter, for national domestic recreational cricket, many of whose younger participants look to emulate their professional 'role' models.

The ICC, like most cricket associations around the world, does nothing to recruit, train or develop its officials. This is left to volunteer bodies like the ICUS and our Association, an Association incidentally that has supplied you with 20% of your Elite panel. We continue to lose those willing to act as umpires due to poor player behaviour, lack of respect and now total disregard for their role in correctly applying the Laws of the game.

The ICC have demeaned the standing and role of the ICC Elite Panel of umpires as well as spectators and your sponsors Global Cricket Corp, Emirates, Getty Images, Octagon CSI, Sportsbrand Media Group, Hyundai Motors and Sony Entertainment Television, all of whom could well be boycotted by those of us who really care.

You and your ICC should all be ashamed of how this has played out.

Yours sincerely,

Tim. M. Donahoo

Chair of the Board — for and on behalf of the Directors, supporters and members who contributed their match payments today to cover the costs of the publication of this letter.

Some interesting points and questions were raised in a forceful and honest way in this letter. Speed later told me he had received some communications from NSWCUSA expressing their concerns about my treatment, that I 'obviously had a lot of friends' and that he intended to respond in detail as soon as he possibly could. He did not respond either in writing or verbally. In fact, he never mentioned it publicly at any time.

There comes a time in life when you need to make crucial decisions. I had enjoyed living in England, partly because travel to fixtures around the world was much easier to manage from there than it was from Australia. I was also lucky to be able to umpire matches for the ECB, and while they were mostly second 11 games, I did officiate at some wonderfully picturesque grounds and was treated superbly by the clubs that hosted the matches.

However, I needed to determine where I was heading with a little more certainty. After all, I had no guarantee of ever being able to return to umpiring at the elite level. My career future was far from certain and I had to consider both what was best for me and my family and how I could continue to participate in and contribute to the game I loved.

I also received encouragement from James Sutherland, CEO of Cricket Australia, who wrote to me that in his view I had much to offer to cricket and umpiring in New South Wales and Australia. James said he would be happy to discuss the nature and extent of this involvement, so I felt increasingly comfortable with the decision I was about to make. Returning to Sydney would, I hoped, enable me not only to resume my on-field umpiring but also to continue my work in umpiring development and keep me closely tied to the game. Amanda was also happy to return to Australia. A very talented businesswoman who was much in demand, she also had many friends in Sydney.

But before departing from Kenya on 7 February 2007 after completing my last match, between Kenya and Scotland at the Gymkhana Ground in Nairobi, I announced publicly that I would be lodging a complaint in the London Central Employment Tribunal against the International Cricket Council for racial discrimination. There would be a battle ahead, that much I knew. But I was determined to win the justice I believed I had been denied following the events of 20 August 2006.

CHAPTER 8

THE TRIBUNAL

To: International Cricket Council FZ LLC,
of: Al Thuraya Tower, 11th Floor, Dubai Media City, PO Box 500070, Dubai, UAE

1. I, Darrell Hair,
of: 96 Mill Road, Lincoln, LN1 3JH
consider that you may have discriminated against me contrary to the *Race Relations Act 1976*.

2. On the 3rd and 4th November 2006, the Respondent, the International Cricket Council 'ICC', took a decision to remove me from the Emirates Elite Panel ('EEP') thus preventing me from maximising my earnings under my 'Consultancy Agreement' (a contract for services) with the ICC.

3. I consider this treatment may have been unlawful because:

The decision to remove me from the EEP arose out of incidents which took place at the Oval Cricket Ground on 20 August 2006. This involved the joint decision which I made with my fellow umpire Mr Billy Doctrove to award 5 penalty runs against the Pakistan cricket team in the Test match that they were playing against England and the subsequent joint decision to award the Test match to England by default after the Pakistan cricket team refused to take the field of play after tea. These decisions were taken entirely in accordance with the rules of cricket.

I have not been given any explanation for my removal. I am currently rated as the second best Test umpire on the EEP and there is therefore no question of my removal being on the grounds of capability.

My removal is an act of racial discrimination because of the fact that no action of any form has been taken against my fellow umpire Mr Billy Doctrove and what appears to have been the driving force behind the voting of the ICC Executive Board on my removal.

24 January 2007

The personal and emotional toll of this affair had been enormous. My family and I had suffered anxiety and distress as a result of the actions of the ICC and the constant negative comment in the media. Family members had experienced the pain of reading headlines such as 'Disgraced former umpire' and 'Sacked International umpire'. I was especially anxious for my mother, who had been ill for some time and became distressed when she read in the newspaper or learned from other family members what was being claimed about me. Much of this might have been avoided were it not for the discriminatory action taken by the ICC board. Since 20 August 2006 no one from the ICC had shown any concern for my welfare or for the welfare of my family. I was denied the opportunity to rebuild the confidence of the board in my abilities as an umpire and had received no assessment of or feedback on the few matches I had umpired. The ICC, in other words, had failed to show any duty of care towards me.

There were times when I felt like giving it all up and walking away from the game. But that would have been both too easy and too hard at the same time. It would have been easy to walk away from the ICC and its board of directors. On the other hand, it would have been very hard to walk away from the game I loved. Umpiring can turn you upside down when things go wrong, but at other times — for instance, at the end of a Test match between the world's best players, when you know how much you contributed to its success — can make you feel like you are walking on air.

If I were to take on the might of the ICC I could not go it alone. I had long been thinking of enlisting legal assistance for the purpose but it can be expensive, and quite obviously the ICC would have the resources to challenge any claims I might make. Through a mutual friend, I had been introduced to Mark Stephens from the London law firm Finers Stephens Innocent. Mark was happy to provide advice and agreed to a preliminary meeting. Paul Gilbert was to take a leading role in the early stages of discussions, along with partners Daniel Marks and Carolyn Brown, who specialised in employment issues. They showed a keen interest in how my earning capacity, not to mention my reputation, had been affected by the ICC's actions. One thing led quickly to another and before I knew it I had a team of passionate professionals on my side who could see the unfairness of the situation and wanted to help me.

I also came across a comment in the daily press from Robert Griffiths QC, who publicly stated his concern that I had not been treated fairly. I had met Mr Griffiths on one or two occasions in the past and he was concerned about how I had been treated then, so naturally I was happy to have him on my side.

I would like to set one thing straight. From the beginning I firmly believed that issues of racism could not have been far beneath the surface at the ICC. Speed's action gave the Pakistan Cricket Board the opportunity to go on a public rampage of a sort never before seen in international cricket.

The PCB demanded (not requested) of the ICC that I never again be appointed to matches involving Pakistan teams. They continually attacked my reputation and standing as an umpire. Shaharyar Khan opened the batting on this, and then left the field to Inzamam, Nasim Ashraf and even Bob Woolmer. Woolmer, who had worked for the ICC in global development of the game, came out with an extraordinary comparison when he claimed on 23 August that I had 'added to the volatile relationship between East and West'. The way an on-field sporting decision could be recast so self-servingly as a political issue was deeply shocking and insulting to me. 'All the Muslim players are sensitive individuals who are very opposed to terrorist activities and to accuse Pakistan of cheating brings these tensions to the fore,' suggested Woolmer. 'I wonder whether Darrell realises the consequences of his actions?'

What consequences? What tensions? Woolmer links two issues that are so far apart on the political and moral compass that even to hear them mentioned in the same thought process insults our intelligence. His irresponsible choice of words was very hurtful to me personally. I was even more surprised that his team did not immediately distance themselves from such comments.

The ICC would defend the case I brought against them by repeatedly suggesting that I was the sole reason for the Test match at The Oval being abandoned. At no stage did they question Billy Doctrove about his view of the forfeiture and ball tampering. (Malcolm Speed would admit this oversight in several interviews and, more importantly, would confirm it in writing in the statement he tendered to the Employment Tribunal.) In addition, all the ICC witnesses cross-examined at the Tribunal would indicate that at no stage did they consider Billy Doctrove had anything to do with the decisions. As far as they were concerned, Darrell Hair bore sole responsibility. Doctrove was in fact no stranger to making judgements on ball tampering. He had penalised a team for ball tampering in the West Indies in 2005. It is clear from his statements both to the code of conduct hearing and later to the Employment Tribunal that the decisions made at The Oval were reached jointly. Somehow this was lost in the campaign to use me as a scapegoat and a distraction from the real issues concerning the behaviour of the Pakistan cricket team and its management.

What was my employer's decision initially based on? Was it bloody-mindedness or was it instead all about revenge by the PCB? Nasim Ashraf had remarked publicly, 'Inzamam has paid the price, now Darrell Hair must pay the price.' More important to me was the fact that when making their decision, after on a five-minute conversation over lunch, the ICC chose not to ask me for my version of events. I did not receive a fair and reasonable hearing and was not given the opportunity to defend myself under the ICC Umpires Code of Conduct before being banished from international cricket umpiring. Among the ICC's stated values, their website carries the following claims:

- **Openness, honesty and integrity**

We work to the highest ethical standards. We do what we say we are going to do, in the way we say we are going to do it.

- **Excellence**

Cricket's players and supporters deserve the best. It is our duty to set the highest standards.

- **Accountability and responsibility**

We take responsibility for leading and protecting the game. We provide outstanding service to our stakeholders. If others are harming the game we take necessary action.

- **Commitment to the game**

We care for cricket. Everything we do and every decision we make is motivated by a desire to serve the game better.

- **Respect for our diversity**

We are an international organisation with a global focus and act at all times without prejudice, fear or favour.

- **Fairness and equity**

  We are fair, just and utterly impartial.

I believe that the way the ICC treated me brought these values into question, and that I was dealt with swiftly and severely — much more harshly, in fact, than players found guilty of corruption. Was it revenge, then, or racism? Was Billy Doctrove never questioned about his role because he was a black West Indian? Two people do the same job and one is singled out for punishment. If that is not racism, then what is it? If racism could not explain the ICC's decision making, then what was behind it? By lodging the action at the London Central Employment Tribunal, I was determined to try to find out. Above all, I wanted to exercise my right to a fair and public hearing, one that the ICC and their directors would not be able to control.

In the weeks following the code of conduct hearing my career had become a roller-coaster ride. Before the hearing I had been included in the appointments for the ICC Champions Trophy scheduled to be played in India during the first few weeks of October. At the end of the hearing, David Richardson spoke to me as I was having lunch with Amanda, and Doug Cowie, who had joined us. Some members of the Pakistan legal team were sitting at the same table. Richardson spoke about the forthcoming Champions Trophy in India and my appointment to it. He bluntly suggested that I withdraw from the tournament for safety and security reasons. I was shocked that the ICC would try to manipulate me in this way, let alone that Richardson would openly discuss such a sensitive issue in front of other people.

I flatly refused to withdraw. Richardson responded that the ICC themselves would be withdrawing the appointment, 'for security reasons', and that ICC media manager Brian Murgatroyd would be making a statement on the reasons later that afternoon.

Once again, without an opportunity for dialogue or input, I was summarily banned from umpiring duties and informed that the ICC were about to make a public statement about me. Had Richardson's course of action been decided on by someone else? Could it have been racially motivated? Richardson said the ICC had received a letter from the Board of Control for Cricket in India (BCCI) citing security concerns. In the letter to ICC president Percy Sonn, dated 25 September, which came to light more than a year later, Sharad Pawar, the president of BCCI, wrote:

> Mr I.S. Bindra has conveyed our views to you on the appointment of Darrell Hair as an umpire for the ICC Champions Trophy. We are of the opinion that, pending enquiry, Mr Darrel [sic] Hair should not be appointed to officiate as an umpire.

First, what 'views' were conveyed between I.S. Bindra and Percy Sonn? Did Sonn steer the BCCI into writing the letter so he wouldn't have to suffer the heat of making the decision himself? In the absence of any denial from the ICC, this is the only conclusion I can arrive at. Percy Sonn was stirring the pot, playing the political game and, I believe, a racist game too. Second, what was this 'pending enquiry' and when would I be told about it? What discussions were taking place? Finally, this letter torpedoed Speed's long-held claim that no country had the right of objection about any umpire's appointment. The letter continued:

> We would like to inform you that in the view of the raging controversy surrounding Mr Hair, there could be some controversy if he is appointed and it could also lead to some unnecessary problems for us in the smooth conduct of ICC CT [Champions Trophy] – 2006.

The letter concluded by requesting that Sonn 'intervene' personally and take 'immediate remedial action'.

I did not know of the existence of this letter when David Richardson told me there were 'security concerns' surrounding my possible appointment. The letter itself does not mention security concerns. The idea seemed laughable. India was a country considered safe enough for the President of the United States and other world leaders to visit regularly but was altogether unsafe for one international cricket umpire?

I could see where Richardson was heading and wanted to dig my heels in, but deep down I felt completely drained by the whole business and a few weeks of quiet time suddenly sounded like an attractive option. It would be good, I thought, to be completely out of the limelight for a while, spend some time with Amanda and our friends in Lincoln, and maybe visit a racecourse or two. I had often looked at cricket as my life and was grateful to be one of the lucky few who could earn a living within the game. Having said that, cricket, or any sport for that matter, should not occupy every waking hour — a good balance of friends, family and other interests is essential.

Finally, then, I told Richardson I would relinquish the Champions Trophy appointments, but not for the limp 'security reasons' he used to justify yet another act of poor governance. In fact, I told him I would never agree to such a ridiculous claim. I had never felt in danger during my previous trips to India and I wasn't about to admit to feeling that way publicly now just to appease him and whoever was pulling his strings. I told him to trump up any other excuse he wanted and I would not challenge him publicly, although later that day I did answer a question from the media honestly by refuting the security excuse used by the ICC.

How ironic it now seemed that while on 25 August I had been accused of attempting to mislead the public by offering to resign, Richardson, evidently under the direction of presumably Speed, was doing the same. Speed happily took to the hustings again on the afternoon of 28 September, read from a statement prepared for him by the ICC media advisory team:

> For Darrell Hair, a decision has been made in consultation with the ICC President Percy Sonn, the ICC general manager David Richardson and myself that he will not umpire at the ICC Champions Trophy 2006 amid concerns over his safety and security and also the safety and security of those around him during the tournament.

On 2 October 2006 I travelled to Dubai to attend the annual ICC umpires conference. Even though I would not be going to India for the Champions Trophy, I maintained the hope of soon getting back to the job of umpiring cricket matches. After all, I was still an Elite Panel umpire and I was looking to the future. Following the session on 3 October, Malcolm Speed requested that I meet him in his office. I was very hesitant at first, expecting another ambush, but part of me still felt I should show some faith in the ICC system. I even wondered if it might be the start of some bridge building between us.

During a brief discussion, Speed again avoided eye contact, and conversation about cricket or umpiring. Then he told me we had something in common — 'The ICC board wants to sack both of us.' Surprised, I asked him on what basis I would be dismissed. Maybe I should have shown some interest in and compassion for his situation, but, at this stage, why would I care? He said he didn't know the reasons but he just wanted to warn me that the ICC board was unhappy with him, and even more unhappy with me. I asked him if it could possibly be performance related, but he agreed that my umpiring since joining the Elite Panel had been generally very good and that I had been regularly ranked among the top three umpires. So how could my career be effectively terminated by the ICC board, unless by a racially motivated and discriminatory process? In telling me this, I think Speed's real message was: the ICC board was clearly divided along racial lines on my removal from the Elite Panel, and the ICC management wanted to appear powerless to counter such a rift, even if they wished to.

As far back as 31 August the BCCI Secretary, Niranjan Shah, made a statement about curtailing umpires' powers, and referred in particular to his board's view of me. Mr Shah stated in an article on Cricinfo that day, 'An umpire who abandons play without sufficient reason should be sacked.' The article also attributed the following to Mr Shah:

> The Indian board will await a ruling on Darrell Hair, the Australian umpire at the centre of the controversy, by Ranjan Madugalle, the Sri Lankan match referee, before taking a stand over Hair's future. The Pakistan and Sri Lankan board have already called for Hair's removal from the ICC's Elite Panel.

There were no calls by the PCB, the BCCI or the Sri Lankan Cricket Board for Billy Doctrove to be removed from umpiring. Shah's comments confirmed for me that there were indeed racially based moves afoot to have me removed from the Elite Panel. And why on earth would the BCCI be waiting on 'a ruling on Darrell Hair ... before taking a stand over Hair's future'? I thought it was Inzamam-ul-Haq who had been charged and that Madugalle was conducting the hearing on those charges alone. What was the BCCI Secretary hinting at when he referred to a 'ruling' on me?

First we had I.S. Bindra, then chairman of the BCCI, asking the ICC to investigate me. Then came Sharad Pawar's letter to Sonn, and now Niranjan Shah's comments. And what did Ranjan Madugalle have to say about all this? Nothing! Was he in on it all too? Talk about rotating the strike! It would appear from subsequent events that Speed was indeed aware of the PCB's pressure on the ICC board to stop me umpiring top-level matches.

On 30 October 2006, with assistance from John Beveridge, I wrote a letter to Speed outlining how disappointed I was by the way things had turned out but reiterating that all I really wanted to do was to return to my job. He replied by asking if I would agree to all or parts of the letter to be read out at the upcoming ICC board meeting. I agreed that the letter should be put before the board (that was one of the main reasons it was written in the first place), but only if it was read out in its entirety. David Richardson confirmed to me at a later meeting in Dubai that in fact none of the letter was read to the board. Speed apparently considered that while some of it might have been helpful, some was not. I was disappointed but not surprised.

I have read the transcript of the ICC board meeting on 3 November that stripped me of my right to umpire elite matches, and it is clear that due process was not followed.

After discussion of the PCB's charges against me, chairman Percy Sonn set up a decision-making subcommittee of Peter Chingoka, Nasim Ashraf and John Anderson. Mr Chingoka, the head of Zimbabwe cricket, has since been totally discredited. He is not allowed visas to travel to many of the cricket-playing nations. Dr Ashraf, the chairman of the PCB, has been connected with various business irregularities in his own country and with inappropriate conduct linked to the Cricket World Cup 2007 held in the West Indies as a result of combining his position on a Pakistan government quango with his chairmanship of the PCB. So at the same time as he was the prime mover in my removal by the ICC, he was also associated with corrupt activities involving unauthorised use of endowment funds. Ashraf had consistently been one of my strongest critics and was the prime mover behind a submission to the ICC board to have me charged under the code of conduct.

In a later statement, Ashraf recorded that his first act on becoming chairman of the PCB on 6 October was to submit a complaint regarding my conduct at The Oval. He admitted that although he had received briefing papers from the ICC, he did not read them before the ICC board meeting of 3 November began. He stated his belief that the ICC did not want to take action against me. Ashraf then recommended that an inquiry be held. Percy Sonn appointed Chingoka, Anderson and Ashraf himself to a subcommittee to 'fast-track' the process and arrive at a quick decision.

During the subcommittee's discussion, they moved away from the idea of an inquiry and instead came up with the idea of loss of confidence in me as an umpire. (It may also have become evident that, according to ICC regulations, any formal inquiry would have been conducted by Cricket Australia as Australia is my home country.) In Ashraf's own words, 'Rather than conduct an inquiry, the outcome of which would be uncertain, Sir John's resolution meant that the issue would be dealt with immediately and without ICC incurring any costs.' Chingoka confirmed that it was Anderson's idea to resolve the matter quickly 'so that a similar incident could not occur again'.

I had never met Nasim Ashraf. I had spoken with Anderson once: for two minutes at a dinner in Auckland some years ago. I had never had any discussion with Chingoka, who presided over cricket in Zimbabwe after the removal of white and Asian (or 'coloured') board members from the Zimbabwe Cricket Union Board on 6 January 2006.

Many articles published in the world media have indicated that the ICC board is controlled along racial lines, with nonwhites in the dominant position. I am not aware of any statement by the ICC refuting such claims. In their defence against the charge of racial discrimination, the ICC would have much to say about my attitude and behaviour, yet I had never received any adverse comment, in writing or verbally, on my skills in these areas from either Chris Kelly or Doug Cowie while they were ICC umpires' managers. I have never been spoken to or received any written notification by any referee about this aspect of my role. And I am unaware of any comment or notification from any captain of a full-member or Associate team that questioned my attitude or communication skills, despite their being required to fill out a captain's report on the umpires following each match.

At last, on 27 January 2007, through my lawyers at Finers Stephens Innocent, I lodged my claim of racial discrimination against the ICC with the London Central Employment Tribunal. Robert Griffiths QC and Stephen Whale QC, from 4–5 Grays Inn Square, offered to represent me. With assistance from the team at Finers Stephens Innocent, especially Paul Gilbert and Carolyn Brown, I felt confident that at last I would be able to get my side of the story across in a forum that could not be controlled by the ICC.

Preparation for the hearing occupied most of my waking hours from February through to October of 2007, during which time Amanda and I left England and returned to live in Sydney. I was determined not to discard any piece of evidence that might assist me. I will be forever grateful for the passionate engagement of Robert Griffiths, Stephen Whale, Carolyn Brown and Paul

Gilbert, who worked hours well beyond what was expected to ensure that the case was thoroughly prepared.

Robert Griffiths began the proceedings with a passionate opening address:

> This case is not about one man. It is actually about two. The first of them, Darrell Hair, is a white Australian man. The second, Billy Doctrove, is a black West Indian man. They have a great deal in common. They are both on the respondent's Elite Panel of cricket umpires.
>
> They are, by common consent, two of the greatest umpires in the world. They were both umpiring the cricket match between England and Pakistan at The Oval ground here in London on 20 August 2006. They made two important joint decisions that day, both entirely in accordance with the Laws of Cricket.
>
> The first joint decision was to award England five penalty runs because they judged that Pakistan had unfairly changed the condition of the ball. Such a decision is rare but is by no means unknown. What happened next was unprecedented. Pakistan, captained by Inzamam-ul-Haq, staged a protest in response to the award of five penalty runs. The team closeted itself in its dressing room and would not take to the field of play.
>
> The umpires explained to Pakistan the ramifications of their protest, but to no avail. The umpires jointly awarded the match to England because in their opinion Pakistan refused to play. Test cricket has been played for well over 100 years. Never before has a match been awarded for this

reason. It is impossible to overstate the fallout from these events, fallout that brings us all here today.

This came from the heart of a man who obviously loves his cricket. Griffiths went on to say that Billy and I had a great deal in common as cricket umpires, but that there the similarities end and the discrimination begins. Griffiths ran the Tribunal through what had happened since that eventful August afternoon. For Billy Doctrove, nothing — no board resolution, no sanction, no harassment, continued ICC support and appointments to umpire elite-level matches. The contrast in treatment between us was indeed striking.

Griffiths then reviewed the several discussions I had had with Doug Cowie in the immediate aftermath of the match, beginning with the dinner we shared on the evening of 21 August during which Cowie himself suggested that I would need to be well compensated if I were to resign. 'This set in train the most extraordinary series of steps, some of which have emerged only on the disclosure and exchange of evidence in the few days leading up to the beginning of the Tribunal. These disclosures were as yet unknown to the world at large and beggar belief,' said Griffiths.

Griffiths now set his sights on Shaharyar Khan, who was in the Pakistan dressing room during his team's protest:

> He is the man who was given by Mr Speed a written final warning for inappropriate media comment about the claimant. He is the man who said to Mr Speed that he did not intend to make public a letter of his criticism of Mr Hair, only for Mr Speed to note the next day that there

had been wide reference to that letter in many publications in the intervening 24 hours.

At the Executive Board meeting of the ICC on 3 November 2006 there were two papers of interest before the Board. The first was from Mr Speed. He recommended to the Board that no action be taken against Darrell Hair and that he continue to be appointed to umpire international matches. He described Mr Hair as one of the best umpires in the world. He recorded an earlier letter to the Pakistan Cricket Board in which he had said that if the ICC wished to take action against Mr Hair, it would be able to do so under the terms of his contract or under the Umpires' Code of Conduct. No doubt Mr Speed was conscious of legal advice he had been given by an Australian sports lawyer that it would be preferable for any sanction against Mr Hair to be pursuant to the Umpires' Code of Conduct, and that any disciplinary charge against him would need to be referred back to his home board, which was Cricket Australia.

Nasim Ashraf was so incensed by Speed's recommendation that no action be taken against me that he asked for the comments to be 'expunged from the record' of the board meeting. The second paper before the board flew in the face of that advice and my procedural rights as the claimant. It was a complaint about me from the Pakistan Cricket Board. It was signed by Dr Nasim Ashraf, by then PCB chairman. Ashraf was in the Pakistan dressing room during his team's protest. He was also the Pakistan representative on the ICC Executive Board. He therefore effectively acted as prosecutor, judge and jury. This had never before been made public.

Speed and Richardson sat in on the board meeting, as did Urvasi Naidoo, the ICC's in-house lawyer, who was there to record the proceedings. Except she didn't. Not when it was most critical.

It was the Indian representative, I.S. Bindra, who first mentioned race, although he omitted to recall the fact in the witness statement he provided. It was Bindra who wrote to the board of racist comments attributed to me. Except that he got it wrong. As was pointed out to him, the alleged comments could not have been made by me because I was not an umpire at the particular game to which Bindra referred. Many ICC witnesses would trot out the mantra that their decision about me had nothing to do with race, and yet it was one of the their own board members who first, wrongly and prejudicially, expressly introduced the issue.

Now to the heart of this case, and revelations that emerged only in the course of the proceedings at the Employment Tribunal and of which the public was unaware. Pakistan led the opposition to Speed's recommendations, as presented by Richardson. Ashraf said Pakistan had never refused to play, an absurd claim. He wanted the ICC to launch an inquiry into my conduct. At the same time, he claimed that no country had ever objected to an umpire's standing, despite the fact that his own Pakistan Cricket Board had written to the ICC on 21 and 28 August 2006 recommending that I be prevented from umpiring any future Pakistan matches.

The ICC disclosed these letters only four days before the Tribunal was due to sit. By then Bindra had built up a head of steam and totally agreed with Ashraf's demands. Peter Chingoka too said he had difficulty with Speed's recommendation. So it went on. There was an impasse over what to do about Darrell Hair. This was when chairman Percy Sonn directed the three board members to fast-track a resolution.

When the board reconvened after lunch there was, according to the ICC's own approved minutes, 'further lengthy discussion' on my future and a discussion of legal issues that might arise from the actions being considered. No written record was kept of this discussion either. That should not matter because the board meeting was tape-recorded and we have two different transcripts. Except one part of the tape recording was missing. That was the part that also covered the passing of the resolution and the simultaneous withdrawal of the PCB's complaint.

These are the circumstances in which the ICC board resolved that I should be cast adrift. No wonder Speed, Richardson and Cowie later admitted to me that there was no logic to the board's position.

Under the *Race Relations Act 1976*, an intention to discriminate is not required for a breach to have occurred. Neither does it depend on the discriminator's subjective reasons for the conduct in question, as would be explained at the Tribunal hearing. The critical question was, would I have received the same treatment had the racial element not existed?

The ICC based their defence on the wider interests of cricket, those being later identified by Sir John Anderson solely as its commercial interests. They would continue to claim that the actions taken could be attributed to my attitude and behaviour. My case was that I was treated the way I was because the ICC bowed to the discriminatory pressures brought to bear by the Asian bloc and their supporters on the board. The ICC board chose to deliberately circumvent the correct procedures for dealing with disciplinary action against an umpire because that might have led to the 'wrong' result. For me, that was the only possible explanation for what happened. But was this done to save Pakistan's reputation and/or to teach a white Australian umpire a lesson and deter any other umpires who might dare to take similar action?

Among the many other unanswered, or unsatisfactorily answered, questions, were these:

1. Why did Inzamam-ul-Haq on 20 August 2006 at The Oval 'raise the stakes' (David Collier) by saying I had a record of ruling against Asian teams?
2. Why did the adjudication of the disciplinary proceedings against Inzamam-ul-Haq switch from the official match referee, Mike Procter (a white South African) to Ranjan Madugalle (a Sri Lankan)?
3. Why was Billy Doctrove (a black West Indian) treated differently from me?
4. Why did Percy Sonn (a non-white South African) so hastily delegate the decision making to Nasim Ashraf (Pakistan), Peter Chingoka (black Zimbabwean) and Sir John Anderson (white New Zealander)?
5. Why, if the view was that I had acted incorrectly or unfairly, were no disciplinary proceedings brought against me in accordance with ICC's own regulations?
6. Why did Indian cricket chief I.S. Bindra tell the board on 3 November 2006 that 'Inzamam-ul-Haq has paid the price, now Darrell Hair must pay the price'?

7. Why did Mr Bindra introduce racial issues into the discussion at the board meeting?
8. Why did Dr Ashraf ask for Speed's/Richardson's comments ('which were supportive of Mr. Hair's position') to be 'expunged from the record' of the board meeting?
9. Why is the vital part of the board's deliberations missing from the record? How long was this discussion? What was said? Why was it not minuted or noted?
10. Why did the ICC keep me on the Elite Panel but give me no Elite Panel work? Was this an attempt to prevent me from bringing court or tribunal proceedings for unfair dismissal?
11. Why was my ability as a player manager and communicator challenged in the board meeting, when I had been praised for those very skills by the ICC's own staff and referees? For example, Sir Clive Lloyd was referee of a match I umpired involving Pakistan on 27 June 2006. On my player management abilities he reported: 'He is always focused and handles all the issues in this section very well.' On my communication skills: 'He is a tremendous communicator and uses everyone effectively.' And on my application of the regulations: 'Do not mess with this guy or you could be up for the high jump.'
12. Why did Speed's witness statement describe me as a 'troublemaker' when in his report to the November meeting he wrote: 'Darrell Hair is one of the best umpires in the world. As I have said to the media on many occasions, I would like to find a way for him to continue umpiring at the highest level'?

There was, I was convinced, a great deal of evidence to support a finding of racial discrimination and/or harassment against the ICC. I had been devastated by the ICC's actions. I felt violated. They had created an environment that was intimidating, hostile, degrading, humiliating and offensive. I had suffered both personally and financially. If the ICC's conduct in this case was taken as a yardstick of how cricket is governed internationally, then I believe the expression 'it's not cricket' takes on a wholly different meaning.

I was in no doubt that the ICC would vigorously defend the charge of racial discrimination. They would surely enlist the best lawyers to prepare their case and it would be gloves off from the start. I expected to be under attack and I was not disappointed.

The first witness statements, from ICC board members, all followed the same line:

> 'Darrell Hair was removed from international umpiring because the Board had lost confidence in him.'
>
> 'Darrell Hair was the sole instigator of the ball-tampering charge, and the subsequent refusal to play was the fault not of the Pakistan captain but of Darrell Hair.'
>
> 'I was initially in favour of acting on the complaint lodged by Nasim Ashraf of the Pakistan Cricket Board, but I was persuaded by Sir John Anderson to take the path of removing the risk of Darrell Hair calling off another game and the subsequent loss of income to the game that would result.'

'I did not think the conduct of Billy Doctrove needed investigation as he was merely playing a following role. Darrell Hair was the leading umpire.'

'Darrell Hair's race was not a factor in arriving at the decision to remove him from international umpiring and race was not mentioned at all.'

The reiteration that race was not specifically mentioned does not necessarily mean that it wasn't a factor, as was pointed out by Robert Griffiths QC in his opening address:

> An intention to discriminate is not required and it does not depend on the discriminator's subjective reasons for his conduct. Would the claimant have received the same treatment leaving out the racial grounds element? It is no defence for the alleged discriminator to show that it discriminated against the claimant to prevent unrest by prejudiced individuals or in the interests of good administration or the best interests from the point of view of chivalry or courtesy. It is no defence in this case to justify discrimination in the best interests of cricket. It is no defence that the intention was to save money or avoid controversy.

Witnesses do not generally advertise their prejudices and very little discrimination is overt or deliberate, but that does not mean it does not occur.

I was happy to fight the case based on what happened on and after 20 August. What I was not prepared for, although with hindsight should not have been surprised by, was the manner in which Malcolm Speed, David Richardson and Doug Cowie tried to dredge up matters dating back ten years or more to try to tarnish my character.

Speed began his witness statement with his 'early dealings with Darrell Hair'. He had known me since 1997, when I was acknowledged as one of the top three umpires in Australia. Our initial contacts related to my role in seeking to negotiate better terms and conditions for Australian umpires. Speed said he understood from other members of the Australian Cricket Board that I 'could be quite difficult' and that there was a general perception that I was 'a troublemaker'.

If the Australian Cricket Board really did think I was a troublemaker, then why did they persist in appointing me to their panel and, more important, why was I entrusted with roles in mentoring and training other umpires, as well as in assisting with writing playing conditions and interpretations of matters involving the Laws of Cricket?

I first became involved with the Australian Cricket Board in 1990, when I was appointed to their National Panel of Umpires. David Richards was then CEO; later, in 1993, he became the first CEO of the ICC. I had plenty of dealings with Richards and other members of the Australian Cricket Board, and I am certain they valued both my abilities as an umpire and my technical knowledge. As far as I know, no one at the ACB considered me a troublemaker, although some board members had misgivings about my calling Muralitharan for throwing in the Boxing Day Test match of 1995. However, when they became aware of the issues I had been raising for several months about Muralitharan's bowling action, they supported their umpires' call. If calling someone who breaches the laws is considered troublemaking, then I put my hand up and admit to being a troublemaker.

Speed said that the first issue to cause him concern related to the derogatory remarks made in my 1999 autobiography, *Decision Maker*, about Muralitharan's action, which I had described as 'diabolical'.

In January 2000 the Australian umpires were under constant pressure from the touring Indian team, and accusations of bias emerged. I had prepared a statement that all on the Australian National Panel of Umpires agreed to sign and read it out in front of Cammie Smith, the ICC referee, at the pre-series meeting. The other umpires were Peter Parker, Steve Davis, Daryl Harper and Simon Taufel.

Speed blamed me for a subsequent leak of information to the media, which meant that 'the incident attracted significant media coverage the next day'. It certainly did. Someone leaked that statement, but it was not me. Apart from the umpires, also present in the room were the team captains, coaches, managers, Tony Crafter, the Cricket Australia umpires' manager, and Brian Murgatroyd, who was working as media manager for the ACB. Murgatroyd said to me later that evening that the matter 'had been well handled' and congratulated me for bringing it out into the open. Murgatroyd changed his tune when Speed unleashed his wrath on me, accusing me of getting involved in cricket politics. My 'punishment' was to be removed from the appointments to the one-day finals. Being sanctioned without having had a fair hearing was something I was going to have to get used to.

Speed said he was initially supportive of my appointment to the

ICC Elite Panel of Umpires when it was formed in 2002, but that he was swayed by Sunil Gavaskar and David Richardson, who convinced him I was difficult to deal with and rude to players. Gavaskar and Richardson also had reservations about my umpiring ability. Speed then dropped a clanger: he detailed a number of occasions on which he spoke with Bob Merriman, the chairman of the ACB. Speed told Merriman that the reason I was not on the Elite Panel when it was formed in 2002 was because I was seen as a troublemaker and that there were concerns about my attitude and behaviour. In a subsequent conversation, Merriman is alleged to have told Speed that he (Merriman) had been assured by me that I would not cause any trouble and that I just wanted to concentrate on umpiring.

I may well have been considered to be tough on poor player behaviour and more than a little harsh with lbw decisions, but I was dedicated to umpiring cricket matches at the highest level, which I firmly believed I could do very well. After all, without self-belief you will never survive as an umpire. I had never told Bob Merriman that I 'would not cause any trouble'. I can recall no conversation in which I assured him of anything concerning my umpiring career.

What do comments such as these have to do with the decision of the ICC board to banish me from umpiring? Actually, nothing at all, but it is the way Speed wanted to paint me: I was always the 'troublemaker'. Perhaps Speed thought that if he succeeded in painting me as the problem child of ICC umpiring, it would impact on my credibility at the Tribunal.

It took a while, but Speed eventually got to the events of 20 August 2006. 'On that day,' he said, 'Darrell Hair was the senior

ICC umpire for the Test match.' This point was later refuted by Chris Kelly, former ICC umpires' manager, along with John Jameson, who was a member of the MCC Laws Working Party on which I sat between 2004 and 2007. Robert Griffiths would cross-examine a procession of ICC witnesses, who would all admit that there is no such thing as a 'senior umpire' who calls all the shots and makes all the important decisions while the other umpire just looks on and nods in agreement.

Speed recalled the call he made to me on my mobile. He said he remembered what I said because he knew it would lead to 'a huge international sporting and diplomatic issue'. Then his memory seems to have become confused. He claimed that I had overruled Billy Doctrove, who had suggested we might wait a bit longer to see if we could identify the culprit(s). I did no such thing. Speed then alleged that in response to requests from both teams that the match resume, I had argued that agreeing to such a course 'would make a monkey out of me'. I have never used such terminology.

Under pressure, I did suggest to Speed that if he was going to direct the umpires to rescind their decision, then he should do so quickly. Speed told me that he would not do that. In his statement he emphatically denied this exchange. Yet the memory is quite vivid in my mind, because I think I was almost hoping at the time that he would agree to override our decision. Although it would have seriously undermined the role of the umpires in any future Test match, it might have eased the pressures on me. But the really damning part of Speed's statement was his conclusion that 'Darrell Hair played the leading role in the umpires' decision to award the game to England, and I saw no reason to telephone Billy

Doctrove.' Why not? Why, if a 'huge international sporting and diplomatic issue' was at stake, did he not pick up the phone again and talk to the other umpire?

On the matter of 25 August, Speed claimed that I was not opposed to the release of the emails to the PCB and the public, yet a couple of paragraphs later he stated, 'Darrell queried why the ICC had to disclose his emails.' Confused? I certainly was.

I was taught in my formative years that the measure of a man is his underlying values — truth, honesty and fairness being at the forefront. My own view is that Malcolm Speed does not measure up to the mark in this respect. If I learn that I have been wrong in my judgement of him, then I will happily apologise, but nothing has happened in the interim to make me change my view. We should expect our leaders in this great game to work hard and lead from the front, not to cave in to pressure groups and politics.

David Richardson began his statement by focusing on my performance in a Test match in Adelaide in 1993. At the time I publicly admitted it had not been my finest moment in the game. 'During the Adelaide Test,' Richardson began, 'he gave a number of controversial lbw decisions against South Africa, and in our view the decisions were clearly wrong. I recall not only the fact that decisions went against us but also the arrogance of his manner.'

Richardson is a very different animal from Speed. Another former lawyer, he has also played Test cricket, which sets him apart as an administrator. He should be an excellent manager. He joined the ICC in 2002 and worked with Speed on the new structure of contracting an Elite Panel of umpires. He was opposed to my appointment, obviously based on what he had experienced of my ability some nine years earlier. He also doubted my suitability, he said, because of a number of allegedly controversial decisions I had made, in particular the no-balling of Muralitharan for throwing. Richardson added that this was one of the main reasons I was not appointed as one of the eight umpires on the first Elite Panel in 2002.

I was 'unsuitable' because I had called it as I saw it. But what about the change in the regulations to permit a bowler to flex his bowling arm by 15 degrees? Did that not vindicate the decisions I made in 1995? Apparently not, as it was because of these calls that I was left off the panel. Richardson went on to admit that I was selected as an Elite Panel umpire in 2003 based on the correctness of my decisions. So I was left off the original panel based on my umpiring decisions, then a year later I was selected for the very same reasons.

But let's not quibble over these matters. I believe a man either has credibility or he doesn't. For me, Richardson falls into the latter category. Why? Well, cast your mind back to the Hansie Cronjé scandal over match and spot fixing, which led to the Commission of Inquiry into Cricket Match Fixing and Related Matters, conducted by Judge E.L. King in Cape Town in 2000. The findings of the inquiry, as presented in the King Commission Report, make interesting reading. Here is an excerpt:

> It had been arranged that on 14 December 1996, two days after the last Test at Kanpur, South Africa and India would play a one-day limited overs match for the benefit of the

former India player Mohinder Amarnath. The South Africans on the eve of their departure for home after a long and arduous tour of the sub-continent, were greatly displeased to hear that the game had been converted into an official one-day international. For various reasons the team, depleted by illness, was far from enthusiastic about the match.

The match was to be played at Mumbai... [O]n the flight from Kanpur to Mumbai, Cronjé came to speak with Derek Crookes, his teammate, mentioning that a money offer had been made to the team to throw the last game; other players were also approached by Cronjé on this flight and on the bus on the way to the hotel; Cronjé told them that he had received an offer dependent on the team playing badly in the one-day international.

Crookes asked his captain whether he was joking or serious. In response to Crookes' enquiry Cronjé told him to think about it and that there would be a (team) meeting later. This would surely have conveyed that Cronjé was serious, as indeed he was.

The King Commission Report then records:

> According to Dave Richardson, a senior player, Cronjé called a meeting of senior players, namely, McMillan, [Andrew] Hudson, Kirsten (vice captain) and himself (Richardson). Cronjé put the proposal. Richardson could not recall the details thereof or the amount of money offered. It was decided that Cronjé would call a meeting of

the whole team. Thus Cronjé's senior colleagues also took the proposal seriously.

Let's get this straight: David Richardson listens to his captain put a proposal to senior members of the South African team to set out to deliberately lose a cricket match. Richardson was a lawyer, so I think it should have been obvious to him that there might be something illegal in what Cronjé was suggesting. Did he reject the proposal outright? Well, he said he could not recall the details or the amount of money offered. Others apparently had a better memory of what was said.

The King Commission Report continues:

> Pat Symcox, a team member, also recalled the incident. He put the offer conveyed by Cronjé at US$250,000. At the team meeting, certain players spoke out against the offer, notably Hudson, Crookes and [Daryll] Cullinan. The whole squad was present at the meeting (excluding [Alan] Donald and [Jonty] Rhodes who had left for home).

How could anyone forget a figure like US$250,000? I think it would be fair to say that if a team were offered a bonus of a quarter of a million dollars to *win* a match, it would be crystal clear to all concerned. Judge King concluded:

> The offer was seriously made and seriously considered. Cronjé's attitude was that the offer had to be accepted by everyone, otherwise it was 'no go'. After the objectors had spoken, the meeting rejected the proposal.

It is not clear who the objectors were, but let's face it, a 20-minute meeting to discuss something so unethical, not to mention highly illegal, must surely have stayed in the memory banks of those in attendance. Apparently not in David Richardson's case. And why did the meeting last 20 minutes anyway? How long does it take to know right from wrong, to say no?

The King Commission Report concludes this little chapter of Cronjé's affairs by recording that after the team meeting a few of the players remained behind in Cronjé's room (where the meeting had been held) and were present when Cronjé telephoned 'MK' and sought an increase in the offer, in which cause he succeeded. MK was prepared to raise the offer by $100,000. 'Well, there's another 100k,' Cronjé informed his colleagues. Whatever the offer really was, according to the evidence available to the inquiry it was not taken up. No evidence was produced to identify the 'few players' who remained behind in Cronjé's room. Richardson has never publicly commented (so far as I can find) as to whether he was or was not present at that later meeting.

ICC lawyer Urvasi Naidoo also acts as company secretary, with the responsibility of sitting in on board meetings and ensuring proper records are kept, a role she said she had fulfilled since 2003. Ms Naidoo qualified as a lawyer in 1992. While she knew the value of good minute taking, she confessed to the Tribunal that she was not actually much good at this particular task. She does not take written notes; rather, she types a record of what is discussed directly onto her laptop. Since she is not a great typist, she takes down a summary of the discussion and outcomes of each agenda item. She also uses a dictaphone to tape the meetings and later refers to the recording to prepare the full minutes.

Under questioning, she said she was aware of how important the minutes of this particular meeting would be. She knew the Darrell Hair issue was 'controversial' and that the ICC directors would later want to check the accuracy of the minutes taken. She said the tapes of the meeting were held in her office until 24 May 2007, when they were provided to the ICC's lawyers in London. Apparently when I issued my claim against the ICC she was asked by the London lawyers to listen to the tapes and produce a transcript of the discussion item relevant to me.

It soon became apparent that the crucial part of the discussion was missing. Ms Naidoo is gallant enough to admit that it must have been an error on her part, although she 'was not exactly sure what happened'. Either she taped over this section or she just plain forgot to turn on the dictaphone after lunch. Finally she suggested that as there was another ICC meeting the next day, perhaps she recorded over the minutes of the previous day's proceedings. 'I just don't know,' she conceded. Now in damage control mode, she recounted what she 'recalled' had been said — that the board had lost confidence in me, and so on. There was apparently some comment that she 'did not think it necessary to minute'.

I do not believe it was for Ms Naidoo to decide what should or should not be included in the minutes of a meeting at which the need for accurate minute taking was so important, as she herself had admitted.

Naidoo stated that no one gave her directions on any aspect of recording the proceedings of the meeting. No allegations were made that she had been instructed to be selective in what she recorded, so I have often wondered why she mentioned that in her statement — did she protest too much? Obviously, though, the missing tape and minutes could lead to an inference that the record was not accurate. Even though her recall of events was a little uncertain, her memory was crystal clear when she insisted that at no point in discussions was my race, colour, ethnicity or nationality mentioned and that 'Darrell Hair's claim that he had been discriminated against on the basis that he is white is completely without merit'.

John Anderson believed firmly that umpires must always act in the best interests of the game. Under cross-examination by Robert Griffiths, however, those best interests turned out to be the revenue streams generated by international cricket. Nothing much else mattered. Anderson's view was that umpires should never invoke the laws if to do so risked conflict or protest. He also had trouble coming to grips with the difference between the responsibility of umpires to make decisions according to the laws and existing playing conditions, and the responsibility of players to act within those laws at all times. He argued that any inquiry would not be in the best interests of the ICC as it would more that likely prove the umpires' decision was correct.

Robert Griffiths asked how the subcommittee of Ashraf, Chingoka and Anderson had come to their conclusions. They did so, said Anderson, through a discussion that lasted less than five minutes. Robert Griffiths was incredulous. 'Five minutes!' he thundered, 'Five minutes! And on that basis Mr Hair lost his status as a Test match umpire!

'How much weight did you give to Malcolm Speed's recommendation not to take further action against Darrell Hair, given his position as chief executive officer of the ICC?' Griffiths asked.

'I disagreed with him,' said Anderson.

'You gave his recommendations no weight, then?' asked Griffiths.

'I disagreed with him,' repeated Anderson.

Under further questioning, Anderson admitted that I was an excellent umpire; that I had not been given due process in this affair; and that the ICC Code of Conduct and the principle of natural justice had been ignored. Griffiths then asked Anderson if he had attended the final of the World Cup in Barbados earlier in the year. Anderson said he had not. Griffiths asked if Anderson believed it was important for an umpire to know the laws of the game. 'Yes it is,' came the response. This led to an obvious question.

'You are aware, of course, that the umpires who officiated in the final made a complete bodge of it? Did they bring embarrassment beyond belief to the ICC?'

'They did,' said Anderson.

'And are they still umpiring?' asked Griffiths, to which Anderson mumbled something resembling a 'yes'.

On my fellow umpire at The Oval, Anderson declared, 'Billy Doctrove was just a follower.' Not only did this show a total lack of respect for Doctrove, but the idea of appointing a senior and a junior umpire was, as he had to admit, an insult to *all* umpires. 'Darrell Hair controlled the events.' How would Anderson know this? He had no knowledge of what had happened, other than what he had been told by others or read in the newspapers. Maybe he actually spoke to Billy Doctrove. It was certainly something that Malcolm Speed had not done.

It was interesting to note that when not 'on the stand', Anderson seemed to be engrossed in a book of Sudoku puzzles. If it was a ploy to ease his nerves or order his thoughts, it seemed to fail miserably. When called to the witness box he fumbled his way through his evidence. Before he left the witness box, he dismissed our crucial umpiring call as 'the most appalling decision I have ever seen', then he went back to Sudoku.

A new, amazing piece of evidence was now presented by ICC president Ray Mali. Under questioning from Griffiths, Mali at first appeared confused. Then came the bombshell. When asked if I was one of the better umpires in the world as a decision maker, given that I had been consistently ranked in the top three ICC umpires, Mali replied, 'I can see no reason why Darrell Hair should not be able to resume umpiring in full-member ICC matches tomorrow.' This answer so stunned Griffiths that he had to ask Mali to repeat it. Mali did so. So why, when the ICC president took this view, were Speed, Richardson and the ICC board members still so keen to sully my reputation? Was it simply personal?

The Tribunal had now been in progress for seven days and the ICC witness list was still a long one. Ten days had been set aside for the case but it was now clear that all the witnesses could not be heard and cross-examined before the time was up. Until now media reporting of the proceedings had been positive towards me, while the ICC, and the manner in which they ran world cricket, was being heavily criticised. Michael Atherton, following the proceedings for the *Telegraph*, had this to say:

I had little sympathy for Hair during the events of The Oval, but I rather hope the tribunal chairman finds a way of recognising that Hair has been treated appallingly. Instinctively I find myself sympathising with the individual and the powerless over the corporate and the powerful. This is not about what happened at The Oval, but what has happened since. There is no doubt that Hair has been treated poorly.

Beyond these narrow confines, perhaps the lasting effects of this case will be to the governance of the ICC. It was clear on Friday that decision-making should be left to the professionals, to the paid executives, rather than to the well-meaning amateurs.

An umpire's role can be a lonely one at the best of times, but there were times during this period when I felt the loneliest man in cricket. That was how I felt when I found out that Billy Doctrove did not intend to fly to London as agreed, although he did send a detailed statement. I had described Billy to the Tribunal as a close umpiring friend, but he still worked for the ICC and may have had second thoughts about sticking his neck out. I had just 24 hours' notice that he had decided against boarding the plane to London, citing matters 'too confidential to explain'. Publicly, the ICC advised that Doctrove had called cricket manager David Richardson to ask for advice on whether he should attend the hearing and that Richardson had left the decision to him. We will never know what was actually said in that conversation. Doctrove himself has never subsequently told me why he bailed out at such short notice.

Looking into the future is always difficult. What lies there is unknown; the prospects can be frightening. But with assistance and advice from Robert Griffiths, Stephen Whale and Carolyn Brown, and after Ray Mali's encouraging comments at the Tribunal, I made the decision to approach the ICC and offer a compromise that might see me umpiring again, in return for dropping the Tribunal claim.

Section 2 of the *Race Relations Act 1976* contains a provision that a person who has lodged a complaint of racial discrimination cannot subsequently be victimised, regardless of the outcome of the proceedings. This would obviously help me in negotiating a new contract in March 2008 — if I was able to prove to the ICC that I was still one of their best umpires.

Discussions took place, and while they must remain confidential (at least on my part) it appeared that I could look forward to a return to Test umpiring. The ICC agreed to my undertaking a management course and I agreed to continue umpiring in second-tier ICC matches. If I were to receive good reports in those matches, the ICC board could have little reason not to renew my contract in March. I was at pains not to jeopardise the arrangement by speaking to the media, but my employment lawyer, Paul Gilbert, said: 'Darrell feels relieved and glad it's all over and he does feel this is in the best interests of all parties. What we have now is a future for Darrell that leads to the possibility of his return to top-level umpiring.'

Malcolm Speed, as always, wanted the last word. 'We had absolutely no alternative but to defend this vigorously,' said the ICC chief executive. A lot will depend on the management and rehabilitation program and how Darrell responds to it.' Determined not to give him the ammunition to be able to say 'I told you so', I let these provocative, highly charged comments pass. It was time to move on.

CHAPTER 9

RETURNING TO TEST CRICKET

The quarterly ICC board meeting was scheduled for 18 March 2008. I knew my 'reinstatement' was on the agenda. However, I had no great confidence that the board would allow it. I expected that Pakistan would oppose me; how India, Sri Lanka and Bangladesh would vote was anyone's guess.

I had complied with the 'rehabilitation program' set out and supervised by ICC umpires manager Doug Cowie. I enrolled in a professionally accredited course in neuro-linguistic programming (NLP), which was something I had always wanted to do. The program satisfied the ICC's requirement that I further develop my people management and communication skills. I completed the program in November 2007 and the results were accepted by Cowie, who then made a submission to senior management through cricket manager David Richardson. I believe Richardson then prepared a paper to be discussed at the ICC board meeting.

It was a long time to wait and I still had little confidence that the board would change their minds. I had not umpired at the highest international level since August 2006, although I never stopped believing I was still capable of doing so. Some 19 months had now passed, so there had been plenty of time for me to think about my future. At the Employment Tribunal the ICC's processes and management had been publicly ridiculed. They remained a very strange organisation, fuelled by political power bases and revenue-making giants, and I still questioned their dedication to the spirit of the game and their acceptance of the primacy of umpires' decisions.

I was taking a walk on a warm Tuesday afternoon when my mobile rang. It was Cowie. As with many international calls, there was a slight delay before Doug introduced himself, and it seemed like an eternity before he spoke again. Still under the familiar clouds of doubt, I felt bad news coming. With all that had happened since August 2006, who could blame me?

As it turned out, my fears were misplaced. Cowie delivered the news that the ICC had agreed to approve my selection to umpire full-member Test matches and one-day internationals again. Were there any strings attached? Cowie said there were none. All that was required of me was that I abide by the ICC Umpires Code of Conduct and umpire matches to the best of my ability. Wasn't that what I had always done? But I left that question unasked — no point fanning the fires now. Cowie told me I would be appointed to matches as soon as he could rearrange various appointments. I asked if I could expect a reasonable quota of matches and he said I definitely could, as 'you are still one of our best umpires'. This rang a little hollow, but I was thankful that I could look forward to getting back onto the field.

The responses from Pakistan were predictable. Inzamam blamed his own board for not speaking out against me. Shaharyar Khan said he was 'shocked' to hear of my reinstatement. But in the time since I had been ostracised, both Inzamam and Khan had passed their use-by dates and were no longer playing or administering. In any case, the many messages of support and encouragement I received far outweighed these minority views. I was excited and couldn't wait to get back.

Old Trafford, Manchester. On 23 May 2008 it was the only place I wanted to be. In the last week of April, Cowie had confirmed my appointment to the 2nd and 3rd Tests between England and New Zealand. This match was also to be Old Trafford's last for at least three years, as the ECB had a commitment to use the grounds at Cardiff and Durham as more regular Test venues. The previous match in the series was played at Lord's under cloudy skies and chilly winds. Today was brighter, although probably a good deal colder. New Zealand captain Daniel Vettori had decided to bat on a dry and bouncy pitch with a bit of a patchwork quilt look about it.

My umpiring partner for this match was Simon Taufel. As we walked down the steps and onto the ground, a freezing gust of wind blew in from the Pennines, a sign of things to come. The next four days would be no warmer than 11 or 12 degrees Celsius, not factoring in the wind chill. Yes, it would make for difficult umpiring conditions, but so what? I had longed for this day and was determined to make it one of my best matches.

Ryan Sidebottom, a left-arm swing bowler, opened the bowling from my end, which got me into the middle of things immediately. It didn't take long before my first big appeal since 20 August 2006. Sidebottom bowled an excellent delivery of good length to New Zealand opening batsman Jamie How. Timed at 85.3 mph, it pitched and straightened down the line of middle stump, rapping How on the pads. There was a huge appeal but I quickly concluded, 'Not out — too high'. It was a great ball from Sidebottom and had it kept a little lower I would have given it out. I knew that all sorts of technology would be replaying the ball, but already Sidebottom was back at the end of his bowling mark and ready to steam in for the next delivery. No time to dwell on it, on to the next ball. As it turned out, technology backed my decision, showing the ball passed just above the bails. It was good to be back, and even better to know I hadn't lost the ability to make correct decisions under pressure.

The game ran its course without incident or questions raised about umpiring decisions. I had invited as my guests the people who had supported me so much the previous year. Knowing that Robert Griffiths, Stephen Whale, Paul Gilbert and Carolyn Brown, along with Amanda, were watching, the last thing I wanted was to give them any cause to wonder if perhaps I wasn't really the umpire of quality they had supported so diligently and selflessly. I did not let them down, and it was very pleasing for me to have them attending my 'comeback' match.

England skipper Michael Vaughan called on his left-arm spinner Monty Panesar in just the tenth over, with New Zealand looking exceedingly comfortable at 80 runs on the board in the opening stand. Vaughan then recalled the trusty Sidebottom, who dismissed Jamie Redmond and Hamish Marshall in quick succession, going round the wicket as he had done with growing frequency on the preceding tour of New Zealand. Brendan Taylor tempered his natural aggression and transformed himself into a cultured, patient batsman, but he soon lost wicketkeeper McCullum, who tried to dominate Panesar in both innings but failed miserably.

Taylor also lost Daniel Flynn who, attempting to hook the fiery James Anderson, was struck on the grille of his helmet at such pace that he lost two front teeth. Bloodied and dazed, he left the field and took no further part in the match. Bad light stopped play just after tea, but next morning Taylor ran himself out, taking on Alistair Cook's deadly aim from backward point. Unbelievably, two balls later Vettori went in similar fashion, neglecting to ground his bat as he completed a second run — a bizarre and embarrassing mistake compounded by the fact that Panesar was the fielder. Bad light again interrupted play after the tea interval.

The next morning, with New Zealand at 6 for 250, Taylor found an ally in Kyle Mills, who looked most accomplished in bringing up his maiden international 50. Taylor's maturity had already resulted in his second Test century, off just 130 balls, before he cut loose in Twenty20 fashion, hitting four of his five sixes, one of which was hooked high over the deep square fielder. It was an almost faultless, responsible and classy knock that saw New Zealand through to a respectable 381 at a healthy run rate of 4.2.

The wind increased to gale force on the third morning, which seemed to suit the Iain O'Brien–Vettori bowling combination:

they skittled England's vaunted middle order with very little fight, dismissing them for 202. Vettori had taken five wickets bowling downwind with his left-arm orthodox spinners. It is not often that a team leading by 179 runs in the first innings find themselves in danger of losing, and losing badly. New Zealand had reached 2 for 85, 264 ahead, thanks to How and Marshall, when Michael Vaughan introduced Panesar to bowl downwind, as had Vettori. Panesar bowled much flatter, faster and more aggressively 'into the pitch', securing four quick lbw verdicts from Simon Taufel as New Zealand crumbled. Six for 37 was Panesar's best Test return, and Taylor became his 100th Test wicket. With Anderson, Stuart Broad and Sidebottom taking turns from the Stretford End into the gale-force winds, England's bowling unit combined with some brilliant fielding to dismiss New Zealand inside 42 overs. Flynn, who had hoped to bat, was rested on medical advice.

England's bowlers had presented their batsmen with the chance to create history, as a winning target of 294 had never before been achieved in the fourth innings at Old Trafford. Andrew Strauss and Cook began with some exciting stroke play and aggressive running between the wickets. This appeared to unsettle New Zealand, whose consistency with the ball began to fade, and although they lost Cook, England reached the close of play at 1 for 76. The lead had been whittled away to just 218.

The fact that 16 wickets were lost on the third day could be put down to exemplary spin bowling and to flawed decision making by the batsmen. The fourth day started with very clear skies but was once again exceedingly chilly; if anything, the wind was even fiercer. Vaughan had accepted the advice of Lancashire groundsman Peter Marron to use the heavy roller, and the pitch played consistently into the afternoon. Whether the rolling meant the pitch played much truer that day we will never know. I have seen enough cricket pitches in my time to know I could never predict if and how they might deteriorate over the course of a match.

Strauss and Vaughan batted positively almost throughout the first session, running quick singles, and the score was 2 for 171 at lunch, with Vaughan the only batsman dismissed. Strauss looked most assured on 73, his third half-century of the series. After lunch, Strauss's precise shot selection saw him through to a superbly worked 106. It was his twelfth Test century, and one of his most important. England had 235 on the board and had clearly assumed control. Kevin Pietersen gave Vettori a helping hand and a small glimmer of hope by running himself out, but Ian Bell and Paul Collingwood, both obviously out of touch, nervously but steadily inched their side towards glory. On the stroke of tea, Collingwood leg-glanced a single and England achieved their fifth-highest run-chase. They had regained the favourites tag, while New Zealand left Manchester perplexed, ruing the one that got away.

Sitting in the umpires' room at the end of the match, I reflected on the last international match I had umpired here — the World Cup semifinal between Pakistan and New Zealand in 1999. I had often cited that match as the highlight of my umpiring career, but now, with all that had happened since then, I rated 26 May 2008 as my most important match.

Episode two of my return to Test umpiring took place at Trent Bridge, a ground I like immensely, having umpired several one-day internationals there. This would be my third Test match at what would have to be the friendliest ground I have been to. It is an excellent ground to umpire on, with a good pitch, and is also what I call a good 'seeing' ground for umpires. I don't know how to really explain that term, but for some reason the ball never gets lost in the crowd and is easy to pick up in flight when you are standing at either end.

My 78th Test match saw England wrap up the series 2–0 with an ultimately comfortable win. But for a few interruptions for bad weather, the match could have ended in three days. Victory looked anything but assured, however, just after lunch on the first day, when England lost three wickets in as many overs and were struggling at 5 for 86. A match-turning stand between Pietersen and Tim Ambrose reclaimed the initiative and a superb spell of swing bowling from Anderson ensured the series win.

This match raised concerns about the balls, which regularly went out of shape at around the 20-over mark. The players thought the current batch of balls provided by the ECB were going soft too early, and that things returned to normal when they got hold of a used ball from the previous year. Officiating in only my second Test since my return, I could probably have done without the fuss. But I thought I handled things well enough and even joked with Vettori and Vaughan when they methodically presented the ball to me for inspection. All I could do was smile ruefully when the cameras zoomed in as my fellow umpire Steve Bucknor and I peered quizzically at the misshapen ball.

A newspaper report later brought to light the fact that, with 77 previous Test matches under my belt and with 123 under Steve Bucknor's, we were the most experienced pair of umpires ever in a Test, our combined total of 200 beating the previous record of 191 set by Bucknor (114) and Rudi Koertzen (77) before the Adelaide Test of the 2006–07 Ashes. I was never one for records, but it seemed bizarre that this statistic was thrown up when only two years earlier various newspaper reports had implied that I had no idea what I was doing!

Whichever ball was used, it swung for both teams early on. Play started on time despite Nottingham having absorbed a month's rain the previous week, a factor that probably led Vettori to decide New Zealand would field first. Some locals thought the new Bridgford Road stand, with its strange, futuristic roof, had helped the ball to swing — another tall tale, and no doubt one that will spread as the years go by. The first ball change coincided with England's 50, and by lunch the score had advanced to 2 for 84. But wickets fell to the last ball of each of the next three overs. Strauss flashed a simple chance to first slip, Bell played across a straight one and then Collingwood gave a harder catch to the diving Taylor at slip. It is an interesting superstition in cricket that certain balls of an over are more likely to take a wicket than others, a little bit like the theory that black and red numbers should come up alternately on a roulette wheel. Total fantasy of course, but it was amusing to hear the New Zealanders chirping up when, for the next half hour or so, the last ball of an over was about to come. When nothing much more happened they turned their efforts to more important things, like trying to separate Ambrose and Pietersen, who eventually put on a sixth-wicket stand of 161.

New Zealand might have wrapped things up quickly next morning had Brendan McCullum, fielding at second slip, held on to a regulation chance given by Broad off Chris Martin, but it bobbled out of his grasp. Broad then went confidently to his first Test half-century, adding 76 with Anderson to stretch the innings past lunch. When England posted 364, it was Trent Bridge's highest total of the season to date by a margin of 85. The score looked even better when Anderson immediately found his rhythm from the Radcliffe Road end. Redmond survived a caught-behind appeal off his first ball, but two deliveries later had no answer to one angled towards the leg then swinging away to hit the off stump as the batsman shaped to play it through mid-wicket. And in Anderson's third over, an even bigger fish fell for the same lure: McCullum tried a similar shot to a similar ball and lost his off stump too. How narrowly escaped when he popped Collingwood up just short of cover, but a change of end and a change of ball seemed to suit Anderson even more. In his second over after tea, Taylor squirted an attempted drive into the gully, then Flynn survived one confident lbw appeal from his second ball only to fall to an even straighter one next up. How followed four overs later, offering a disappointingly limp bat to an outswinger after two hours. Just before bad light ended play for the day, Anderson went round the wicket to Jacob Oram and moved one away enough to take the edge. At stumps James Anderson had taken all six wickets for 42 runs — his best Test figures, to follow his batting best earlier in the day.

New Zealand crumbled early the next morning to be all out for just 123 and were asked to follow on. The main destroyer in the second innings was Ryan Sidebottom, who had seemed out of sorts in the first innings, apparently suffering from a back spasm that kept him off the field for a time. With their main batsmen gone, and still trailing by 64 overnight, New Zealand needed the weather to intervene if they were to survive. Instead, they got the best weather of the match. I walked out to start the fourth morning in brilliant sunshine and the warmest temperature (around 19 degrees) in nearly a month. A surprisingly large crowd watched local hero Sidebottom lead the way as the last five wickets tumbled in 41 balls. Sidebottom finished with 6 for 67, taking his tally in six Tests against New Zealand in 2008 to 41.

I felt mixed emotions when the last wicket fell. I was thrilled to have successfully completed two more Test matches but also quite sad that it might be the last time I umpired a match on this beautiful and friendly ground.

Now I had some thinking to do. One question in the back of my mind was whether the ICC would extend my contract in March 2009. There were regular leaks from faceless ICC 'sources' suggesting it was unlikely that I would be offered a continuation. No matter how well things seemed to be going, I always felt a nasty undercurrent not far beneath the surface. David Richardson, now ICC general manager, had made it known through his statement to the Employment Tribunal that he was not a fan of my style, and it was Richardson who made decisions on future contracts. I had no confidence that he would take into account my latest on-field performances when making up his mind. Would he be influenced by my temerity in publicly challenging the ICC's management style and handling of umpires? As a lawyer, he would know that it would be illegal to base his decision on that, wouldn't he?

Another thing on my mind was the total lack of communication in the lead-up to the Old Trafford Test. Normally the ICC like their umpires to be fully prepared, especially if they have not umpired for some time. Back in the early days of ICC umpiring appointments, there was always an offer of 'warm-up' matches in second eleven county cricket fixtures. My last competitive match had been on 15 July 2007, when Ireland played Scotland in Belfast. Having been off the field for nine months, I would have liked to do some preparatory games before I walked out onto Old Trafford for the Test. But no such offer was made. It gave me the feeling that someone might have wanted to see me fail.

The question that most occupied my thoughts was Doug Cowie's promise that he would be appointing me to as many matches as possible. Despite this assurance, I now had no prospects other than the possibility of some matches in South Africa in November/December. So I would have had just four matches in the nine months between 18 March, when I had been reinstated, and the end of December. Were the ICC deliberately restricting my appointments and opportunities? Maybe I was wrong, but lacking a reasonable run of matches to look forward to, my thoughts turned increasingly to retirement from international cricket. There was much for me to think about over the next few days.

PART 3

DECISION MAKING

CHAPTER 10

THE CONTROVERSIAL UMPIRE

My umpiring career began in October 1985 at Tunks Park, Cammeray, New South Wales. The match was a fourth-grade fixture between one of my old clubs, North Sydney District Cricket Club, and neighbouring Manly Warringah Cricket Club. I knew many of the players. I recall the occasion vividly. It was a fine, sunny spring day with a gentle north-easterly breeze wafting across the ground from Cammeray Marina in Long Bay, one of the many bays and inlets that dot Sydney Harbour. Tunks Park is situated on the bayside of a stretch of open parkland incorporating several playing fields and public walking tracks that run for about three kilometres through Flat Rock Gully, finishing at Hallstrom Park near Willoughby Road. The ground has a peaceful outlook and a wonderful view of The Northbridge, a sandstone suspension bridge built in 1892 specifically to carry trams and to open access to the (then) far northern suburbs of Sydney.

My partner was Andrew Miles, who is still a member of the New South Wales Cricket Umpires and Scorers Association. Andrew, who no longer umpires in Sydney grade matches, had eased me into umpiring with kind words and sound counsel. Dave Ford, from Manly, who was later to become a colleague at Cricket NSW, was run out for being too slow between the wickets. Steve Taylor, a former fast-bowling teammate from North Sydney but now many kilos heavier, stood at first slip giving a running commentary of the day, as he usually did. (Steve was a fearsome sight back in 1972, when there were not many batsmen who enjoyed facing his first few aggressive overs.)

It was an unremarkable beginning to my career as an umpire. There were no arguments about our decisions. Indeed, there was nothing controversial at all for the umpires — just 22 players and two umpires enjoying a day out in the sun. It was an opportunity to maintain friendships with the people and the game that had dominated my memory of summer days as far back as I could recall. By day's end I felt I had made the right decision to continue my involvement with cricket.

The term 'controversial' was first attached to my name in the newspapers and electronic media a little over ten years later, in 1995, solely on the basis of a decision I had made about one bowler's illegal action. But on that day in Tunks Park, Cammeray, the only meaningful decision I had to make was how many beers to drink back at Percy's Hotel, North Sydney, after the close of play. It was the way of club cricket in Sydney that both teams would later gather to down a few cool drinks and discuss the day's game.

Here's a dictionary definition:

Controversial (adjective)
Causing argument — provoking strong disagreement or disapproval, e.g. in public debate
Argumentative — enjoying or habitually engaging in controversy

I have also been described as 'contentious', 'notorious' and 'divisive', all gibes I find annoying and inconsistent with the values and spirit of the game. I have had to learn to live with the 'controversial' tag, but what does it really mean when applied to the things I have done? In a nutshell, I believe that if I am considered controversial for doing something that is right, even if few of my peers choose to do the same, I can wear that. If penalising a violation of the laws of the game is considered controversial, then so be it. All I have ever had to ask myself is, 'Is this the right thing to do?' I was brought up always to do what was right. To ignore wrongdoing would put me at odds with my values and beliefs. In the context of the game, doing that would 'reward' a player or team that contravenes the Laws of Cricket, thereby penalising the team that upholds the laws.

Newspaper journalists and media commentators have delighted in playing the 'controversial' card when describing me or my decisions. These 'experts', who show a blithe disregard for the distress their commentary can cause, invariably claim that I have deliberately sought out controversy. The plain truth is that in 22 years of umpiring I never made a decision or followed a path of action *because* it was controversial. Rather, I made decisions I believed to be right *despite* their being controversial. For this I make no apologies and have no regrets.

Here's another take on one of those 'controversial' stories:

> Umpire Darrell Hair yesterday rightly penalised Danish Kaneria of Pakistan for damaging the pitch on his follow-through. Kaneria, bowling in the second innings when India were batting, had been issued two prior warnings and was removed from the attack when he transgressed the third time.
>
> In an official statement issued at the close of the day's play, an ICC spokesman said Darrell Hair had acted correctly and as a result the Pakistan team would have to bowl for the rest of the innings without their star leg spinner.
>
> 'The Laws are quite clear,' added the ICC spokesman, 'in ruling that there must be a severe penalty to dissuade bowlers from damaging the pitch and thereby gaining an advantage for their team. We fully support our umpires when they act promptly in the interests of the game to prevent further damage to the pitch.'
>
> It should be noted that this is not the first time Kaneria has found himself in trouble for damaging the pitch and the ICC feels that he should work with the coaching staff to eliminate this flaw in his bowling technique.

Of course the above media release is pure fantasy! As good as it sounds, it has never happened and probably never will. The ICC seems to permit their employees to be maligned. A cloak of secrecy descends like a pea soup fog whenever the handling of mostly unjust criticism of cricket umpires is raised. These media assaults amount to a direct slap in the face for umpires around the world. Is it any wonder that recruitment and retention of umpires at grassroots level has been falling for decades in most parts of the world?

Here are some real headlines, the type effectively condoned by Malcolm Speed and the regiment of ICC media and public relations staff:

'Controversial Australian umpire Darrell Hair was on Monday subjected to ridicule and scorn by Sri Lankan cricket experts …'

'Pakistan says that it was Hair who controversially adjudged Pakistan skipper Inzamam-ul-Haq run out and unnecessarily warned Danish Kaneria and Salman Butt for running on the pitch during the last England–Pakistan series.'

'Umpire Darrell Hair, the man at the centre of the controversy …'

'Darrell Hair has been a controversial figure for a long time in Asian cricket circles and it was insensitive and unwise to appoint him for the last two matches of this series …'

'Former Pakistani Test batsman Shafqat Rana said Hair's role in the "biased" decision on Sunday made it look as if the Australian was looking to settle a score with Pakistan ...'

'Rameez Raja described Hair — who called Sri Lanka off-spinner Muttiah Muralitharan for "chucking" in Melbourne in 1995/6 — as seemingly biased against players from the subcontinent ...'

'Rameez Raja claimed that subcontinental players universally feel that he is biased even to the extent of being racist.'

Public abuse and racially biased comments like those from Rameez Raja are, of course, themselves controversial as well as extremely disrespectful of the game's adjudicators. Raja was never called on by the ICC to substantiate his criticisms, even though they also implicitly targeted the ICC for appointing me to matches. The MCC Spirit of Cricket calls on all participants to respect the role of the umpire, yet the ICC, with all its media resources, does little to support their umpires who come under attack. By refusing to confront the issue they do the game itself a disservice.

I have applied the same principles throughout my umpiring career: that the umpire's role is to ensure fair play according to the laws; that the umpire is the sole judge of fair and unfair play; and that it is the umpire's duty to the game and the players to make those decisions without fear or favour. When players do not break the laws, few decisions, 'controversial' or otherwise, need to be made. So is it the players or the umpires who provoke controversy?

'Rewarding' the non-offending team is surely a basic principle of fairness in sport. Commit a foul in football or a dangerous tackle in rugby and your team is penalised, which benefits the other side. Why should it be any different in cricket? Throwing is not permitted in cricket. Neither is ball tampering, deliberate pitch damage, time wasting or any other behaviour that is against the spirit of the game. Any umpire worth his salt does not tolerate such offences.

I have never sought confrontation or conflict with any player, team or country, although certain countries, or the sports bodies that represent them, have sought conflict with me. If any of my decisions have been generally accepted as correct in interpretation and application, but have subsequently become 'controversial', then maybe we need to scratch the surface a little to see what lies underneath. If a breach of the Laws of Cricket goes unpenalised, it can be for one of only two reasons: either the umpires did not detect it or they did detect it but chose to ignore it.

Ponder, now, the fact that the ICC have changed the Test match and one-day international playing conditions to permit bowlers to straighten their arm by up to 15 degrees. This change implicitly confirmed that Muttiah Muralitharan was employing an illegal bowling action on 26 December 1995 as the Laws of Cricket then stood. It is important to point out that under the Laws of Cricket 2000 Code (amended 2010), Muralitharan's action (along with those of some other bowlers) is still illegal.

What does that say about other umpires who officiated in the period between 1995 and 2003? It was clear enough to me, but not many of my colleagues, Ross Emerson and Tony McQuillan aside, were willing to stand up and be counted. Did they do the game a disservice by their inaction, or is this just Darrell Hair being controversial again? I recall Steve Dunne commenting in the dressing room at the MCG that I must be either very brave or very stupid. He said publicly that it was not up to him to 'play God' with someone's career. Maybe I was both brave and stupid, Steve, but I felt I had a duty to be true to myself and to the game. I was not prepared to wait until after I had retired to state my views in print.

The 'controversial' tag was recycled by journalists every time a player or team did not like a decision I made. Someone lays an egg and the newspapers and that unruly rogue called the internet cackle in delight. Am I the only umpire to have intervened to stop the pitch being illegally damaged? Have I been the only umpire to report players for dissent or other code of conduct breaches? Most definitely not, but you can be sure I am in the headlines when I do.

I like the way sport in the USA is administered. The governing bodies there cherish the history and heritage of their sports. They employ panels of full-time professional umpires and referees, and they publicly back those umpires and referees in the face of unjust media criticism. Baseball in particular manages its television rights to perfection. They insist that their broadcasters do not show endless replays of an umpire's decision. Balls and strikes are the sole domain of the home plate umpire. If his judgement is challenged, there is normally one replay; the commentators lament that this player or that team might have been lucky or unlucky to get that particular call, then the game moves on.

Broadcasters pay huge sums for the rights to show elite sporting events. Why, then, do many cricket broadcasters try to drag their own product down by highlighting poor or 'controversial' judgement calls by umpires? It doesn't make sense to ask viewers to watch a game that the broadcaster's own presenters then disparage by harping forever on an umpire's questionable decision. It's time cricket officials took control and supported and fostered their sport rather than allowing broadcasters to abuse it.

I have mostly been known as a straight shooter. I got plenty of decisions wrong in my career, but I managed to get a good number right as well. But a basic principle that holds the game together is the acceptance of the umpire's decision, right or wrong, without dissent. The behaviour of some players who are unhappy when decisions run against them can be appalling.

Steve Bucknor made a decision in good faith in a Test match in Sydney during India's 2007–08 tour, and suddenly the Indian team were threatening to abort the tour and hire a plane to go home. The problems began when Bucknor failed to pick up an edge from Andrew Symonds. Michael Clarke didn't help the situation when he refused to walk after being caught at slip in the second innings and then claimed a disputed low slip catch himself on the final day. Mark Benson gave Sourav Ganguly out, honouring the pre-series agreement between the captains that the fielder's word would be accepted. In all the acrimony that developed over a couple of umpires' decisions, the pre-series agreement was jettisoned immediately.

An allegation by Symonds, the only non-white player in the Australian side, that Harbhajan Singh had racially abused him only added fuel to the fire. The decision of referee Mike Procter to suspend Harbhajan incensed the Indians, and there was talk of the tour being called off if his appeal was unsuccessful. The ICC initially banned Harbhajan for three Test matches, but faced with a significant loss of revenue they folded like a pack of cards. The ICC's subsequent decision to delay the appeal until after the Tests, leaving Harbhajan available for selection, smacked of political expediency. Australia's victory was overshadowed by the row.

The match had begun so well for India, who reduced Australia to 6 for 134 in excellent batting conditions. Then the umpiring decisions went against India and the frustration turned to anger and allegations of racism. It was clear that Bucknor's decision to give Symonds not out caught behind had a major influence on the match's outcome. But let's face it, India had batted themselves into an almost impregnable position with a lead of 69 runs at the end of the third day. Ricky Ponting was overcautious in setting India 333 to win with just 72 overs to bowl.

With the might of India's batting facing Brad Hogg as the only recognised spinner, the game should have been safe for India. The luck of Clarke, bowling his left-arm spinners just when M.S. Dhoni and Anil Kumble looked untroubled, resulted in a miraculous win for Australia. Then the real sparks began to fly. India accused Australia of being poor sports for celebrating the win on the field. Well, they were entitled to celebrate such an unlikely victory. And then came Harbhajan Singh's three-Test suspension and India's threat to go home if it was not overturned on appeal.

The irony that Mike Procter was the ICC referee judging the case was not lost on me. Had he been willing to act decisively at

The Oval in August 2006, maybe things would have ended differently. Procter's decision in Sydney was overturned by the ICC, but not until 29 January 2008, when the Test series had been completed. All very well then, you might say. Not really, because between all the allegations of racism and unsportsmanlike behaviour and threats to abandon the tour, Malcolm Speed told the ABC's *7.30 Report* on 8 January:

> We were faced with a number of issues that when joined together created a serious problem for the game of cricket. One of the issues was some unhappiness, some dissatisfaction with the standard of the umpiring. By bringing in a new team of umpires for the Perth Test we believe that we will take away one of those issues and I think it gives us a better chance to solve the other issues that we face.

When asked if this was, in effect, a back-down to head off a nasty confrontation and loss of revenue, Speed replied:

> I think we had a choice. We could have taken a hard line. We could have said we will abide by the letter of what we do where we appoint the umpires or we could respond to requests, unhappiness about the umpiring. It's a relatively easy solution to bring in another umpire, to bring in a new team of umpires to take this issue away so that we can focus on the other issues we face.

But doesn't this set a precedent by sending a message that if complaints are loud enough, the ICC can always sack the umpire?

Speed said he didn't think it created this precedent; the power still resides with ICC to appoint the umpires:

> I think this is a very unusual set of circumstances where we have issues that relate to the playing of the game, a code of conduct issue, the racism issue, umpiring issues. We can't solve all those issues but we can put in a new team of umpires for the Perth Test. So we solved the issue that confronted us there. I don't think we'll have this set of circumstances again.

How could Speed be confident it wouldn't happen again? Was it because he had ushered in his troubleshooter, Ranjan Madugalle, to 'calm things down in Perth'? It sounded very familiar to me. Speed removed Procter from hearing the ball-tampering case at The Oval, sending Madugalle into the fray — and suddenly there was no evidence of ball tampering. Send Madugalle to Perth and all the issues of the Sydney Test may be easily resolved too.

But what about Bucknor? Speed publicly ridiculed him by saying that mistakes had been made in Sydney and that Bucknor would be replaced 'to ease the tensions between the two teams'. Bucknor faced the same political expediency that I had encountered in August 2006. He had made an honest mistake. But the tensions between the two teams were not caused by umpiring decisions; they were caused by players' refusing to accept the umpire's decision even if it was mistaken. Steve Bucknor became a public scapegoat, and that must have hurt deeply.

★

Mike Denness, a former England player who later became a dignified and popular ICC referee, found six Indian players guilty of various offences during a Test between India and South Africa played in November 2001 at St George's Park, Port Elizabeth. Denness's decisions initiated protests by the Indian team. Penalising six players from one team was unprecedented in Test cricket and the matter is still viewed as controversial in some parts of the world. The players sanctioned were:

- Sachin Tendulkar (ball tampering): 1 Test match suspended ban
- Virender Sehwag (excessive appealing): 1 Test match ban
- Sourav Ganguly (inability to control the behaviour of his team): 1 Test match and 2 one-day international matches suspended ban
- Harbhajan Singh (excessive appealing): 1 Test match suspended ban
- Shiv Sundar Das (excessive appealing): 1 Test match suspended ban
- Deep Dasgupta (excessive appealing): 1 Test match suspended ban.

These suspensions resulted in a subsequent Test match being deemed 'unofficial' by the ICC. Virender Sehwag was made to serve his one-match ban.

Denness was heavily criticised for failing to explain his actions at a press conference, thus infuriating the Indian cricket establishment and precipitating a political and administrative crisis in international cricket. In India protesters took to the streets and burnt effigies of Denness. I can relate to that! The matter was raised in the Indian Parliament, the popular press termed Denness a racist and the ICC was accused of discriminating against the emerging Third World. The public face of the protest was former India cricketer and commentator Ravi Shastri, who asked at the press conference, 'If Mike Denness cannot answer questions, why is he here? We know what he looks like.' The BCCI threatened to call off the South African tour unless Denness was replaced as match referee for the third Test. The ICC backed Denness but the South African board supported the BCCI's position and replaced Denness, who was not even allowed to enter the stadium. Denis Lindsay, a South African who was also on the ICC Referees' Panel, was appointed by Cricket South Africa as his replacement. The ICC declared the match to be 'unofficial', reclassifying it as a 'friendly five-day match'.

Mike Denness served as match referee in only two more Test matches and three more one-day international matches — all in the West Indies vs Pakistan series in Sharjah during January and February 2002. An ICC Disputes Resolution Committee hearing headed by Michael Beloff QC (then chairman of the ICC Code of Conduct Commission) was scheduled to hear the case on 6–7 June 2002. The committee never met to consider the issue, as the BCCI decided to forgo the hearing in view of Denness's impending heart surgery.

Mike Denness was one of the better ICC referees I had worked with. The background to the suspensions he handed out in that particular series has probably never seen the light of day. However, I can state confidently that all umpires and referees had been issued with instructions to stamp out unnecessary and excessive appealing. Denness carried out those instructions, but once again the ICC deserted one of their umpires when confidence in that umpire was urgently required. The ICC permitted merciless criticism and racist allegations against Denness to go unanswered. No wonder Mike's health suffered.

In March 2002 Denness's role as a match referee came to an end when the ICC failed to select him for their newly formed Elite Panel of Referees, even though he had been put forward by the England and Wales Cricket Board as a candidate. Mike Denness was treated appallingly simply for doing his job. If you believe the excessive appealing did not happen, watch the video footage of that match in November 2001 and make up your own mind. Interestingly, Ganguly was penalised for failing to control his own team, which is one of the main responsibilities of any captain. The other players? Well, they just kept on appealing.

I know Mike Denness was carrying out instructions issued by the ICC to clamp down severely on excessive appealing. I umpired the West Indies playing Pakistan in Sharjah during February 2002 and he showed me the written directions. I believe he was acting honestly and was left unsupported by the ICC, who once again failed to do the right thing.

The World Cup in 2003 was fraught with problems. New Zealand refused to play in Kenya on safety grounds, and England refused to play in Zimbabwe on security grounds, although everyone knew the reasons were really political. In the match in Harare between Zimbabwe and India, Henry Olonga and teammate Andy Flower wore black armbands to protest against the policies of Zimbabwe's government led by Robert Mugabe. They released a statement on 10 February, stating in part:

> In all the circumstances, we have decided that we will each wear a black armband for the duration of the World Cup. In doing so we are mourning the death of democracy in our beloved Zimbabwe. In doing so we are making a silent plea to those responsible to stop the abuse of human rights in Zimbabwe. In doing so we pray that our small action may help to restore sanity and dignity to our nation.

This act led to a warrant being issued in Zimbabwe for Olonga's arrest on charges of treason, which carries the death penalty in Zimbabwe, forcing him to retire from international cricket and temporarily go into hiding. With the world's eyes focused on South Africa and Zimbabwe during the preliminary rounds, Olonga and Flower knew they were safe as long as their team remained in the competition. Bad things had a habit of happening to Mugabe's enemies, but making two of the country's highest profile cricketers disappear might not be the wisest option.

Olonga was convinced that his best chance of escaping the reach of Mugabe's henchmen was for Zimbabwe to qualify for the Super Sixes stage, because they would then have to fly to South Africa to play those matches. Incredibly, Zimbabwe did make it through, thanks in no small measure to being awarded the points for a win when Nasser Hussain and his England team refused to travel to Harare to play Zimbabwe. The Zimbabweans were quickly eliminated from the Super Sixes, however, and suddenly Olonga, who had been allegedly shadowed by his own country's security forces, was on his own. He stayed with friends in Johannesburg until a mysterious South African benefactor paid for his flight to London.

The ICC continued to support Zimbabwe cricket despite clear evidence that the Zimbabwe Cricket Union was powered by political appointees of Mugabe's regime. Money went unaccounted for and the team was floundering. Eventually their Test status was withdrawn. I umpired two of their last Test matches, in which they were soundly beaten by New Zealand, in August 2005. In the first, in Harare, Zimbabwe lost by an innings and 294 runs in less than two days. The next Test, in Bulawayo, saw an improved performance, but Zimbabwe were again beaten by an innings and 46 runs, this time in less than three days.

Henry Olonga and Andy Flower made a brave protest under quite obvious threats to their personal safety. No one could doubt their sincerity. I was the third umpire for that match — it must have been a very difficult time for them. Sometimes the truth really hurts, but it's much better for it to be out there. The pressures on 'controversial' umpires are trifling in comparison with those faced by others. Give me centre stump anytime, and not a bit either way!

CHAPTER 11

15 DEGREES OF TOLERANCE

Deep in the ICC website is a document called 'ICC Regulations for the Review of Bowlers Reported with Suspected Illegal Bowling Actions'. This document outlines the terms of reference and definitions relating to how the bowling review system works. It details the process for dealing with players suspected of bowling in a manner that constitutes an 'illegal bowling action'. It also contains the following statement: 'Nothing contained herein shall override an Umpire's responsibility and discretion to apply Law 24 of the Laws of Cricket.' There is a contradiction of some significance here, one would think.

In deciding whether to cite a player, the regulations say, umpires and match referees should first study the action with the naked eye, viewing it live and/or on television at normal speed.

Slow-motion television replays should be used only to confirm initial suspicions. Umpires are 'encouraged' (the ICC's word) to describe in their report whether just one specific type of delivery is involved, for example a fast, short-pitched bouncer or a reverse-swinging yorker. From this starting point, the matter is referred to a panel of human movement experts for independent analysis. Once their testing has taken place, a report is produced with a recommendation on whether or not the bowler's action is, in fact, illegal.

There are two very big flaws in this process, and basically it comes back to the umpires themselves. On the one hand, they are 'encouraged' to use the review process if they believe a bowler is responsible for an illegal action. On the other, they are told there is nothing in the regulations to override the umpire's responsibility to apply Law 24. I also take exception to the ICC's use of the word 'discretion' with reference to the application of the laws. In effect, it encourages a weak culture in umpires, inviting them to take the easy way out and not call it as they see it, or to ignore the issue and leave it to someone else to clear up.

Most of the bowlers reported under this system have been seen to have a serious problem, yet they all resume their careers following a 'rehabilitation' process. I'm sorry, but it stinks! The bowler can bend the rules to gain an advantage knowing that in the unlikely event of his being caught, all he needs to do is undergo testing and then he can return, probably to bowl illegally once again. The umpires may not report him again. The word gets out that this bowler has been 'cleared', so the umpires can salve their consciences with the knowledge that someone else has done their job for them. But what about the batsmen who have been dismissed or had their scoring ability curtailed by bowlers who, in effect, get away with cheating? Don't the batsmen deserve the opportunity to play to the best of their ability against bowling that is legal in every sense?

Since Boxing Day 1995, little effort has been made by umpires to improve their skills in judging whether a bowler is throwing. It is not all that hard to arrive at your own conclusions. Even the wording of the MCC Laws of Cricket has been made much clearer. Now the umpire need only judge the arm in the delivery swing from the point of being level with the shoulder (horizontal to the ground) up to the point of release. It is only a small area to focus on, but it seems to be too much for most umpires to bother about.

There is a simple solution to this simple problem: back up the umpiring panels when important calls are required. Then it becomes the player, rather than the umpire, who is on trial for not abiding by the laws, not the umpire. That is the ideal response to such an important problem.

It is interesting to revisit my 1998 book *Decision Maker*, which did in fact cause me just a little grief. My views on throwing landed me in a code of conduct hearing arranged by Malcolm Speed, then chief executive of the Australian Cricket Board. In 1998 Speed was unable to make much stick, as umpires were not then specifically bound by the ICC code of conduct. As soon as the hearing was over, the ICC introduced a regulation specifically gagging umpires from publicly expressing their views. According to Speed and the then chairman of Cricket Australia, Denis Rogers, you could think what you liked about a bowler's action but you were not actually allowed to say it in public. Terms like 'extremely emotive' and 'politically insensitive' were used against me, but I believe administrators do themselves a disservice when an umpire is effectively gagged because he has the audacity to say what everyone else believes.

Back in 1995, if an umpire had any doubts about the legality of a bowler's action, the procedures the ICC had in place were simple. If he was unsure if a bowler was throwing, the umpire could pass on those concerns to the ICC referee, who would review footage of the bowler in the next match of the series. If that was not possible, the ICC referee would approach the broadcaster to obtain videotape from the match just completed.

In the case of Sri Lankan bowler Muttiah Muralitharan, I was one of the three umpires officiating in one of those meaningless one-day tournaments in Sharjah in October 1995. The referee was Raman Subba Row from England and the other two umpires were Nigel Plews from England and Steve Dunne from New Zealand. Nigel and Steve were both to play a part in the events surrounding my 'controversial' throwing calls. I didn't know at the time how different their values were with regard to umpiring. Nigel became a great mentor and friend, and I can honestly say I would not have had the courage or strength to get through that dire period in my life between August 2006 and May 2008 without Nigel's words of advice: 'If you believe it happened, stick to your guns.' Nigel was too ill to be at the ground on my return to Test match umpiring at Old Trafford, but he was with me in spirit.

Steve Dunne would not play much of a part in the throwing calls of December 1995 and had not shown much enthusiasm for any involvement in the affair, even though he had agreed just a few months earlier in Sharjah that Muralitharan had problems with his bowling action. I believe Steve deliberately distanced himself from the issue when he told the world that he did not believe in 'playing God' on the field. For me that could be construed in one of two ways: either he thought I made the wrong call, even though he had agreed a few months earlier that Muralitharan had a problem; or he believed that no umpire should make a call for throwing.

The umpire quickly became the target following my calls on Boxing Day 1995. I did everything possible to resolve the matter before it came to a head. Apart from the reports jointly made by Nigel Plews, Steve Dunne, Raman Subba Row and myself in Sharjah, I spoke at length with ICC referee Graham Dowling following a one-day international played in Sydney on 8 December 1995. Dowling told me that our reports had been passed on to the Sri Lankan Cricket Board and it was up to them to decide if Muralitharan should modify his action. I told Dowling that from what I had observed during the match just completed, there was no evidence of any change in Muralitharan's action since the tournament in Sharjah in October. Dowling said he would not be pushing the Sri Lankan team management, and in any case the umpires had options under the laws for dealing with throwing.

Yes, we certainly did and still do. But why were the ICC steering us towards reporting our concerns while also telling us to deal with them on the field as we saw fit? It was seriously confusing. I had just watched Muralitharan bowl his full quota of 10 overs in a one-day international in front of a large crowd and a huge television audience, and very few balls were, in my opinion, legal. Later that week came confirmation of my appointment from Cricket Australia to umpire the Boxing Day Test. My partner was to be Steve Dunne.

On the morning of the match I turned over in my mind the idea of discussing my concerns with Dunne. But I didn't want to be seen to be putting pressure on another umpire, so I dropped the thought. I also wanted to be in my normal relaxed state of mind when 11 a.m. rolled around, so I spent most of the morning focusing on the day ahead. It was going to be a rather cool day in Melbourne with a forecast top temperature of 18 degrees, which would at least make for a comfortable day on the field. Much better than heatwave conditions, which make concentration more difficult to maintain.

Many things went through my mind when Muralitharan came on to bowl midway between lunch and tea on that first day. I decided to watch his first few overs in the hope that his action had somehow miraculously changed, but I watched in vain. Muralitharan's first couple of overs were nothing special: his arm was bent but it remained so right up to the point of release. Also, he was not getting very much spin off the pitch. However, in his third over things changed considerably. He was getting more 'work' on the ball, applying more spin; more important, his arm was bent in his wind-up but straightening just before release.

I struggled within myself for a solution. I explored the option of telling Sri Lankan captain Arjuna Ranatunga that I considered Muralitharan's action illegal and asking him not to bowl him for the remainder of the day. Some breathing space at least, I thought. I also considered speaking with Steve Dunne to see what he would do if I started to call no balls. My mind raced back to the conversations with Raman Subba Row and Nigel Plews, who believed that Muralitharan's action was illegal. Finally, I recalled the conversation with Graham Dowling just a few weeks before.

Muralitharan's fourth over began. The first three deliveries were all illegal and I called 'no ball' on the fourth. It was a strange and eerie feeling, almost like something happening in slow motion but without any sound. I signalled to the scorers and the light in the scorers' box flashed in acknowledgement. It was a sequence that had happened time and again during my career; watch the play, make a call if required, get an acknowledgement from the scorers and the game moves on.

This was different, though. Before the Laws of Cricket were amended in 2000, there was no official warning process and no need for the bowler to be informed. If a bowler were to be no-balled on the field today — and it is a very big if — the bowler would be cautioned for each throw, and after three illegal deliveries the captain would be required to remove the bowler from the attack, and he would not be permitted to bowl again in that innings. But in 1995 everyone probably thought my call was 'just a foot fault'.

The next ball was the same as the previous one, but I let it go — to this day I don't know why. The next ball, the last of the over, the arm was bent in the delivery swing and straightened just prior to the release of the ball. I called it as another no ball. The over ended and the game moved on. Muralitharan said nothing, Ranatunga ignored me and Steve Dunne seemed none too keen to make eye contact. After being no-balled another five times during the next two overs, Muralitharan finally asked whether it was 'the foot'. I said it was not — it was for throwing. He snatched his cap and Ranatunga left the field. He returned a few minutes later and moved Muralitharan to Steve Dunne's end.

Dunne refused even to look at the bowler's action. Clearly, he wanted none of this controversial business, even though I knew he felt that Muralitharan's action was suspect. During the tea break I spoke with Dowling again, informing him officially that the no-ball calls were for throwing. I almost pleaded with him to go to the Sri Lankan team management as they, not Ranatunga, were obviously in charge. Dowling said it was not for him to intervene. So there I was, alone in the middle of a Test match, having made what I still believe to have been the correct calls, but without support from my on-field partner or the ICC referee. It would not be the last time I felt isolated, but I was certain I was 100 per cent correct. This was reinforced when, a few years later, the ICC introduced their '15 degrees of tolerance', which ensured that most of Muralitharan's deliveries would now be deemed legal under ICC regulations (although, importantly, not the MCC Laws of Cricket), an implicit admission that they had previously been illegal.

So what was the official response from the Sri Lankan Cricket Board? Anura Tennekoon, the secretary of the board, said:

> Tour management and officials of the Board of Control for Cricket in Sri Lanka will view the video tape on slow motion and if we feel that his action has not flouted the Laws then we will consider playing Murali in whatever match in future games.

From that moment on, the official snub of the ICC by Sri Lankan authorities placed me in the position of the villain. To ICC chief executive David Richards' credit, he told the world that the ICC had been aware for some time of speculation as to the legitimacy of Muralitharan's bowling action. He revealed that in 1993 and again in 1995 ICC referees Peter Burge and Barry Jarman had both raised concerns directly with the Sri Lankan board and that those steps were taken 'in the player's best interests'. Richards also told the world of the concerns raised by umpires Hair, Plews and Dunne and by ICC referee Raman Subba Row in Sharjah.

It appears that very few were willing to listen. Any reasonable person would take heed of warnings given and concerns raised over a two-year period. But in the end it was left to an umpire to bring the matter to a head. Richards concluded his press release with the following:

> Notwithstanding, it is every umpire's duty to apply the Laws of Cricket fully and impartially and we stand in full support of those umpires who execute this responsibility to the best of their ability. The relevant Law is clear and the game of cricket cannot accept any breach of this Law.

Sri Lankan management fed information to the media in an attempt to ensure that I never umpired any of their future matches. They said they had lodged an official complaint with Cricket Australia. Richard Watson, operations manager for Cricket Australia, responded:

Any request to have Hair replaced will be rejected. They can have whatever they want on their wish list, but playing conditions state that neither team will have the right to object to an umpire's appointment.

The statements by the ICC's David Richards and Cricket Australia's Richard Watson would effectively be the last time that I was fully supported by cricket's administration. Do I agree with the 15 degrees rule? No! It has not stemmed the flow of bowlers entering international cricket with suspect bowling actions, but the ICC wants a framework within which everyone can work — preferably one that makes no waves.

Since the mid 1990s, when Pakistani off spinner Saqlain Mushtaq pioneered the 'doosra' (which means 'the other one'), a ball that imparts leg spin and is bowled with the back of the hand facing the batsman at the release point, other off spinners who have bowled with a non-classical action that can produce this delivery have routinely been reported and investigated for throwing. Those bowlers include Harbhajan Singh, Shoaib Malik, Marlon Samuels, Mohammad Hafeez and Johan Botha. Of these only Botha was banned from bowling (in February 2006), although he was subsequently allowed to bowl again in international matches from November 2006. Unfortunately, he must have later fallen into old habits as he was reported again in April 2009 and his doosra was banned.

Any delivery that cannot be legally delivered must be a no ball. The bowler gains an unfair advantage by being able to deceive the batsman about which direction the ball will spin off the pitch. It is not a matter of a bowler having variety in his bowling toolkit; it is purely about what he can do legally. If it is not legal, the batsman must be protected, and every delivery the umpire believes is not fair should be called a no ball.

Throwing will always be a matter for discussion, and some umpires may see the same bowler differently, as is their right. Implying that only certain countries or types of bowlers are targeted is a smokescreen. I see nothing in the laws that supports bending the rules to suit certain cultures or countries. Referring to my decision to no-ball Muralitharan, Bruce Yardley, then bowling coach for Sri Lanka, said, 'We should be celebrating his action, not trying to run him out of the game. There is no way that Murali has to change his action.' I don't buy the argument that bowlers with 'different' actions (i.e. actions that do not conform to the laws) are good for the game. Reckless and uninformed or professionally biased comments like Yardley's do nothing for the sport. I wonder how he feels now, some 15 years on, when we see an explosion of young kids trying to emulate Murali's doosra. Ashley Mallett expressed a different view when he said he thought Muralitharan's action looked very suspect and that he definitely straightened his arm.

Muralitharan was reported by match referee Chris Broad during Australia's tour of Sri Lanka in 2004 for illegal straightening of the arm at the elbow during his bowling action. Tests on 1 April 2004 at the University of Western Australia revealed that he straightened his arm by an average of 14 degrees, which was 9 degrees in excess of the tolerance level for spin bowlers mandated by the ICC at the time. On 5 February 2005 the ICC's Chief Executive Committee approved proposals aimed at ending the 'malaise' over illegal bowling actions. Under the new proposals, the tolerance limit for straightening of the arm for all bowlers was to be set at 15 degrees, which studies had shown is the point at which the naked eye can make out excessive straightening. Amazingly, this was one degree more than the average of Muralitharan's arm straightening!

The changes were suggested by an expert panel chaired by former Indian opening batsman Sunil Gavaskar and came into effect on 1 March 2005.

The new regulations would be based on the findings of the ICC's research program, which discovered that most bowlers are likely to straighten their arm to a level undetectable by the naked eye during the bowling action. But that's fine. If the umpire cannot detect a straightening of the arm, then it is not a throw.

There would be a shorter, independent review process under the central control of the ICC, with immediate suspensions for bowlers found to employ an illegal action, which was one positive thing to come out of these changes. The ICC also promised increased commitment to working with the problem at the junior level, and to changing in the testing, analysis and review procedures then employed. But such an approach works only if each ICC member country embraces the commitment. As we approach 2012, it is patently obvious that some have not.

As Cricinfo reported on 5 Feburary, 2005:

> ICC chief executive Malcolm Speed admitted at the time that there might be a strong reaction from sections of the cricket community, but he insisted that the radical overhaul in the laws was necessary to deal with a problem that has plagued cricket ever since the near epidemic of chucking in the late 1950s.

★

You will be unsurprised to hear that I disagree with Speed's comments. First, he talks about overhauling the laws, but the MCC Laws of Cricket have not changed to reflect the ICC's changes. Speed clearly did not understand the difference between the MCC Laws of Cricket and the special regulations the ICC wanted to introduce in international cricket. (The MCC Laws of Cricket are the blueprint for how the game is played from the grassroots to the elite level. The ICC cannot change the Laws of Cricket, only the MCC can approve any changes. Therefore the ICC have a special set of regulations that vary the laws but only for matches played at international level.) The laws do not permit throwing, yet the ICC regulations have made it legal in ICC-sanctioned matches. According to Speed:

> This issue has afflicted the game for over 60 years. Try as it might, the sport has never properly come to terms with it. Every time it comes up there are emotional reactions from people around the world based on fear and ignorance and I've no doubt we will see them all again this time.
>
> The reality is that this new process provides the game with a sensible way forward to properly protect against people breaking the rules while providing every opportunity for players with illegal actions to remedy any problems and return to the game.

How can a sport maintain its integrity if it protects players who break the rules rather than penalising them? It is not the sport of cricket itself that has failed to come to terms with chucking. It is the administrators who are at fault for failing to support and encourage umpires simply to do their job.

In July 2009 a spin summit held at Cricket Australia's Centre of Excellence in Brisbane decided against teaching the doosra to young spinners. The delegates at the meeting included former Test spinners Shane Warne, Stuart MacGill, Jim Higgs, Gavin Robertson, Terry Jenner, Peter Philpott and Ashley Mallett. According to them, the doosra cannot be bowled legally, and unless the ICC decides to legalise all forms of chucking, it would not be taught in Australia. But that was before Australia lost the Ashes and the investigations began into what Australian cricket could do to restore the Australian team to the number one spot.

On 9 February 2011 it was revealed that the man whom Australia once treated as an outcast, Muttiah Muralitharan, could now help them unearth a match-winning spinner. According to a report in the *Daily Telegraph*, the controversial off spinner was about to be signed on as a guest spin coach with the Centre of Excellence. Muralitharan confirmed to the newspaper that he had been approached for the job and that negotiations were ongoing. 'They want me to come for two weeks in a year and help them with the Academy,' Muralitharan said. 'They want me to come in May but there is the IPL so we have to finalise the dates. We are still in the process of talks.'

Muralitharan retired from Test cricket in 2010 with a haul of 800 wickets, many of them taken with the doosra, bowled with an illegal action. I could not believe the double standard by Cricket Australia. It was just 18 months since Cricket Australia's Centre of Excellence revealed that they would not countenance their elite young players being taught the doosra. In the meantime panic must have set in. Maybe Cricket Australia just thought, 'If you can't beat 'em, join 'em.' I would like to think that idea was not behind their motivation.

Muralitharan advised, 'Australians have to change their mindset. In Sri Lanka, every kid wants to bowl spin. It's the same in the subcontinent. Younger Australians must also mentally want to do that, like they focus on fast bowling.' Muralitharan said Australian wickets favoured pace men and conditions are challenging for aspiring spinners. 'They [Australian coaches] need to train younger bowlers to bowl more spin,' he said. 'I feel more programs for spinners in cricket academies and perhaps at the state level will nurture interest among younger players. Let's see how I can help them get there.' But the opportunity to learn the dreaded doosra would also be there, and you could not fault young players tempted to follow that route — if it can be done legally, and I still don't believe it can.

Australian selector Greg Chappell told the *Daily Telegraph*: 'It is not just Murali's obvious physical skill that will be a huge benefit for our young spinners; it is also his physical toughness, his cleverness, his cunning and his ability to be able to set a batsman up and bowl 10–15 overs to a plan.' No problem with that, Greg, as long as it involves teaching a variety of off spinners and maybe the arm ball — which, incidentally, Muralitharan does not bowl.

As it turned out, the dream ended quickly. On 1 March 2011 the *Daily Telegraph* reported that at the eleventh hour Muralitharan had turned his back on a coaching cameo at the Cricket Australia Centre of Excellence, instead opting to play Twenty20 cricket in India and England. 'The Sri Lankan legend was also expected to record a spin coaching tutorial during his visit so his remarkable knowledge would never be lost to the Australian system,' said the report.

'Cricket Australia wanted him to come down for a particular period of time but it doesn't go down well with the IPL [he was contracted by the Kochi franchise for the 2011 season] and Gloucestershire assignments,' Muralitharan's agent, Kashil Gunasekera, told the *Telegraph*. 'They [Cricket Australia] wanted him to come at the end of May. They were trying to figure out another time, but it just couldn't be finalised. The IPL starts on April 7 and goes until the end of May, and by June 1 he has to go to Gloucestershire.'

All I can say is, thank heavens for the IPL and English County Cricket.

The following players have been reported to the ICC by umpires because of concerns about their bowling actions but subsequently 'cleared' to continue bowling without sanction: Saeed Ajmal (PAK), Kumar Dharmasena (SL), Mohammad Hafeez (PAK), Jermaine Lawson (WI), Brett Lee (AUS), Shoaib Malik (PAK) and Harbhajan Singh (IND). Bowlers reported to the ICC and subsequently sanctioned in some form or another are:

- Shoaib Akhtar (PAK) in December 1999 (overturned almost immediately)
- Shabbir Ahmed (PAK) in December 2005 (banned for 12 months)
- James Kirtley (ENG) in October 2005 (by England and Wales Cricket Board)

- Johan Botha (RSA) in February 2006 (by ICC; lifted in November 2006)
- Abdur Razzak (BAN) in December 2008 (lifted in March 2009).

During World Cup 2011 I noted that Harbhajan Singh, Shoaib Akhtar, Mohammad Hafeez, Johan Botha and Abdur Razzak all bowl with a highly suspicious action that may or may not fall within the 15 degrees of tolerance. But the chances of their being reported are slim. As to the chances of their being actually called during a match? Yes, you're right again — absolutely zero.

CHAPTER 12

THERE ARE THREE SIDES TO EVERY ARGUMENT

THE DECISION REVIEW SYSTEM

The old saying 'There are two sides to every argument' is not true in cricket. When an appeal is made to the umpire there are actually three sides to the disagreement. Both the batting and bowling sides will lay claim to the unvarnished truth, but the third side — that of the umpires — after all the evidence is considered, is more often than not correct. Before the era of television replays, every umpiring disagreement was always won by the umpires. 'Look in the scorebook' was the expression commonly used. But that was in the old days.

Television coverage to assist umpires in their decision making was first applied in 1995. Its introduction was discussed in June of that year by the international umpires nominated by each country at the second National Grid ICC Umpires Conference, where all present raised concerns that the innovation would be 'the thin end of the wedge'.

Initially, the umpires could refer only line decisions, such as a stumping or run-out appeal. Later, television footage came to be much more widely used as the unruly system grew its own heart and lungs to become a monster, and sometimes a blight on the game. Umpires would begin to use it as a crutch, and simple decisions they alone were responsible for making suddenly became too hard and were sent 'upstairs', as it became known. In this I believe umpires abdicated their responsibilities. Down the track this would come back to bite them — and bite very hard indeed.

My introduction to the system came in Perth during a Test between Australia and New Zealand. My on-field umpiring partner was Tony McQuillan and the third, or TV, umpire was Terry Prue. The day before the match we assembled at the WACA Ground for a run-through with the host broadcaster, Channel 9, of how the system would work. It was very simple: the television feed was hooked up to a 15-inch monitor; to refer a decision to Terry, all we had to do was signal to him using the now-familiar ritual of sketching out the shape of a screen in the air. Following that signal, Terry would pick up the phone and call the Channel 9 director to request a replay, after which he would make his decision. By switching on a red or a green light positioned above the third umpire's box he would communicate to us, and inform the world, whether the batsman could keep batting or had to make the long trudge back to the pavilion. But there was also a white light! This was to be switched on when the third umpire lost the television pictures through some sort of blackout or power failure.

The white light was illuminated early on in the Perth Test when, on the Saturday afternoon, Channel 9 began their coverage of the daily double races from Sandown, Victoria. For three anxious minutes the Test match continued while the third umpire at watched race six at Sandown. Such was the way sport was broadcast around Australia at the time. Some years later the third umpire was provided with a direct feed from the outside broadcast van, which meant unwanted interruptions such as horse racing and advertisements were not fed into the third umpire's box.

The white light was never meant to be used just because the third umpire could not make a decision based on the pictures alone and was therefore throwing the problem back to the on-field umpires, yet that is how it developed. Another misconception among viewers at home was the belief that the system accessed TV footage that was available only to the third umpire. In fact, all that the third umpire had access to, and this remains the case to this day, was the host broadcaster's coverage that went out to every home tuned to that channel.

The restriction to referring for line decisions only didn't last long. Soon catches taken low to the ground and boundary-line decisions were added to the list. Then the decision as to which batsman was out on a run-out if they both ended up at the same end, and who should face the next ball, also became part of the third umpire's domain.

The use of television replays to decide whether a catch was legitimate was a hot topic in the ICC before they decided to introduce it. Naturally, some teams felt hard done by when a television replay clearly showed a ball making contact with the ground before being 'caught'. But what the ICC failed to recognise was that a two-dimensional picture provides a foreshortened view of the action, and for each replay that clearly showed a ball not carrying to the fielder, there would be another nine or ten that were inconclusive. If the third umpire finds the evidence inconclusive, he can only arrive at one decision — not out.

The players agreed to the use of technology in the first place because of a few isolated occasions when a replay showed that a player, knowingly or not, had claimed a catch that was subsequently given out by the umpire. So it was ironic that the technology-based decisions led some players to accuse others of cheating. Over time several captains, including Steve Waugh, Brian Lara, Ricky Ponting and Michael Vaughan, openly stated their preference for the umpires on the ground to make the final decisions. There was talk of urging teams to agree to accept each other's word — for example, agreeing that the batsmen accept the fielder's word that a clean catch was taken. In a perfect world, that would indeed be the ideal solution. But I can cite two instances when the best intentions of captains and players alike failed to deliver the ideal outcome.

The one-day international between Australia and South Africa in Perth on 3 February 2003 provided me with a difficult decision to make as third umpire. In the opening stages of the match Adam Gilchrist, who was on 22 at the time, appeared to be caught at the wicket off an inside edge. Mark Boucher dived low to his right to take the chance one-handed off Pollock. Gilchrist, it seemed, was prepared to walk if Boucher confirmed the catch, but the South African wicketkeeper indicated he too was not entirely sure he had taken it cleanly.

That really should have been the end of it. If a fielder is not certain he caught the ball, then the umpire should give the batsman not out and continue the match. But not in this era, when everyone wants to shove the decision somewhere else — not least the players, who believe technology should be able to sort out the whole mess.

So off it went to the third umpire. But in the crucial angle, at the critical moment, Boucher's glove was off screen for all but those with expensive widescreen TV sets. As third umpire I did not have that luxury, and my small monitor was not about to make the decision easy for me. I asked for every conceivable angle to try to ascertain if and when the ball went into Boucher's glove. If television is so keen to involve itself in the game, the least the broadcaster could do is to supply the third umpire with adequate replays and equipment!

In the end, I could not see the 'catch' being taken and as the on-field umpires Bob Parry and Steve Davis had referred it for a decision, I was left with one option only — to give Gilchrist not out. I flashed the green light; Gilchrist continued his innings but added only another seven runs before he was bowled in bizarre fashion, when a ball from Makhaya Ntini went off his thigh pad and by way of his shoulder onto the top of his helmet before looping over him and onto his leg stump, thankfully removing a bail. It was a gratifying postscript to a decision that would have been argued long and loud had Gilchrist gone on to make a big score.

How did this reliance on technology come about, and why did we let it encroach on our job? Mostly I think we, as umpires, accepted it too quickly and without much thought about what our true role is. There was no resistance from within umpiring at international level. It was a matter of 'Let's get the decisions correct so we cannot be criticised.' I take another view, however. We were not confident or united enough to fight the gradual erosion of our traditional role. I believe we agreed to take the easy way out. This came about in several ways.

First, we didn't stand up and say, 'Give us more resources and training and we will provide you with better decisions.' If that had occurred, all the extra funding now being soaked up flying third umpires around the world (because they too must be considered independent) could have been channelled into improving the overall standard of world umpiring. Second, despite their long training in making decisions confidently, some umpires welcomed the changes as a way of passing on difficult decisions. Finally, there were umpires who were not good enough, lacked confidence and, more importantly, lacked the ability to think, train and make themselves better decision makers. These umpires were only too happy to draw on video assistance in making their decisions.

Much has been written and said about the latest innovation, the umpire decision review system or UDRS. The ICC's own regulations state, 'The Decision Review System (DRS) will be used in all matches.' But it isn't! Matches have been played in Bangladesh, India, Zimbabwe and New Zealand in which the DRS has not been used. It never will be universally adopted unless all the Test-playing nations agree on what type of technology provides the best results. The simple answer to that, though, is that no system is going to be perfect, because any technology has to be operated and interpreted by humans.

The DRS includes two sections: in the first the umpires refer decisions to the third umpire; in the second the process is initiated by the players. Rather strangely, though, where consent has been granted for the matches not to be broadcast, the home board is still required to ensure that certain television camera specifications are met as a minimum requirement, and only the umpires themselves can ask for a review. Even if a series is not being broadcast, then, the cost of making footage available to the umpires is still to be borne by someone. Confused yet?

In situations where the umpires themselves have the option of referring a decision, nothing much has changed. Run-out, stumping and hit-wicket decisions, caught decisions (clean catches) and boundaries can still be referred if the umpire is unsure. In reviewing the television replay, the third umpire must also check the fairness of the delivery on no-ball decisions and whether the batsman has hit the ball on caught and lbw decisions. If it was not a fair delivery, then that is the end of it. The batsman is automatically not out, unless of course the referral is for a run-out. For a caught decision, if it is clear to the third umpire that the batsman did not hit the ball, then the batsman is not out.

Finally, when reviewing the TV replay, if the third umpire believes that the batsman may instead be out by *any other mode of dismissal* beyond that initially consulted upon, he can rule the batsman out. So what started out as an appeal for a catch could end up being given out lbw, stumped or run out. Phew!

It just doesn't make any sense. Yes, I know the ICC emphasises the idea that it is better to get the decision correct than to persist with a blunder. But whatever happened to having umpires well prepared, trained and confident enough to make the majority of decisions correctly? If the aim is the elimination of 'the clanger' in international matches (a decision that is too outrageous to be allowed to stand), then I say the umpire should never have been permitted to get that far. How was he trained and assessed before being elevated to international matches? What training was he provided with to ensure he was able to cope with the high pressure of Test cricket contests? The ICC's insistence on implementing the Decision Review System indicates a couple of trains of thought: either they believe that umpires are doing their best, considering that the training provided is less than satisfactory; or they believe that umpires are incapable of providing the service cricket deserves. I think the latter is the one they favour.

According to the second part of the DRS, the players may request a review of any decision taken by the on-field umpires concerning whether or not a batsman is dismissed. But only the batsman involved in a dismissal can request a review of an out decision, and only the captain (or acting captain) of the fielding team may request a review of a not out decision. Interestingly, the total time that may elapse between the ball becoming dead and the review request being made should be no more than a few seconds, and if the umpires believe that a request has not been made sufficiently promptly, they may decline to review the decision. This particular requirement is certainly a dubious one, and one that is not being adhered to by the players. Time after time we see the fielders discussing a decision or insisting to the captain that a review take place. It is a poorly written regulation. How long is a few seconds, anyway?

The third umpire is then required to 'work alone, independent of outside help or comment, other than when consulting the on-field umpire'. The consultation process is to investigate whether the third umpire can see or hear anything that would indicate that the on-field umpire should change his decision. But before the third umpire goes to work on the decision he must check whether the delivery is fair, and not a no ball because the bowler overstepped the popping crease or delivered a fast full toss passing above waist height. Again, it is only the front foot of a no ball that is checked, not whether the bowler has touched the return crease with his back foot, so it is only a half measure in checking the fairness of the delivery.

If the available technology does not show conclusively that the on-field umpire has made a mistake, the original decision stands. This leads to some doubtful decisions being allowed to stand even though 'Hawk-Eye' or a similar tracking system indicates that they may be incorrect. Say Hawk-Eye shows that part of the ball may have just clipped the top of the stumps. In the past, if the decision was given as not out, it was readily accepted as giving the batsman the benefit of the doubt. But now, should the original decision be out, then that decision also stands. In other words, the umpire now seems to get the benefit of the doubt.

Of course the status of the game now is partly the fault of the players. Instead of using their review option to overturn obviously poor decisions, they are actually using it in an effort to dodge a bullet and maybe have a marginal decision go their way. This was never what the system was meant to produce, but unfortunately that has been the result. The review system also has the capacity to undermine the confidence of the umpires and make them more reluctant to give a batsman out. It encourages a 'You challenge it if you feel I am wrong!' mentality.

Problems in the implementation of the DRS continue to bamboozle me. Here's another illustration of a nonsensical system. Following an unsuccessful lbw appeal, the striker sets off for a run but is sent back and there is an appeal for his run-out. The fielding team request that the lbw decision be reviewed. In the meantime the umpire at the striker's end requests that the run-out be reviewed, which is his right under the 'normal' referral system. Incredibly, the ICC now directs that the run-out referral be determined first. Should the decision on the referral for run out be out, then there is no requirement for the lbw review to take place.

If I were a bowler, I would not like this innovation much at all! The lbw appeal certainly happened first, and as that particular type of dismissal means the bowler gets credit for the wicket, it seems a little unfair on the poor bowler not to give it precedence. What would be wrong with dealing with the appeals as they occur? If the lbw appeal is dismissed, the run-out can be reviewed. And there is another small problem. What if the batsman is given not out lbw, the ball runs far enough into the field for the batsmen to attempt two runs and he is then run out trying to make his ground for the second run? The fielding side should still have the right to request that the lbw be reviewed, and if that is successful, any runs completed will not count. If the ICC's way of dealing with the appeal is perpetuated and the batsman is judged to be run out, then the first run must count. All very confusing to me; I only hope it is clearer to you!

The review system now itself needs a review. This is not to argue that the system ought to be junked, but the results so far have been mixed. On certain occasions it allows edges to be detected with greater certainty. In recent times the ICC decided to allow the use of the Hot Spot technology, which has in some cases looked to be the most foolproof system for detecting the impact of the ball; lbw decisions are far more complicated. There is simply no technology available to remove the subjective element. Indeed, if every ball that would go on to graze a stump were to be given out, matches might well regularly finish in less than five days.

The recent tendency for umpires to make their own referral, even when there are clear-cut grounds for dismissal, just to check that a no ball has not been bowled, cannot be good for the game. I can understand their wish to ensure that they don't make incorrect decisions, but that is a confidence factor that can be fixed, along with umpire performances overall at the elite level. They can all be improved, and it's not rocket science either. I don't believe enough training support is given to umpires as they come up through their own country's umpiring system. I am a supporter of the idea that 10,000 hours of practice is needed to become an 'expert'. In practice, however, it is not really possible to practise cricket umpiring at all. Most of our learning takes place out there on the field; we experience something that hasn't happened before and we store up that experience so we are well armed to use it again later.

In reality, to rack up 10,000 hours would require an umpire to practise his skills for six hours a day for 166 days each year for

10 years! In today's world most people don't have that sort of time. Instead, more time should be devoted to deliberate practice of specific aspects of umpiring — the issues that crop up most often in a cricket match. These are lbw and catches by the wicketkeeper or by fielders in the slips and close to the wicket in front of the batsman.

The importance of experience in the development of expertise, as opposed to an expectation that umpiring talent is somehow ingrained, must be recognised. But while there is a high correlation between hours of practice and the learning of new skills, hours alone do not determine improvement in performance. The essential ideas are 'deliberate' and 'practice', but it is the conditions that surround each of these that are critical for turning average performers into world-class performers. Many factors are involved in skill acquisition. How the umpire uses his time at practice defines how quickly he will improve. As a simple example, merely attending net practice to 'get your eye in' or 'get into the groove' will not guarantee improvement in decision making.

Habits and skills are developed through many repetitions of the activity. Most critically in cricket umpiring, the behaviour you want to develop must be reinforced. Repetition alone is not enough. It is the conditions that surround that repetitive practice that will determine how long it will take to learn to perform better under pressure. It is all about becoming addicted to information that will help you improve. Simple things like counting the balls and deciding where each ball pitched, and what it did after it pitched, are skills many umpires take for granted. But the more often you practise them, the easier they become under match conditions — and the more often you will make the right judgement when the appeal goes up. Net practice involving lining up the sound of any noise as it passes the bat is crucial to developing the ability to decide whether the batsman actually hit the ball on its way through to the wicketkeeper.

We hear often that someone needs more time in a job before he or she will be ready for a promotion. It is not time; it is not mere experience either. Benjamin Franklin said, 'Experience keeps a dear school, but fools will learn in no other.' It is a special kind of experience that is important. What we know is that skill acquisition requires many repetitions where correct behaviours are identified, where information on results is readily available and where small improvements are positively reinforced.

The business world has to get away from time-based performance criteria and begin to focus on rate and accuracy of behaviour as the criteria for workplace recognition and reward. Thousands of studies have demonstrated the superiority of ratio-based performance schedules of reinforcement over time-based schedules. In spite of what is known about how to improve performance, business, industry and government continue to pay for time rather than performance. Ultimately, world economic conditions will force a change from paying for time to paying for performance. The bottom-line difference is too great to be ignored. Whether in training or in daily work activity, it is performance, not time, that should be reinforced, recognised and rewarded.

We often talk about our plans to do something we have always wanted to do 'when we get the time'. I recall some very good advice one of my old captains from Molong offered when his son complained that he didn't have enough time to do a certain job. He replied, 'Son, you've got all the time there is. If you can't fit something in, get out of bed an hour earlier.' Creating enough time to efficiently and effectively learn and improve is the key. And so it is with learning how to improve your umpiring skills.

PART 4

INSPIRATIONS

CHAPTER 13

THANKS, MISS MURRAY!

We don't understand much about the world when we are young. Yes, we are aware of our surroundings — family life, school, sport, making friends and generally growing up. But how much of this do we really understand during our early years, and how does it prepare us for what lies ahead? Mostly we don't realise what we have until it's taken away. Some parts of our life come back to us in our quieter moments when we take the time to think deeply, but as we go about our daily lives, important past events fade from our minds, becoming remote or even surreal. There are times we can almost convince ourselves that it all happened to someone else.

There were many times after August 2006 when I felt deeply unhappy about the events that had turned my life on its side. I just wanted to feel that ultimately some sort of fairness would emerge. Of course I knew I could wait a long time, or in vain, to feel that way. Other people's perceptions, whether right or wrong, are difficult to change. You cannot control them.

You can't replace the days you feel you have lost out of your life, but you can move on to something new — something that in time will grow its own story and acquire its own pedigree and tradition. Umpiring for me was not an obsession based on livelihood or material things. It was about being in a position to influence fair play based on the beliefs and values that had been, unknowingly to me at the time, planted in my teenage days.

It was 1966, a rainy Saturday afternoon in Orange, a city located beneath Mount Canobolas in the central west of New South Wales, when my older brother, Denis, with the *Central Western Daily* neatly folded open at the sports section, said to me, 'Look at this ad: "Cricketers wanted for new club".' So we jumped into his car and drove around to visit the advertiser. It was a typical August day, heavy rain dashing against the windscreen. When we arrived at the address in Franklin Road, Denis said, 'You wait in the car.' It dawned on me. The advertisement, still displayed on the seat between us, ended with the words 'Orange District Association Men's Competition'. It looked like this 13-year-old would again miss out on the fun. I always seemed to be too young to do what the adults did.

The advertiser was a gentleman called Carl Sharpe, who was later to become a big influence on my values, not only in the game of cricket but in life in general. According to Denis, their first conversation went something like this:

DENIS: I'd like to come along and play some cricket with your new team.

CARL: OK, you're in. Sign this registration form. Practice starts next Saturday. By the way, who's that young fellow down there in your car?

DENIS: Oh, that's my little brother, but don't worry about him — he's only 13.

CARL: Doesn't matter. We'll have him too. Just get him to sign the registration form.

And so began my career playing in men's competitions in wonderful country towns like Molong, Cargo, Gulgong, Mudgee, Parkes, Forbes and Lake Cargelligo, the last a four-hour drive from Orange. A few years later I was chosen to represent Molong in the Grinstead Cup, a challenge trophy that is greatly coveted around the western districts of New South Wales and is commonly known as 'the Sheffield Shield of the West'. How lucky was I to be given an opportunity to play in the senior competition at such a young age?

Much later, international umpiring would take me to many places I had dreamed of visiting, and some I didn't necessarily want to, but Lord's, Trent Bridge, Old Trafford, Wanderers, Newlands, Kensington Oval Barbados, Queen's Park Trinidad, the SCG, the MCG, Adelaide Oval, the Gabba in Brisbane and the WACA in Perth have all been a dream come true. Umpiring has also taken me to Scotland, Ireland, Italy, Kenya, Malta, Malaysia, Hong Kong, Fiji and Papua New Guiea. All a long way from Orange and our futile efforts to win the Grinstead Cup with Molong when we played Forbes or Parkes. Yet I owe much of my success to the values I learned in those early days. Ordinary people do make it to the top. Perhaps it didn't happen in the way I thought it would, but it happened all the same. I feel proud of my achievements, but I'll always remember the simplest of lessons: take something positive out of every day. People have labelled my umpiring style as, among other things, tough, determined, uncompromising and hard-nosed, but I have never tried to be anything other than fair, intent on ensuring that both teams have the chance to win on their merits.

In October 1959 I had just turned seven and Denis was just 13 when he was struck down with polio. The diagnosis was *poliomyelitis*, known then as 'creeping paralysis'. It paralysed the nerves and muscles in the legs and lower back. There was no known cure. My mother was told to expect Denis to be restricted to a wheelchair for the rest of his life. He would never walk again. The news was devastating for both my mother and Denis, who was a keen cricketer and a more than capable rugby league player and was doing exceptionally well academically too, having just started at Orange High.

Doctors tried new surgical procedures — operations on his leg muscles that involved nerve grafting and tendon lengthening. He was sent to Sydney Hospital for six months for these operations and then transferred back to Orange Base Hospital for rehabilitation. It would take time to gauge the results.

Denis remained in Orange Base Hospital for 18 months with no obvious signs of improvement in his condition. There he first met Ros Murray, the resident physiotherapist. She visited every week day to test his recovery progress, but there seemed to be nothing much for Denis to feel confident about. The doctors told Mum she had better get used to coping with a 'polio victim', which seemed such a heartless way of getting the message across. Leg braces known as calipers, and corrective shoes to which these braces could be attached, were ordered. The doctors suggested that using these braces sometimes assisted recovery, if and when the affected muscles started to respond again.

When Mum went to see Denis in hospital during visiting hours each day, I used go with her, although I was not actually allowed into the ward. In public hospitals at that time it was thought that young children either could be carrying a disease or could pick one up, so children under 12 were not permitted to visit. But the nurses showed me how to reach the window outside the ward. They would push his bed close to the window and I would stand in the flowerbed talking to Denis about cricket and league, or whatever else was the topic of the day, while Mum sat quietly inside. Strange days indeed! Denis used his time in hospital to continue his high school studies, and just before he was released he completed his Intermediate Certificate, passing with flying colours.

Miss Murray was a returned servicewoman who had seen the horrors of World War II, having served as a nurse in the Middle East and Papua New Guinea. On Anzac Day she marched proudly down Summer Street, Orange, wearing her service uniform, along with the rest of the returned soldiers, my father among them, to the cenotaph in Robertson Park, where they would lay wreaths. I know from my father's own scars that the war was horrific. He served as a signalman in the Middle East and then in 1942, just when he thought he was coming home, the Japanese swarmed into Papua New Guinea. He saw most of his service in New Guinea, but he never spoke about his time there. Unfortunately, my father turned to alcohol and violence. I never forgave him for his violent attitude towards his family, but for him the horrors of war just never went away. I came to understand that while I couldn't condone his behaviour, there must have been deep-seated reasons for it, most of which I could never begin to comprehend.

Other ex-service people, like Miss Murray, came home and worked away selflessly at their chosen profession. For our family, she just happened to be in the right place at the right time. After his spell in hospital Denis visited her at her practice three times a week for ongoing physiotherapy. Mum was never one to stand on ceremony and could often be seen pushing Denis's wheelchair down the main street to Miss Murray's consulting rooms. After several visits she offered to take him swimming, which she thought might help stimulate his body. Conventional medical treatment had not had much impact, so my mother agreed. Anything was worth a try, she must have thought, after two years of hell. But the Orange Olympic Swimming Pool was a good distance from our house, and Mum did not drive. No problem at all for Miss Murray. She would pick Denis up at 6 o'clock each morning, fold the wheelchair into the boot of her car and drive him to the pool for an hour of swimming therapy, then drop him back home. I joined them on many mornings, sitting quietly in the back seat while Miss Murray's calm conversation and kind manner seemed to give Denis the confidence that better times were ahead.

Whatever motivation Denis needed to aid a recovery the doctors had no faith in, he found within his own body. And Miss

Murray was instrumental in it. I believe that without her encouragement and dedicated work, Denis would not have made the remarkable recovery he did.

Denis told me recently how he would listen to the Test matches on his crystal radio when he was in Orange Base Hospital in the summer of 1960–61, and how he remembered vividly the unmistakable voice of the ABC's Alan McGilvray as he described the tied first Test in Brisbane between Richie Benaud's Australians and Frank Worrell's West Indies team. Fresh in his memory even to this day are names like Rohan Kanhai, Garfield Sobers, Wes Hall, Charlie Griffith, Alan Davidson, Wally Grout and Lindsay Kline — and the game's exciting finale.

In his own mind, Denis remained determined that his dream of playing cricket again would be fulfilled, no matter what it took. With Miss Murray's help, his physical improvement was remarkable, if not miraculous. Within a few months Denis was able to pick himself up out of his wheelchair and take a few steps. Our neighbours were always supportive, the Matheson family who lived next door and the Bowman family, two doors down, providing moral support whenever they could. Their cheery greetings each day as they passed our door were a welcome antidote to the gloom that had descended over the household. There was a standing offer to help with the shopping or other household chores, something I know Mum was forever grateful for. Kindness and consideration were all they could offer, but these came by the truckload.

It was only recently that I found out about one act of kindness by the Bowmans that was right out of the box. The day before Denis was due to travel to Sydney for the start of his series of operations, the Bowmans asked, or to be truthful they insisted, that we join their family for afternoon tea. Granny Grace Bowman, a proud woman who commanded respect from all who entered her home, had baked some biscuits and the tea was brewing over the open fire. The Bowmans were a large family and everyone was there to wish Denis luck for his trip. During the course of the afternoon, a hat was passed around and coins collected, then wrapped in a handkerchief and given to Denis, 'just in case he needed to buy some sweets in the hospital canteen'. When Mum told me recently about this collection, she said she was overcome with emotion. She knew the Bowmans were not well off and never had much for themselves, yet they still gave to their neighbours when it mattered. It wasn't the money, Mum recalled, but the genuine willingness to help someone in need that had really amazed her.

Denis was forever at me and Mum to let him play backyard cricket with some of my friends, as we had done during the early summer of 1962. Mum worried that he might get hit by the ball because his reflexes were slow, but Denis insisted 'he could look after himself'. She eventually relented and we returned to playing our regular 'Test matches' in the backyard, emulating all the stars of the era. Denis would sit in his wheelchair in front of the stumps and pretend he was opening batsman Colin Cowdrey or Bob Simpson. If a wicket fell early, Norm O'Neill would stride to the crease. And I would be Graham McKenzie, Brian Statham, Fred Truman or Alan Davidson (except I bowled right-handed) charging in from the Paddington end at the SCG. Cover drives off the middle of the bat had to be four runs, even though I had my fielders astutely placed! A single to square leg was always possible because, Denis told me, 'you can't have fielders everywhere'. The scores each day were copied from real matches that Denis had read about in the many cricket books given to him as birthday and Christmas presents. So it just wouldn't do if Norm O'Neill had scored a century at the SCG and I tried to claim him lbw for a duck at No. 2 Molong Road.

At 10 years old I was totally unaware of how rapid Denis's recovery was. It became very clear, though, to our neighbours the Mathesons. One time Denis pulled a short ball over 'mid-wicket' that went straight through the Mathesons' kitchen window — which was closed at the time, I might add — and landed in the sink. Mrs Matheson threw the ball back to us without complaint, and Denis swears that it still had soapsuds on it for a few balls afterwards. Keith Matheson told Mum the smashed window was a small price to pay to see such a huge improvement in Denis's condition and that he would gladly see another window go each day.

Denis eventually cast the wheelchair aside completely and began to make his way with the aid of walking sticks. The wheelchair sat idly in the laundry for some months, with Mum unable to make the decision to get rid of it as easily as Denis had. But eventually it was sent back to the hospital for reuse. In late 1962 Denis threw away the walking sticks for good as a Christmas present to himself. Early the following year he started work at the Westinghouse factory in Orange as a clerk in the office. He just wanted a normal life — no small thing for someone who had spent three of his 17 years wondering what sort of hand fate had dealt him.

Many others apart from Miss Murray and our neighbours helped in countless small ways. Jack Moroney, who had played seven Test matches for Australia and had represented New South Wales in 57 first-class games during the 1950s, was working as a schoolteacher in Orange at the time. Jack was not playing much by then, so he would often come and pick Denis up on Saturdays or Sundays, when there was a district representative match being played at Wade Park, Orange. Jack would park the car in a spot around mid off so they could see how much the bowlers were swinging the ball. They would sit in the car and talk about the match all afternoon. Occasionally I joined them. Denis watched every ball with interest, talking about this or that bowler's 'side-on action'. He must have been turning over in his mind how his 'comeback' to actually playing cricket would occur, and when.

While the doctors told my mother they were wasting their time, Mum and Miss Murray and a host of others believed otherwise. The Mathesons, the Bowmans and all the neighbourhood boys who joined our 'Test matches' during the summer of 1962–63 all played their part, albeit unknowingly.

I knew Denis had summoned all his willpower to climb those few steps to Carl Sharpe's front door. As I watched him I wondered if he really knew what he was doing. I should never have doubted him. Denis was utterly determined. Nothing was going to stop him playing cricket again. His brief conversation with Carl Sharpe that day changed his life and, although I did not realise it at the time, mine also changed.

In just under seven years since contracting polio, Denis was playing with the Orange Waratahs. He wanted to open the batting, and he got his way. He wanted to field and chase balls towards the boundary, and he got his way. He wanted to bowl his right-arm, medium-paced nagging deliveries, and so he did. Many years later he began to tire easily but he refused to stop playing. So he thought he would try wicketkeeping, a less energetic role! And he got his way. Then he decided to take up umpiring. He officiated in District Representative matches on Sundays whenever he wasn't required to play.

His career statistics bear commenting on. He was a foundation member of the Waratahs and Orange City when it was formed in 1967. Most of his cricket was played in third grade, where he captained the side for a number of years. He played from 1966 to 1982. During those 16 years he scored 1813 runs from 143 innings, at an average of 12.68. He bowled 805 overs, with 82 maidens, and took 198 wickets for 3838 runs at an average of 19.38. On his retirement in 1982 he was the leading wicket taker for the Orange City Cricket Club. Denis also played several seasons (between 1967 and 1971) in the Molong Sunday competition, but with plenty of young players coming on he more often turned his hand to umpiring on Sundays.

He was made a life member of the Orange City Cricket Club in 1976. He was a club selector for his entire period with the club and served at various times as vice-president and assistant secretary. Denis dedicated all his waking hours to the club that gave him the chance to live out his dream. Whether on or off the field, 'City' was his team; he wore the green-and-white quartered cap proudly every moment he was on the ground, and even on occasion in the Hotel Canobolas bar until closing time.

He may have thought about playing on for one more season to take those two more elusive wickets to reach his double century, but he had nothing to prove to anyone. Many thought he was dreaming to believe he would ever play again following his early retirement from the crease in 1959. But he was only 'retired hurt' for seven years, and once he resumed his innings in 1966 he wasn't about to let any more opportunities slip by. He asked for no special treatment and he received none. He was a dogged opening batsman who enjoyed occupying the crease and taking the shine off the new ball. His job was to make things easier for the middle order, and he took the job seriously. His teammates appreciated everything he did for them. His gentle seamers and outswingers outfoxed many an unsuspecting opposing batsman into playing the cover drive, and more often than not he found the edge to the slips.

He valued his wicket while batting but he never disputed a decision on being given out. He was always thrilled to take a wicket with his outswinging seamers but he never appealed unless he was sure it was really out. He treated his teammates and opposing players with respect because he knew that without them he would not have been able to fulfil his dreams. Cricket gave him a lot and he gave it back threefold.

Walking up those stairs to sign up to play cricket displayed great strength and courage. I have never met a tougher or more determined man in my life, and I thank him for passing on a small share of those qualities to me.

When you are looking for inspiration, you often don't need to look very far. You will probably find it close to home — in a family member, a friend or a workmate. You may even find a Miss Murray or neighbours like the Mathesons or the Bowmans. Of course they were not the only unselfish people in the world or even the only ones who influenced my brother during his battles.

Everyone has what I call 'everyday courage', be it a resolution to battle against all odds or just a desire to survive. Denis Hair's story is true and ends happily. He achieved his dream and did what he always wanted to do — play cricket and be treated fairly and equally. It took me many years to fully understand the meaning of courage, fairness and equality. I couldn't have got by in my own life without my brother's example. Thanks, Carl Sharpe. And thanks, Miss Murray. But above all, thanks Denis Hair.

CHAPTER 14

IT WOULDN'T HAPPEN IN MUM'S BACKYARD

The backyard at home was a special place when I was growing up. It was where we played our cricket matches in summer and soccer or rugby league in winter. A standard of behaviour applied in this sporting arena. We made up our own rules, but there was one person who decided whether all was fair and above board, who adjudicated when a dispute arose, and who generally made sure everyone was safe and happy. If there was any argument about who was out and how or whether a four or six had been hit, the umpire's voice would thunder from the kitchen, 'Stop all that arguing or I will confiscate the bat and ball.' That settled things quickly!

This 'backyard academy' gave me an ideal grounding in the principles of fair play before I moved on to playing with the

Orange Waratahs, later to become Orange City Cricket Club. I have often thought about how Mum would have viewed some of the cricketing events I have experienced during my career. Here is how I believe she would have reacted to a few of the dilemmas the cricket world has faced in recent years, followed by some pertinent family history.

Changing the Result

When one team decides they no longer wish to play, no matter what their reasons, then that would be the end of it. Mum would declare the match over and the game forfeited. There was only one result that mattered in our games — the one that was declared at the close of play. Both teams accepted the result and then looked forward to the next match.

In 2008 the ICC bowed to political pressure from Pakistan, changing the result of the Test at The Oval to a draw. The MCC, the guardian of the Laws of Cricket, informed the ICC that the result could not be changed once it had been legitimately reached. It was another 12 months before the ICC decided to change the result back to a forfeit. I am as satisfied with the result now as I was in August 2006, and I know Mum would feel the same.

Nigel Plews Bows Out

As an umpire, Nigel Plews may not have had many international matches to his credit, but he lived for cricket and had a wonderful mind for interpreting and explaining the Laws of Cricket. When the ICC introduced the Duckworth/Lewis system for calculating target scores in one-day internationals interrupted by weather, Nigel was one of the umpires they relied on to relay the message to each Test-playing country. He travelled around the world for no fee to talk to individuals and associations. The Duckworth/Lewis calculations can make anyone's eyes glaze over, but Nigel could make it all sound simple.

Nigel devoted a vast amount of time to assisting the ICC not only with the Duckworth/Lewis educational program but also with communicating the never-ending changes to the playing conditions and their effect on the laws of the game. He was one of the founding members of the International ICC Umpires Panel formed in 1994 and was probably the most highly respected expert on the MCC Laws. Even in retirement he served on the MCC Laws Committee.

In 2007, after being diagnosed with incurable cancer, Nigel was told of a new drug. It was not listed in the UK's National Health Benefits Scheme, and so the cost was out of his reach. I sent out messages to the ECB and the ICC to ask what type of assistance might be available to Nigel. The ECB, in conjunction with the Hornby Trust, immediately swung into action, but the response from the ICC, and in particular from general manager David Richardson, was perplexing. Richardson argued that such a case was really a 'home board' responsibility and that the ICC could not set a precedent by making a financial commitment.

Eventually Nigel received his treatment. It certainly extended his life.

In Mum's backyard you could expect that any reward you got would be determined by the effort you put in. She never forgot the Bowman family's kindness during my brother's illness, and she expected the same of me. In Mum's backyard, Nigel would have been welcome anytime.

The Blame Game

Ijaz Butt, chairman of the Pakistan Cricket Board, started the blame game when he attempted to deflect the fallout from the 'no balls for cash affair' in 2010:

> This is not a conspiracy to defraud bookies but a conspiracy to defraud Pakistan and Pakistan cricket. We have taken it in hand to start our own investigations. We will shortly reveal the names of the people, the parties and the bodies involved in this sinister conspiracy and we also reserve the right to sue them for damages. There is loud and clear talk in bookie circles that some English players have taken enormous amounts of money to lose the match [the third one-day international].

This all fell flat a few months later when three Pakistan players, captain Salman Butt (no relation), Mohammad Asif and Mohammad Amir, were suspended by the ICC for ten, seven and five years respectively for arranging to bowl deliberate no balls in a Test match against England.

Ijaz Butt's attempt to blame someone else for the predicament Pakistan cricket found itself in was shameful. It came after Pakistan captain Shahid Afridi had decided to bite the ball during a match against Australia. Afridi's explanation was that 'he was trying to do something to help his team win'. The ICC responded by suspending him for a couple of one-day matches. He was soon back as captain of Pakistan's national cricket team for the showcase World Cup tournament.

When you were caught playing unfairly in Mum's backyard, the sanctions could be severe. Anything from a severe verbal berating to a permanent ban could be expected. Pakistan's cheats would not have been welcome.

Removing the Up-and-comers

As World Cup 2011 was about to commence the ICC confirmed their decision to reduce the 50-over World Cup from 14 to 10 teams, despite protests from the Associate countries who are likely to be left out of the tournament in 2015. 'We have felt in the past few years that Twenty20 is the best format to develop the game world-wide and it provides a better environment for competition,' said the ICC. 'The 50-over format is more skill-based and suitable for the top teams.'

The decision was released, following no consultation whatsoever with the teams affected, with impeccable timing. A few days later, Ireland, one of the countries that would suffer most, having built up a strong team and a development system that most Associate countries would die for, defeated England. And it was not just a win. Chasing 327, Ireland got the runs with several balls to spare, and with one of their players, Kevin O'Brien, scoring the fastest ever World Cup hundred — from just 50 balls faced. How much egg do you need on your face?

Once again ICC's decision making seems to be at odds with the best interests of the game. The skills needed to score a century in

50 balls could not be found even in Twenty20 cricket, where runs are scored at an average of 9 or 10 per over. O'Brien's century was scored at the amazing rate of 12 runs an over against a team that featured several of the world's best bowlers.

To compensate for the loss of places in the 50-over tournament, the ICC decided to add four spots to the Twenty20 World Cup, making it a 16-team event, but the Associate countries that have worked so hard to develop cricket in their own countries could be forgiven for believing that the ICC was not acting in the best interests of the game by locking the smaller teams out of the next World Cup.

How can Ireland be expected to develop players like Kevin O'Brien when they are forced to play an even shorter version of the game? How do you improve standards by denying countries such as Ireland, Scotland, Kenya, Holland and Canada the opportunity to compete at the top level? *The Wisden Cricketer* called the decision 'scandalous and bloody ridiculous. It's all about money, power and votes — and that's not good for cricket.' Mum would be perplexed by this style of decision making. It certainly wouldn't happen in her backyard.

Sledging

When I talk cricket with people at dinners or functions, one of the first questions I am often asked is, 'What are the best sledges you've heard during your career?' I have a standard answer now: I don't repeat anything that is detrimental to the spirit of the game. About 95 per cent of so-called sledging fits into that category. It is against the spirit of the game to do or say anything that might bring cricket into disrepute, and that covers a wide range of behaviour. Anything that is said or done on the field that undermines the unique character and enjoyment of the game should not be condoned and should not be permitted to continue.

It is written clearly in the preamble to the MCC Laws of Cricket that the spirit of the game involves respecting your opponents, your own captain and team, the role of the umpires and the traditional values of the game. There are many things that are not written down, though. Take, for example, the way the players take and leave the field at the start and end a session of play. At the start of play the umpires are first on the field, followed by the fielding team and finally the two batsmen. When play ceases, whether for an interval or at the close of play, the sequence is reversed: the two batsmen leave first, followed by the fielding team and then the umpires.

The umpires will provide bowling markers, hold the bowler's sweater, help the batsman on strike find his guard, and ensure that the sightscreens are aligned to the batsman's satisfaction. These duties are performed continually throughout the day's play, with batsmen checking guard regularly and with bowlers changing ends or changing their delivery (say, from over to around the wicket), thus requiring more sightscreen realignment. All these routines should be carried out with courtesy and professionalism by all involved.

It used to be common practice to acknowledge your opponents' performances and achievements and to show respect for their captain by giving a brief round of applause when he came in to bat. I know this still happens in the central west of New South Wales, where I learned the values of the game, but it never happens in the competitive grade competitions in the cities. Why not? Without the opposing team there would be no game to enjoy. Why do bowlers and fielders say things to batsmen or use gestures that they wouldn't use on a public street? I cannot accept that it is simply gamesmanship, because it just demeans the perpetrator and lowers the tone of the game. Umpires and captains set the tone for the conduct of the match and every player should be expected to contribute to the spirit of the game.

Good-natured banter is fine but personal abuse or aggressive body language used to intimidate another player is not good for the game. I once heard an Australian player say to South African Adam Bacher, 'You're only in the team because of your uncle,' a reference to Dr Ali Bacher, who played a leading role in South Africa's return to international cricket following the apartheid era. At face value, it may sound like a harmless comment, but it was delivered with a genuine sneer. The player responsible did not play very much for Australia afterwards, so I suppose you could say that what goes around comes around.

Players at all levels today devote a truckload of energy to gaining a psychological edge. When a bowler boils over I often sympathise with him. Bowling is a tough job; it always has been. But I finish by saying, 'Would you speak to you mother/father/brother/sister that way?' Sometimes that gets a grunt of acknowledgement or recognition that he could have handled his frustration better.

One of the greatest fast bowlers I umpired was Curtly Ambrose. For batsmen he was a fearsome sight. He bowled a lethal bouncer and just as lethal a yorker. But when a batsman miss-hit a drive and it flew over slips for four runs, Ambrose never said a word. He would just stand mid-pitch and play with his gold neck chain, which held a crucifix. After a few seconds spent glaring at the batsman, Ambrose just tucked the crucifix back in side his shirt, turned on his heel and walked briskly back to his mark. The intimidation was silent but very effective. I not once saw a batsman smile back. All the batsman could do was wait, tapping his bat nervously on the crease, while Curtly bounded in to unleash another thunderbolt towards them. Would it be a bouncer? Would it be a yorker aimed at the toes? Or would it be another slightly short ball climbing up around chest height? He'd find out soon enough. That's much more effective than sledging!

A good illustration of the ineffectiveness of sledging occurred during a one-day international at the SCG between Australia and the West Indies on 17 January 2001. Brian Lara produced a magnificent century and threatened Australia's hold on a game it had previously dominated, but a typical Sydney January thunderstorm intervened. The skies released a torrential downpour of rain that ruined what might have been one of the greatest run-chases in history as the West Indies pursued Australia's imposing tally of 4 for 277. It would have required something of a miracle for them to overtake Australia, but then miracles are something that can happen when a player of the calibre of Brian Lara is at the crease. Few batsmen can change the course of a match as easily as Lara, who produced his breathtaking 14th one-day hundred in just 97 balls.

Coming in with the score at 2 for 31, Lara found a long-term partner hard to find, with Sherwin Campbell, Marlon Samuels and Jimmy Adams all departing by the 25th over, and the scoreboard limping to 5 for 94. For the next 16 overs Lara took absolute control, scoring 83 of the last 117 of the West Indies total. You could be excused for thinking this was just Lara doing his normal thing. But it was all in the face of relentless chirping from none other than Shane Warne. The West Indies had dropped several simple catches during Australia's innings, and with wickets tumbling around him Lara was on the receiving end of Warne's constant chatter, most of which meant nothing at all other than passing the time of day. Warne hardly drew breath after each ball he bowled to Lara, who produced sweeps and pull shots regularly. 'Watch out, Brian. You miss one of those and this man here will have to give you out,' said Warne, indicating in my direction. Of course every utterance contained several expletives.

Lara mostly let his batting do the talking, as Warne's frustration grew and Lara raced closer to his century with a deft paddle down to fine leg. When Lara completed the single, which as the last ball of the over also meant he kept the strike, Warne blew up. He screamed at Lara that his luck had just about run out and predicted he would be out lbw next over. 'How's that going to happen?' asked Lara quietly. 'You got one big problem, Warnie. You keep hitting the middle of my bat.' It was a great put-down of the greatest leg spinner the world has ever seen. And what was most amazing was that Warne knew it was true. Lara never looked like getting out, and although a West Indies win was still remote, Warne knew that if anyone could do it, Lara was the man.

Lara was particularly severe on Warne's bowling that night, with the great man conceding 63 runs off his 10 overs, something unheard of in Warne's long career. Lara continued to cleverly harvest the strike to thrash shots over and through the in-field. It was a dangerous time for Australia and the war of words dried up in the tension of the situation.

The thunder that had been growling in the distance all evening now grew closer, and a torrential downpour ended play with the West Indies on 8 for 211, Lara on 116, and needing 66 more runs off eight overs to win. Lara had hit ten fours and two sixes, but it was his absolute dominance of Shane Warne that was most memorable. It was an unfulfilling end to the match, though, with no thrilling last few overs and no fairytale win. We can only wonder what might have been. The dreaded Duckworth/Lewis system calculated a win for Australia, but it was a sobering night for Warne. It also demonstrated how useless sledging can be when directed against great players.

Sledging should also be discouraged at the grassroots level. If cricket is to continue growing as Australia's number one summer sport, there can be no place for acts of boorishness, rudeness or sheer bloody-mindedness. Kids need to learn how to play tough and to become strong mentally, and cricket is the ideal game to teach these skills, but there is no place for personal abuse, foul language and other offensive behaviour. No one should condone sledging, which violates cricket's traditional values. The game deserves better. So let's stop it, I say, before we lose sight of why we play, umpire and coach the sport. As Mum would say, it is only a game, after all.

My Family — Behind the Backyard Academy

Doreen Pearl Menchin was born on 11 June 1922 into a large farming family at Wilbertree Flat on the banks of the Cudgegong River, a few miles out of Mudgee. It was a large family and she had nine siblings. Living in such a close-knit family environment, she learned the important family values at an early age. She first met Ronald Hair in 1940, when she was 18, then waited five long years for their marriage on 4 April 1945, before the war had ended.

During the war she travelled to Lithgow a few days each week to work in the Lithgow Small Arms Munitions Factory, where Lee-Enfield rifles, Vickers machine guns, Bren guns and bayonets were manufactured. When I asked her how much she was paid, she replied, 'Not much, but it was something we just did without asking questions — our bit for the war effort.' The bus trip from Mudgee took more than two hours, and after a nine-hour shift she would catch the bus home again.

In 1941 my father left his family home in Wollar, a sleepy little township on the Wollar Creek 50 kilometres northeast of Mudgee, to join the army. He served in the Middle East from September 1941 until March 1943. When he was shipped back to Australia he must have been hoping the war was drawing to a close, but after a few short months back home and further training at the Bonegilla Army Camp he was sent to New Guinea, where he served from August 1943 until the war ended. He was finally demobilised on 30 October 1945.

Along with thousands of other young Australians, he served his country with pride. He was in New Guinea when the fighting against the advancing Japanese forces was at its fiercest. He was a signalman, a vital part of army communications. His role was to ensure communication lines remained intact at all times. It was a dangerous job, and the lives of his fellow soldiers depended heavily on his efforts. His war experience must have been traumatic. He never spoke about it, though, instead bottling it up inside. As a result, as the years went by he changed from a loving husband and father to a troubled alcoholic prone to mood swings and violence. This returned soldier couldn't find permanent work and couldn't cope with his life.

In the late summer of 1975 he was admitted to Royal North Shore Hospital in Sydney to undergo surgery. He had been seeing a succession of doctors and during a routine scan a shadow had been discovered near the base of his skull behind the right ear. The operation removed a small piece of grenade shrapnel. He had never once complained about being in any pain. There is nothing in his army record of his being wounded. We never found out how it happened, as any questions we dared to ask were met with a stony and surly silence. Maybe he saw his fellow soldiers suffer in more horrific ways and knew his was just a 'minor' injury. He must have put it behind him and just carried on. As was the way back then, you mostly absorbed the pain without complaint.

His pain was over when he passed away suddenly of a heart attack on a late summer morning in March 1989; he was 68 years old, although his army record gave him as 70. As many had done before him, he had lied about his age on his Attestation Form when enlisting to fight 'His Majesty's enemies'.

I also learned recently that during my father's brooding periods, the ones that usually took hold before something deep inside him exploded, he would take himself off to the room at the back of the garage and scribble things on notepads. I never knew what he wrote — we were afraid to ask — until Mum showed them to me two years ago. Many pages showed his attempts at poetry — often just a verse or half a page, unfinished. Many sheets had been scrunched up and cast aside, but not totally discarded. Maybe he half intended to come back to them later. He persevered, though, and a few reached fruition. I cherish those fragments of verse. Mostly they bring me down to earth when I think things in my life have not worked out the way I'd hoped they would.

I have often wondered what might have been going on in the mind of that troubled returned soldier as he wrestled with his demons. As a family, we never looked forward to Anzac Day or any other military milestone, as it always signalled the beginning of my father's spiral into very dark moods. I could understand little of this at the time, but I would like to think it has become a little clearer to me as the years have gone by. In those roughly written poems he took himself away to labour on, he was trying to find expression for his experiences and what they all meant in the end. And that's all that matters.

Mum's backyard was always a safe and happy place for us to play, but it's only in the past few years that I have begun to understand how she must have struggled to shield her children from the violence that threatened us. Her efforts to keep her family together were further tested when Denis contracted polio. She must have wondered what other trials would be sent to test her resilience. Probably she thought not much else could happen that she hadn't already been through, and that outlook kept her focused on passing on to her children the life skills they would need.

CHAPTER 15

THE BEST OF THE BEST

Great Umpiring Mentors

The best umpires I have stood with share a special place in my heart. Without the counsel of experienced peers, you will learn nothing about the rigours of international cricket umpiring. I was lucky to learn from some masters of the profession and was grateful to be able to draw on their knowledge and experience when building my own career. Here, in no particular order, are the umpires from whom I learned most.

Peter Willey

Having played Test cricket himself (he represented England between 1970 and 1986), Peter had an excellent feel for the game and was a great team man. This playing experience showed in his decision making under pressure. His sense of humour helped too.

Sadly, Peter tired of travelling the world and in 2003 retired from international umpiring after officiating in 25 Test matches. His last match was in Perth on the occasion that Matthew Hayden scored 380 against Zimbabwe to pass Brian Lara's then record of 375.

Steve Bucknor

Steve's dry sense of humour shone through in the tense stages of a Test match. I had the pleasure of joining Steve in his 100th Test: in Kolkata between India and Pakistan in March 2005. It was a memorable match for both of us, with 30 of the 39 wickets falling to spinner bowling. India had Harbhajan Singh and Anil Kumble, while Pakistan's spinners included Danish Kaneria and Shahid Afridi. It's an understatement to say it was probably the most difficult match I had umpired, but it was a privilege to be part of Steve's 100th. He was an exceptional umpire and did not deserve the criticism he received for making an honest mistake in not giving Andrew Symonds out in Sydney against India a few years later.

David Shepherd

Shep lived for cricket and was without doubt the most respected umpire ever to stand in international matches. His knowledge and experience were exceptional, his enthusiasm infectious. Shep was always great fun to stand with. As another milestone I was lucky enough to be associated with, I stood with him in his last Test match, in Jamaica in June 2005. Shep passed away in October 2009.

Nigel Plews

It was my loss that I never had the pleasure of standing with Nigel in a Test match. He officiated in 11 Tests and 16 one-day internationals. His main value to cricket was in his phenomenal knowledge and understanding of the laws and his ability to impart that knowledge leavened with a good dose of common sense and humour. I first met Nigel at a conference in England in 1994, when the inaugural ICC Independent Umpires Panel was formed. I umpired with Nigel in ICC Associate games in Malaysia in 1997, in the semifinal between Kenya and Ireland, which Kenya won in a very close finish. Bangladesh and Kenya eventually qualified for the World Cup. Bangladesh went on to attain Test status, and Kenya and Ireland continue to qualify for the ICC World Cup tournaments.

We formed a wonderful friendship over the years. Nigel was a great listener and someone I bounced thoughts and ideas off for the rest of my career. I always cherished his measured response to a ticklish question on the nuances of the MCC Laws. After he retired from international cricket in 1997 we kept in touch, and during my visits to Stanmore Gardens, Nottingham, we would reminisce over cups of tea on how good we used to be. I learned something new with each visit and telephone conversation — pleasures I miss to this day. On 19 October 2008, Nigel succumbed to the cancer he had fought bravely for more than a year. It was a sad day in my life.

Tom Brooks

The only occasions I ever umpired with Tom were club matches in the Sydney Cricket Association competitions not long after I began my career. He was a major early role model for me. Not many rookie umpires have the privilege of standing in matches with a Test umpire. I soaked up the opportunities, and sitting listening to Tom talk about his career over a beer at the close of play at Chatswood or Waitara Oval was a priceless experience. Tom had played 16 matches for New South Wales between 1946 and 1953. His integrity as an umpire was beyond reproach and he was only too willing to pass on his experience — all you had to do was ask. I learned more in four club matches with Tom than I had in my previous four years of umpiring.

The current crop of international umpires are very good. They need to be. Every move they make is heavily scrutinised and subject to challenge under the Decision Review System. I hope they enjoy their careers as much as I did, but somehow I doubt it. Many of them seem to lack confidence in making on-field decisions and appear, at least on the surface, to be happy to delegate the task to someone off the field. But the attitude that any mistake they might make can be 'corrected' by someone else is a self-defeating one. I umpired because I enjoyed the challenge. I'm not convinced that international umpires today do it for the same reason.

The Best Teams in the World

As with all 'best ever' selections, the relative quality of each player I have picked, and many I have not, will no doubt inspire vigorous debate. There are players who appear high in the rankings of the ICC system who, some would argue, should not be there; equally, some players who are omitted deserve selection. I have drawn my teams solely from players I umpired in Test matches and one-day internationals between 1991 and 2008.

In selecting these teams, sometimes I have focused on pure statistics — how many wickets they took in their careers or how many runs they compiled. That can often be sound logic, as players are never going to be considered the greatest of their era unless their figures support it. However, I picked my teams mainly based on what I saw in the matches I umpired. I have compiled three teams — a World Test Match side, a World One Day International squad and an Australian team that I believe would have performed best in both these formats.

The World Test Match Team

Here is my World Test Match team, in batting order:

Sachin Tendulkar
Rahul Dravid
Brian Lara
Steve Waugh
Allan Border (captain)
Jacques Kallis
Kumar Sangakarra
Shaun Pollock
Shane Warne
Curtly Ambrose
Glenn McGrath
Mohammad Yousuf (12th man)

All four of the bowlers selected figure in the top ten of the fastest to 400 Test match wickets and played a minimum of 120 Tests. The six bowlers to miss out were Richard Hadlee, whom I never umpired, Kapil Dev, Anil Kumble, Courtney Walsh, Wasim Akram and Muttiah Muralitharan. I did consider the last five, but ultimately decided that with Ambrose and McGrath to open the bowling, any opposition batsmen would have their work cut out scoring runs quickly. Bringing in Shaun Pollock, with his deceptively quick swing and seam, to bowl first change would keep the pressure on the batsmen. With Shane Warne to unleash at any stage of the game on any pitch in the world, my dream-team attack is complete. In the unlikely event that the attack came under pressure, Jacques Kallis, with his fast, medium-swing bowling, would be there to give the bowlers a rest.

The wicketkeeper is Kumar Sangakarra, who is also one of the current top five batsmen in the world. What a luxury to have him coming in at number 7! Sadly, Adam Gilchrist misses out.

The top six batsmen I have selected have scored more than 10,000 runs, with Ricky Ponting just missing out. The opening pair of Dravid and Tendulkar might seem to be playing out of position, but out of the six they were the ones most suited to taking guard in the opening overs. Lara, Steve Waugh, Allan Border and Jacques Kallis are the most dominating batsmen I have ever witnessed. They can all play fast and spin bowling equally well. The luxury of Kumar Sangakarra at number 7 really tops off the team.

Mohammad Yousef just misses out in the eleven. He is currently averaging 52 runs in Test matches, most of which have been played away from home, which indicates his ability to adapt to all types of conditions and bowlers.

Allan Border would be my captain. His tenacious batting and ability to astutely read the flow of the game and change his field and bowlers accordingly are arts that not many players possess. He would also lead from the front, and his high expectations of his teammates would give them confidence and the determination not to let him down.

The One-Day International Team

The one-day international team has a slightly different look. The Test match squad would make a formidable one-day, limited-overs side too! Some players, though, would not only adapt a little better to the shorter form of the game but also make the game more exciting to watch. Here is my one-day team:

Chris Gayle
Virenda Sehwag
Adam Gilchrist
Ricky Ponting
Brian Lara (captain)
Jonty Rhodes
Jacques Kallis
Daniel Vettori
Shane Warne
Curtly Ambrose
Glenn McGrath
Wasim Akram (12th man)

The top of the order is sensational, all three having strike rates of 100 runs per 100 balls. Gilchrist can also take on the wicketkeeping duties. Sehwag and Gayle are explosive and heartbreaking to bowl at. Their range of shots and power all around the ground would confound the fielding captain trying to decide where best to place the field, regardless of the line or length the bowlers were aiming for.

Ponting and Lara are somewhat steadier, but their ability to score at 5 runs per over would keep the pressure on the bowlers. Jonty Rhodes is a selection that might raise eyebrows, but he played an important part in the evolution of limited-overs cricket, his brilliant fielding cutting off many potential boundaries as he patrolled the area between point and cover. It is impossible to say how many runs he was really worth, but his batting strike rate of 80 runs per 100 balls, his ability to bat with the lower order and still maintain the momentum of the innings, and his frustration of opposition batsmen in the field, all mean Jonty Rhodes is a must in my team.

Jacques Kallis takes on the all-rounder's role. His ability either to increase the tempo coming in at number 7 or to bat out the innings under any circumstances means he is pivotal to any team's balance. Daniel Vettori bats at number 8 and is able to bowl his left-arm orthodox spin on any pitch and in any conditions. Vettori is one the few spinners in the world to have an economy rate of 4 runs per over, actually bettering Shane Warne's 4.25 rate. Warne had a better strike rate for wickets, taking them at 25 runs each as opposed to Vettori's 31, but they would be a formidable partnership in this team.

The three fast bowlers are all extraordinary, with economy rates below 4 runs per over, but Curtly Ambrose and Wasim Akram combine that with taking their wickets at, respectively, 23 and 24 runs per wicket. Glenn McGrath, however, is the best I have seen in the limited-overs format. His 389 wickets were collected at a miserly average of 22 runs per wicket, and his economy rate of 3.88 is second only to Ambrose.

Brian Lara would be my captain. Arguably, though, the team would not really need a leader, as they all have the confidence and experience just to go about their jobs. If each individual plays his part in batting, bowling and fielding, then the results take care of themselves.

As most of these matches are played over a series of more than five games, the 12th man gives the selectors the option of resting a bowler and rotating the talent.

The Australia Team

The Australia team is a little easier to pick. I have picked just one team to play in both formats. I believe there would be no reason to make changes between the Test and one-day international teams, as each player has proven himself playing for his country. Here is my line-up:

Mark Taylor (vice-captain)
Matthew Hayden
Allan Border (captain)
Steve Waugh
Ricky Ponting
Adam Gilchrist
Ian Healy
Shane Warne
Craig McDermott
Brett Lee
Glenn McGrath
Michael Hussey (12th man)

What's this I hear? Picking two wicketkeepers can't be right! But let's face it, how could I leave out Adam Gilchrist? In his 96 Test matches he effected 416 dismissals with the gloves. But his batting made him a true all-rounder. He averaged 48 runs per innings and produced 17 centuries, many of which are vividly implanted in our memories. His 202 in Johannesburg turned the match on its head. He was explosive and a match winner with the bat alone. The fact that he was also classy enough to keep wicket made him indispensable. Actually he was my first pick and he is in the team solely as a batsman.

Ian Healy was a valuable member of the national team throughout his career of 119 Test matches, in which he effected 395 dismissals and batted solidly at number 7 or 8. Healy kept the team going with his energy and was an integral member of the dominant Australia sides captained by Mark Taylor and Steve Waugh.

Mark Taylor and Matthew Hayden open the innings and are perfect foils for each other. Well known for his power and strength, Hayden could also occupy the crease for long periods, depending on the situation of the game. Taylor could read the game exceptionally well and knew how and when to change the tempo, as he proved when he filled the captain's role between the reigns of Border and Steve Waugh. His positive attitude and insistence on working his side into a winning position gave the team the best chance to wrap up the game.

Allan Border comes in at number 3. There could be no player more suited to this spot in the batting order. And, although not famous for it, he could handle fast bowling with ease; his footwork to the spinners was always good, and he could settle in for a long, hard fight when the need arose. Border is also captain.

Steve Waugh's dogged determination makes him ideal for the number 4 spot. He had an exceptional appetite for grinding the opposition into the ground. He was afraid of no bowler and could respond with equal potency to spin or speed.

Ricky Ponting, at number 5, would be heartbreaking for any opposition. His power and timing have seen him rise to the number 2 spot in world cricket (second only to Sachin Tendulkar), with an average of more than 53.

Shane Warne, at number 8, is undoubtedly the greatest leg spinner of them all. Warne was often criticised for lack of fitness, but he could bowl 25 overs in a day and never tire to the extent of bowling too many loose balls. His longevity in the game speaks for itself. No batsman was safe when Warne was summoned to bowl.

The fast bowlers McGrath, McDermott and Lee are all standouts, and each bowls differently, so the variety is always going to be difficult for batsmen to counter. McDermott and Lee were express pacemen and while McGrath was slightly slower, he was no less effective and dangerous. This attack would be good enough to win against all comers on any pitch and in all conditions.

Mike Hussey, sadly, performs 12th man duties, but would be a strong backup at any time if a rotation was considered.

Without any doubt in my mind, these are the best players I have seen in the matches I have been privileged to umpire. Of course I have left out many brilliant players, some of whom may have even better statistics, but I believe each of my selections could, more often than not, turn a game from a losing position to a winning one.

CAREER MATCHES

First Class Matches

Date	Competition	Match	Venue
22 February 1989	Sheffield Shield 1988/89	New South Wales v Tasmania	Sydney Cricket Ground
15 December 1989	Sheffield Shield 1989/90	New South Wales v Victoria	Lavington Sports Oval, Albury
6 January 1990	Sheffield Shield 1989/90	New South Wales v Western Australia	Sydney Cricket Ground
15 February 1990	Sheffield Shield 1989/90	New South Wales v South Australia	Sydney Cricket Ground
9 March 1990	Sheffield Shield 1989/90	New South Wales v Tasmania	Sydney Cricket Ground
22 November 1990	Wellington in Australia 1990/91	New South Wales v Wellington	North Sydney Oval, Sydney
13 January 1991	England in Australia 1990/91	New South Wales v England XI	Lavington Sports Oval, Albury
31 January 1991	Sheffield Shield 1990/91	New South Wales v Western Australia	Sydney Cricket Ground
7 March 1991	Sheffield Shield 1990/91	New South Wales v Queensland	Sydney Cricket Ground
8 November 1991	Sheffield Shield 1991/92	New South Wales v Victoria	Sydney Cricket Ground
25 January 1992	India in Australia 1991/92	Australia v India	Adelaide Oval
7 March 1992	Sheffield Shield 1991/92	New South Wales v Western Australia	Sydney Cricket Ground
6 November 1992	Sheffield Shield 1992/93	New South Wales v Victoria	Sydney Cricket Ground
14 November 1992	West Indies in Australia 1992/93	Australian XI v West Indians	Bellerive Oval, Hobart
20 November 1992	West Indies in Australia 1992/93	New South Wales v West Indians	Sydney Cricket Ground
11 December 1992	Sheffield Shield 1992/93	New South Wales v Queensland	Sydney Cricket Ground
2 January 1993	West Indies in Australia 1992/93	Australia v West Indies	Sydney Cricket Ground
23 January 1993	West Indies in Australia 1992/93	Australia v West Indies	Adelaide Oval
3 February 1993	Sheffield Shield 1992/93	New South Wales v Western Australia	Sydney Cricket Ground

First Class Matches continued.

Date	Match	Teams	Venue
11 March 1993	Sheffield Shield 1992/93	New South Wales v South Australia	Sydney Cricket Ground
26 March 1993	Sheffield Shield 1992/93	New South Wales v Queensland	Sydney Cricket Ground
29 October 1993	New Zealand in Australia 1993/94	New South Wales v New Zealanders	No 1 Sports Ground, Newcastle
12 November 1993	New Zealand in Australia 1993/94	Australia v New Zealand	Western Australia Cricket Association (WACA) Ground, Perth
26 November 1993	New Zealand in Australia 1993/94	Australia v New Zealand	Bellerive Oval, Hobart
18 December 1993	Sheffield Shield 1993/94	New South Wales v Victoria	Sydney Cricket Ground
26 December 1993	South Africa in Australia 1993/94	Australia v South Africa	Melbourne Cricket Ground
28 January 1994	South Africa in Australia 1993/94	Australia v South Africa	Adelaide Oval
17 March 1994	Sheffield Shield 1993/94	New South Wales v Queensland	Sydney Cricket Ground
25 March 1994	Sheffield Shield 1993/94	New South Wales v Tasmania	Sydney Cricket Ground
8 April 1994	England in West Indies 1993/94	West Indies v England	Kensington Oval, Bridgetown
16 April 1994	England in West Indies 1993/94	West Indies v England	Antigua Recreation Ground, St John's
12 November 1994	England in Australia 1994/95	New South Wales v England XI	No 1 Sports Ground, Newcastle
18 November 1994	Sheffield Shield 1994/95	New South Wales v Queensland	Sydney Cricket Ground
1 January 1995	England in Australia 1994/95	Australia v England	Sydney Cricket Ground
27 January 1995	Sheffield Shield 1994/95	New South Wales v Victoria	Sydney Cricket Ground
4 March 1995	South Africa in New Zealand 1994/95	New Zealand v South Africa	Eden Park, Auckland
24 March 1995	Sheffield Shield 1994/95	Queensland v South Australia	Brisbane Cricket Ground

First Class Matches continued.

26 October 1995	Sheffield Shield 1995/96	New South Wales v Tasmania	Sydney Cricket Ground
2 November 1995	Sheffield Shield 1995/96	Tasmania v Queensland	Bellerive Oval, Hobart
17 November 1995	Pakistan in Australia 1995/96	Australia v Pakistan	Bellerive Oval, Hobart
30 November 1995	England in South Africa 1995/96	South Africa v England	New Wanderers Stadium, Johannesburg
26 December 1995	Sri Lanka in Australia 1995/96	Australia v Sri Lanka	Melbourne Cricket Ground
13 February 1996	Sheffield Shield 1995/96	Victoria v South Australia	Melbourne Cricket Ground
23 March 1996	Sheffield Shield 1995/96	Victoria v Queensland	Melbourne Cricket Ground
30 March 1996	Sheffield Shield 1995/96	South Australia v Western Australia	Adelaide Oval
6 June 1996	India in England 1996	England v India	Edgbaston, Birmingham
20 June 1996	India in England 1996	England v India	Lord's Cricket Ground, St John's Wood
6 November 1996	Sheffield Shield 1996/97	Queensland v Tasmania	Brisbane Cricket Ground
15 November 1996	Sheffield Shield 1996/97	Western Australia v Tasmania	WACA Ground, Perth
29 November 1996	West Indies in Australia 1996/97	Australia v West Indies	Sydney Cricket Ground
2 January 1997	India in South Africa 1996/97	South Africa v India	Newlands, Cape Town
1 February 1997	West Indies in Australia 1996/97	Australia v West Indies	WACA Ground, Perth
14 February 1997	England in New Zealand 1996/97	New Zealand v England	Lancaster Park, Christchurch
13 March 1997	Sheffield Shield 1996/97	Queensland v South Australia	Brisbane Cricket Ground
21 March 1997	Sheffield Shield 1996/97	Western Australia v Queensland	WACA Ground, Perth
15 October 1997	Sheffield Shield 1997/98	South Australia v Tasmania	Adelaide Oval

First Class Matches continued.

31 October 1997	Sheffield Shield 1997/98	Tasmania v Western Australia	Bellerive Oval, Hobart
20 November 1997	New Zealand in Australia 1997/98	Australia v New Zealand	WACA Ground, Perth
2 January 1998	South Africa in Australia 1997/98	Australia v South Africa	Sydney Cricket Ground
13 February 1998	England in West Indies 1997/98	West Indies v England	Queen's Park Oval, Port of Spain
27 February 1998	England in West Indies 1997/98	West Indies v England	Bourda, Georgetown
12 March 1998	Sheffield Shield 1997/98	Victoria v Tasmania	Melbourne Cricket Ground
20 March 1998	Sheffield Shield 1997/98	Western Australia v Tasmania	WACA Ground, Perth
18 June 1998	South Africa in British Isles 1998	England v South Africa	Lord's Cricket Ground, St John's Wood
21 October 1998	Sheffield Shield 1998/99	Queensland v Western Australia	Brisbane Cricket Ground
20 November 1998	England in Australia 1998/99	Australia v England	Brisbane Cricket Ground
10 December 1998	Zimbabwe in Pakistan 1998/99	Pakistan v Zimbabwe	Gaddafi Stadium, Lahore
19 December 1998	Sheffield Shield 1998/99	Western Australia v South Australia	WACA Ground, Perth
2 January 1999	England in Australia 1998/99	Australia v England	Sydney Cricket Ground
4 March 1999	Sheffield Shield 1998/99	New South Wales v South Australia	Sydney Cricket Ground
19 March 1999	Sheffield Shield 1998/99	Queensland v Western Australia	Brisbane Cricket Ground
27 October 1999	Pura Milk Cup 1999/00	New South Wales v South Australia	Sydney Cricket Ground
11 November 1999	South Africa in Zimbabwe 1999/00	Zimbabwe v South Africa	Harare Sports Club
26 November 1999	Pakistan in Australia 1999/00	Australia v Pakistan	WACA Ground, Perth
2 December 1999	India in Australia 1999/00	New South Wales v Indians	Sydney Cricket Ground

First Class Matches continued.

Date	Series	Match	Venue
2 January 2000	India in Australia 1999/00	Australia v India	Sydney Cricket Ground
14 January 2000	England in South Africa 1999/00	South Africa v England	Centurion Park
9 March 2000	Pura Milk Cup 1999/00	New South Wales v Western Australia	Sydney Cricket Ground
17 March 2000	Pura Milk Cup 1999/00	Queensland v Victoria	Allan Border Field, Brisbane
12 September 2000	New Zealand in Zimbabwe 2000/01	Zimbabwe v New Zealand	Queens Sports Club, Bulawayo
25 October 2000	Pura Cup 2000/01	Victoria v New South Wales	Richmond Cricket Ground, Melbourne
7 November 2000	Pura Cup 2000/01	Tasmania v New South Wales	Bellerive Oval, Hobart
15 November 2000	England in Pakistan 2000/01	Pakistan v England	Gaddafi Stadium, Lahore
15 December 2000	Pura Cup 2000/01	Western Australia v New South Wales	WACA Ground, Perth
2 January 2001	West Indies in Australia 2000/01	Australia v West Indies	Sydney Cricket Ground
14 February 2001	Pura Cup 2000/01	New South Wales v Tasmania	Sydney Cricket Ground
2 March 2001	Pura Cup 2000/01	New South Wales v Queensland	Sydney Cricket Ground
9 March 2001	Pura Cup 2000/01	Western Australia v Tasmania	WACA Ground, Perth
17 March 2001	South Africa in West Indies 2000/01	West Indies v South Africa	Queen's Park Oval, Port of Spain
29 March 2001	South Africa in West Indies 2000/01	West Indies v South Africa	Kensington Oval, Bridgetown
17 May 2001	Pakistan in England 2001	England v Pakistan	Lord's Cricket Ground, St John's Wood
29 August 2001	Asian Test Championship 2001/02	Pakistan v Bangladesh	Multan Cricket Stadium
7 September 2001	South Africa in Zimbabwe 2001/02	Zimbabwe v South Africa	Harare Sports Club
17 October 2001	Pura Cup 2001/02	New South Wales v Tasmania	Sydney Cricket Ground

First Class Matches continued.

Date	Match	Teams	Venue
30 November 2001	New Zealand in Australia 2001/02	Australia v New Zealand	WACA Ground, Perth
14 December 2001	Pura Cup 2001/02	New South Wales v Western Australia	Sydney Cricket Ground
26 December 2001	South Africa in Australia 2001/02	Australia v South Africa	Melbourne Cricket Ground
7 February 2002	West Indies in United Arab Emirates 2001/02	Pakistan v West Indies	Sharjah Cricket Association Stadium
1st March 2002	Pura Cup 2001/02	New South Wales v Queensland	Sydney Cricket Ground
21 March 2002	England in New Zealand 2001/02	New Zealand v England	Basin Reserve, Wellington
8 November 2002	Pura Cup 2002/03	New South Wales v Tasmania	Sydney Cricket Ground
14 November 2002	Pura Cup 2002/03	New South Wales v South Australia	Sydney Cricket Ground
5 June 2003	Zimbabwe in British Isles 2003	England v Zimbabwe	Riverside Ground, Chester-le-Street
27 June 2003	Sri Lanka in West Indies 2003	West Indies v Sri Lanka	Sabina Park, Kingston
31 July 2003	South Africa in British Isles 2003	England v South Africa	Lord's Cricket Ground, St John's Wood
14 August 2003	South Africa in British Isles 2003	England v South Africa	Trent Bridge, Nottingham
17 October 2003	South Africa in Pakistan 2003/04	Pakistan v South Africa	Gaddafi Stadium, Lahore
4 November 2003	Pura Cup 2003/04	New South Wales v Western Australia	Sydney Cricket Ground
12 December 2003	West Indies in South Africa and Zimbabwe 2003/04	South Africa v West Indies	New Wanderers Stadium, Johannesburg
26 December 2003	West Indies in South Africa 2003/04	South Africa v West Indies	Sahara Stadium, Durban
1 April 2004	England in West Indies 2003/04	West Indies v England	Kensington Oval, Bridgetown
10 April 2004	England in West Indies 2003/04	West Indies v England	Antigua Recreation Ground, St John's

First Class Matches continued.

20 May 2004	New Zealand in England 2004	England v New Zealand	Lord's Cricket Ground, St John's Wood
29 July 2004	West Indies in British Isles 2004	England v West Indies	Edgbaston, Birmingham
19 August 2004	West Indies in British Isles 2004	England v West Indies	The Brit Oval, Kennington
17 December 2004	England in South Africa 2004/05	South Africa v England	Sahara Oval, Port Elizabeth
26 December 2004	England in South Africa 2004/05	South Africa v England	Sahara Stadium, Durban
8 March 2005	Pakistan in India 2004/05	India v Pakistan	Punjab Cricket Association Ground, Mohali
16 March 2005	Pakistan in India 2004/05	India v Pakistan	Eden Gardens, Kolkata
4 April 2005	Sri Lanka in New Zealand 2004/05	New Zealand v Sri Lanka	McLean Park, Napier
11 April 2005	Sri Lanka in New Zealand 2004/05	New Zealand v Sri Lanka	Basin Reserve, Wellington
27 April 2005	Frizzell County Championship 2005	Warwickshire v Middlesex	Edgbaston, Birmingham
26 May 2005	Pakistan in West Indies 2004/05	West Indies v Pakistan	Kensington Oval, Bridgetown
3 June 2005	Pakistan in West Indies 2004/05	West Indies v Pakistan	Sabina Park, Kingston
26 July 2005	Bangladesh A in England 2005	Glamorgan v Bangladesh A	Pen-y-Pound, Abergavenny
30 July 2005	Australia in British Isles 2005	Worcestershire v Australians	County Ground, Worcester
7 August 2005	New Zealand in Namibia and Zimbabwe 2005/06	Zimbabwe v New Zealand	Harare Sports Club
15 August 2005	New Zealand in Namibia and Zimbabwe 2005/06	Zimbabwe v New Zealand	Queens Sports Club, Bulawayo
20 November 2005	England in Pakistan 2005/06	Pakistan v England	Iqbal Stadium, Faisalabad
29 November 2005	England in Pakistan 2005/06	Pakistan v England	Gaddafi Stadium, Lahore

First Class Matches continued.

13 January 2006	India in Pakistan 2005/06	Pakistan v India	Gaddafi Stadium, Lahore
9 March 2006	England in India 2005/06	India v England	Punjab Cricket Association Ground, Mohali
18 March 2006	England in India 2005/06	India v England	Wankhede Stadium, Mumbai
5 May 2006	New Zealand in South Africa 2005/06	South Africa v New Zealand	New Wanderers Stadium, Johannesburg
17 May 2006	University Centres of Cricketing Excellence 2006	Cambridge University Centre of Cricketing Excellence v Kent	FP Fenner's Ground, Cambridge
25 May 2006	Sri Lanka in England 2006	England v Sri Lanka	Edgbaston, Birmingham
2 June 2006	Sri Lanka in England 2006	England v Sri Lanka	Trent Bridge, Nottingham
6 July 2006	Pakistan in British Isles 2006	England A v Pakistanis	St Lawrence Ground, Canterbury
19 July 2006	Liverpool Victoria County Championship 2006	Yorkshire v Warwickshire	Nor Marine Road Ground, Scarborough
4 August 2006	Pakistan in British Isles 2006	England v Pakistan	Headingley, Leeds
17 August 2006	Pakistan in British Isles 2006	England v Pakistan	The Brit Oval, Kennington
28 June 2007	ICC Inter-Continental Cup 2007/08	Canada v Neerlands	Maple Leaf South-East Ground, King City
23 January 2008	ICC Inter-Continental Cup 2007/08	United Arab Emirates v Namibia	Sharjah Cricket Association Stadium
29 January 2008	ICC Inter-Continental Cup 2007/08	Kenya v Namibia	Sharjah Cricket Association Stadium
23 May 2008	New Zealand in England 2008	England v New Zealand	Old Trafford, Manchester
5 June 2008	New Zealand in England 2008	England v New Zealand	Trent Bridge, Nottingham

One-day Internationals

14 December 1991	Benson and Hedges World Series Cup 1991/92	India v West Indies	Adelaide Oval
11 January 1992	Benson and Hedges World Series Cup 1991/92	India v West Indies	Brisbane Cricket Ground
14 January 1992	Benson and Hedges World Series Cup 1991/92	Australia v India	Sydney Cricket Ground
8 December 1992	Benson and Hedges World Series Cup 1992/93	Australia v West Indies	Sydney Cricket Ground
17 December 1992	Benson and Hedges World Series Cup 1992/93	Pakistan v West Indies	Sydney Cricket Ground
12 January 1993	Benson and Hedges World Series Cup 1992/93	Australia v Pakistan	Melbourne Cricket Ground
18 January 1993	Benson and Hedges World Series Cup 1992/93	Australia v West Indies	Melbourne Cricket Ground
14 December 1993	Benson and Hedges World Series Cup 1993/94	Australia v South Africa	Sydney Cricket Ground
9 January 1994	Benson and Hedges World Series Cup 1993/94	Australia v South Africa	Brisbane Cricket Ground
23 January 1994	Benson and Hedges World Series Cup 1993/94	Australia v South Africa	Sydney Cricket Ground
25 January 1994	Benson and Hedges World Series Cup 1993/94	Australia v South Africa	Sydney Cricket Ground

One-day Internationals continued.

Date	Series	Match	Venue
6 December 1994	Benson and Hedges World Series Cup 1994/95	Australia v England	Sydney Cricket Ground
15 December 1994	Benson and Hedges World Series Cup 1994/95	England v Zimbabwe	Sydney Cricket Ground
11 October 1995	Singer Champions Trophy 1995/96	Sri Lanka v West Indies	Sharjah Cricket Association Stadium
13 October 1995	Singer Champions Trophy 1995/96	Pakistan v West Indies	Sharjah Cricket Association Stadium
15 October 1995	Singer Champions Trophy 1995/96	Pakistan v West Indies	Sharjah Cricket Association Stadium
17 October 1995	Singer Champions Trophy 1995/96	Pakistan v Sri Lanka	Sharjah Cricket Association Stadium
20 October 1995	Singer Champions Trophy 1995/96	Sri Lanka v West Indies	Sharjah Cricket Association Stadium
21 December 1995	Benson and Hedges World Series Cup 1995/96	Australia v Sri Lanka	Sydney Cricket Ground
7 January 1996	Benson and Hedges World Series Cup 1995/96	Australia v West Indies	Brisbane Cricket Ground Brisbane
12 January 1996	Benson and Hedges World Series Cup 1995/96	Australia v Sri Lanka	WACA Ground, Perth
16 January 1996	Benson and Hedges World Series Cup 1995/96	Australia v Sri Lanka	Melbourne Cricket Ground
18 January 1996	Benson and Hedges World Series Cup 1995/96	Australia v Sri Lanka	Melbourne Cricket Ground
8 December 1996	Carlton and United Series 1996/97	Australia v West Indies	Sydney Cricket Ground
12 January 1997	Carlton and United Series 1996/97	Australia v West Indies	WACA Ground, Perth
16 January 1997	Carlton and United Series 1996/97	Australia v Pakistan	Melbourne Cricket Ground

One-day Internationals continued.

18 January 1997	Carlton and United Series 1996/97	Pakistan v West Indies	Sydney Cricket Ground
7 December 1997	Carlton and United Series 1997/98	Australia v New Zealand	Adelaide Oval
17 December 1997	Carlton and United Series 1997/98	Australia v New Zealand	Melbourne Cricket Ground
18 January 1998	Carlton and United Series 1997/98	Australia v South Africa	WACA Ground, Perth
23 January 1998	Carlton and United Series 1997/98	Australia v South Africa	Melbourne Cricket Ground
26 January 1998	Carlton and United Series 1997/98	Australia v South Africa	Sydney Cricket Ground
27 January 1998	Carlton and United Series 1997/98	Australia v South Africa	Sydney Cricket Ground
15 January 1999	Carlton and United Series 1998/99	Australia v England	Melbourne Cricket Ground
17 January 1999	Carlton and United Series 1998/99	Australia v England	Sydney Cricket Ground
5 February 1999	Carlton and United Series 1998/99	Australia v England	Sydney Cricket Ground
10 February 1999	Carlton and United Series 1998/99	Australia v England	Sydney Cricket Ground
13 February 1999	Carlton and United Series 1998/99	Australia v England	Melbourne Cricket Ground
8 April 1999	Coca-Cola Sharjah Cup 1998/99	India v Pakistan	Sharjah Cricket Association Stadium
9 April 1999	Coca-Cola Sharjah Cup 1998/99	England v India	Sharjah Cricket Association Stadium
11 April 1999	Coca-Cola Sharjah Cup 1998/99	England v India	Sharjah Cricket Association Stadium
13 April 1999	Coca-Cola Sharjah Cup 1998/99	India v Pakistan	Sharjah Cricket Association Stadium
16 April 1999	Coca-Cola Sharjah Cup 1998/99	India v Pakistan	Sharjah Cricket Association Stadium
16 May 1999	ICC World Cup 1999	Pakistan v West Indies	The Royal & Sun Alliance County Ground, Bristol
21 May 1999	ICC World Cup 1999	Bangladesh v West Indies	Castle Avenue, Dublin

One-day Internationals continued.

Date	Match	Teams	Venue
25 May 1999	ICC World Cup 1999	England v Zimbabwe	Trent Bridge, Nottingham
29 May 1999	ICC World Cup 1999	England v India	Edgbaston, Birmingham
31 May 1999	ICC World Cup 1999	Bangladesh v Pakistan	County Ground, Northampton
5 June 1999	ICC World Cup 1999	Pakistan v South Africa	Trent Bridge, Nottingham
12 June 1999	ICC World Cup 1999	India v New Zealand	Trent Bridge, Nottingham
16 June 1999	ICC World Cup 1999	New Zealand v Pakistan	Old Trafford, Manchester
2 September 1999	Coca-Cola Singapore Challenge 1999	West Indies v Zimbabwe	Kallang Ground, Singapore
4 September 1999	Coca-Cola Singapore Challenge 1999	India v Zimbabwe	Kallang Ground, Singapore
7 September 1999	Coca-Cola Singapore Challenge 1999	India v West Indies	Kallang Ground, Singapore
8 September 1999	Coca-Cola Singapore Challenge 1999	India v West Indies	Kallang Ground, Singapore
23 January 2000	Carlton and United Series 1999/00	Australia v Pakistan	Melbourne Cricket Ground
25 January 2000	Carlton and United Series 1999/00	India v Pakistan	Adelaide Oval
28 January 2000	Carlton and United Series 1999/00	India v Pakistan	WACA Ground, Perth
30 January 2000	Carlton and United Series 1999/00	Australia v India	WACA Ground, Perth
16 August 2000	Super Challenge 2000	Australia v South Africa	Colonial Stadium, Melbourne
20 August 2000	Super Challenge 2000	Australia v South Africa	Colonial Stadium, Melbourne
5 October 2000	ICC KnockOut 2000/01	Bangladesh v England	Gymkhana Club Ground, Nairobi
10 October 2000	ICC KnockOut 2000/01	England v South Africa	Gymkhana Club Ground, Nairobi
14 January 2001	Carlton Series 2000/01	Australia v West Indies	Brisbane Cricket Ground

One-day Internationals continued.

Date	Series	Teams	Venue
17 January 2001	Carlton Series 2000/01	Australia v West Indies	Sydney Cricket Ground
25 January 2001	Carlton Series 2000/01	West Indies v Zimbabwe	Adelaide Oval
28 January 2001	Carlton Series 2000/01	Australia v Zimbabwe	Sydney Cricket Ground
2 February 2001	Carlton Series 2000/01	West Indies v Zimbabwe	WACA Ground, Perth
9 February 2001	Carlton Series 2000/01	Australia v West Indies	Melbourne Cricket Ground
11 January 2002	VB Series 2001/02	Australia v New Zealand	Melbourne Cricket Ground
19 January 2002	VB Series 2001/02	New Zealand v South Africa	Brisbane Cricket Ground
22 January 2002	VB Series 2001/02	Australia v South Africa	Sydney Cricket Ground
29 January 2002	VB Series 2001/02	Australia v New Zealand	Melbourne Cricket Ground
1 February 2002	VB Series 2001/02	New Zealand v South Africa	WACA Ground, Perth
15 June 2002	Pakistan in Australia 2002	Australia v Pakistan	Colonial Stadium, Melbourne
17 December 2002	VB Series 2002/03	England v Sri Lanka	Brisbane Cricket Ground
22 December 2002	VB Series 2002/03	Australia v Sri Lanka	WACA Ground, Perth
11 January 2003	VB Series 2002/03	Australia v England	Bellerive Oval, Hobart
13 January 2003	VB Series 2002/03	England v Sri Lanka	Sydney Cricket Ground
25 January 2003	VB Series 2002/03	Australia v England	Melbourne Cricket Ground
13 February 2003	ICC World Cup 2002/03	New Zealand v West Indies	St George's Park, Port Elizabeth
16 February 2003	ICC World Cup 2002/03	England v Netherlands	Buffalo Park, East London
23 February 2003	ICC World Cup 2002/03	Canada v West Indies	Centurion Park

One-day Internationals continued.

26 February 2003	ICC World Cup 2002/03	Bangladesh v New Zealand	De Beers Diamond Oval, Kimberley
8 March 2003	ICC World Cup 2002/03	New Zealand v Zimbabwe	Goodyear Park, Bloemfontein
17 June 2003	National Westminster Bank Challenge 2003	England v Pakistan	Old Trafford, Manchester
20 June 2003	National Westminster Bank Challenge 2003	England v Pakistan	The AMP Oval, Kennington
22 June 2003	National Westminster Bank Challenge 2003	England v Pakistan	Lord's Cricket Ground, St John's Wood
3 October 2003	South Africa in Pakistan 2003/04	Pakistan v South Africa	Gaddafi Stadium, Lahore
5 October 2003	South Africa in Pakistan 2003/04	Pakistan v South Africa	Gaddafi Stadium, Lahore
7 October 2003	South Africa in Pakistan 2003/04	Pakistan v South Africa	Iqbal Stadium, Faisalabad
10 October 2003	South Africa in Pakistan 2003/04	Pakistan v South Africa	Rawalpindi Cricket Stadium
12 October 2003	South Africa in Pakistan 2003/04	Pakistan v South Africa	Rawalpindi Cricket Stadium
10 January 2004	Pakistan in New Zealand 2003/04	New Zealand v Pakistan	Jade Stadium, Christchurch
14 January 2004	Pakistan in New Zealand 2003/04	New Zealand v Pakistan	McLean Park, Napier
17 January 2004	Pakistan in New Zealand 2003/04	New Zealand v Pakistan	Westpac Stadium, Wellington
25 January 2004	West Indies in South Africa and Zimbabwe 2003/04	South Africa v West Indies	Sahara Park Newlands, Cape Town
30 January 2004	West Indies in South Africa and Zimbabwe 2003/04	South Africa v West Indies	Sahara Stadium, Kingsmead, Durban
4 February 2004	West Indies in South Africa and Zimbabwe 2003/04	South Africa v West Indies	New Wanderers Stadium, Johannesburg
24 April 2004	England in West Indies 2003/04	West Indies v England	Queen's Park Oval, Port of Spain

One-day Internationals continued.

Date	Series	Match	Venue
28 April 2004	England in West Indies 2003/04	West Indies v England	Queen's Park (New), St George's
1 September 2004	National Westminster Bank Challenge 2004	England v India	Trent Bridge, Nottingham
3 September 2004	National Westminster Bank Challenge 2004	England v India	The Brit Oval, Kennington
5 September 2004	National Westminster Bank Challenge 2004	England v India	Lord's Cricket Ground, St John's Wood
14 September 2004	ICC Champions Trophy 2004	Kenya v Pakistan	Edgbaston, Birmingham
17 September 2004	ICC Champions Trophy 2004	England v Sri Lanka	The Rose Bowl, Southampton
22 September 2004	ICC Champions Trophy 2004	Pakistan v West Indies	The Rose Bowl, Southampton
1 December 2004	England in Namibia, South Africa and Zimbabwe 2004/05	Zimbabwe v England	Harare Sports Club
5 December 2004	England in Namibia, South Africa and Zimbabwe 2004/05	Zimbabwe v England	Queens Sports Club, Bulawayo
7 May 2005	South Africa in West Indies 2004/05	West Indies v South Africa	Sabina Park, Kingston
11 May 2005	South Africa in West Indies 2004/05	West Indies v South Africa	Kensington Oval, Bridgetown
15 May 2005	South Africa in West Indies 2004/05	West Indies v South Africa	Queen's Park Oval, Port of Spain
21 May 2005	Pakistan in West Indies 2004/05	West Indies v Pakistan	Beausejour Stadium, Gros Islet
7 October 2005	Johnnie Walker Super Series 2005/06	Australia v ICC World XI	Colonial Stadium, Melbourne
9 October 2005	Johnnie Walker Super Series 2005/06	Australia v ICC World XI	Colonial Stadium, Melbourne
10 December 2005	England in Pakistan 2005/06	Pakistan v England	Gaddafi Stadium, Lahore
12 December 2005	England in Pakistan 2005/06	Pakistan v England	Gaddafi Stadium, Lahore
31 December 2005	Sri Lanka in New Zealand 2005/06	New Zealand v Sri Lanka	Queenstown Events Centre

One-day Internationals continued.

Date	Match	Venue
3 January 2006	Sri Lanka in New Zealand 2005/06	New Zealand v Sri Lanka	Jade Stadium, Christchurch
6 January 2006	Sri Lanka in New Zealand 2005/06	New Zealand v Sri Lanka	Westpac Stadium, Wellington
8 January 2006	Sri Lanka in New Zealand 2005/06	New Zealand v Sri Lanka	McLean Park, Napier
13 June 2006	England in Ireland 2006	Ireland v England	Civil Service Cricket Club, Stormont, Belfast
17 June 2006	Sri Lanka in England 2006	England v Sri Lanka	Lord's Cricket Ground, St John's Wood
20 June 2006	Sri Lanka in England 2006	England v Sri Lanka	The Brit Oval, Kennington
27 June 2006	Pakistan in British Isles 2006	Scotland v Pakistan	Grange Cricket Club Ground, Raeburn Place, Edinburgh
18 January 2007	ICC Associates Kenya Tri-Series 2006/07	Canada v Scotland	Mombasa Sports Club Ground
20 January 2007	ICC Associates Kenya Tri-Series 2006/07	Kenya v Canada	Mombasa Sports Club Ground
21 January 2007	ICC Associates Kenya Tri-Series 2006/07	Kenya v Scotland	Mombasa Sports Club Ground
23 January 2007	ICC Associates Kenya Tri-Series 2006/07	Canada v Scotland	Mombasa Sports Club Ground
30 January 2007	ICC World Cricket League Division One 2007	Ireland v Scotland	Gymkhana Club Ground, Nairobi
2 February 2007	ICC World Cricket League Division One 2007	Bermuda v Canada	Gymkhana Club Ground, Nairobi
4 February 2007	ICC World Cricket League Division One 2007	Kenya v Scotland	Gymkhana Club Ground, Nairobi
7 February 2007	ICC World Cricket League Division One 2007	Kenya v Scotland	Gymkhana Club Ground, Nairobi
3 July 2007	Netherlands in Canada 2007	Canada v Netherlands	Toronto Cricket, Skating and Curling Club
4 July 2007	Netherlands in Canada 2007	Canada v Netherlands	Toronto Cricket, Skating and Curling Club
11 July 2007	Quadrangular Series 2007	Ireland v Netherlands	Civil Service Cricket Club, Stormont, Belfast

One-day Internationals continued.

13 July 2007	Quadrangular Series 2007	Netherlands v Scotland	Civil Service Cricket Club, Stormont, Belfast
15 July 2007	Quadrangular Series 2007	Ireland v Scotland	Civil Service Cricket Club, Stormont, Belfast
18 August 2008	Scotiabank Tri-Series 2008	Canada v Bermuda	Maple Leaf North-West Ground, King City
20 August 2008	Scotiabank Tri-Series 2008	Bermuda v West Indies	Maple Leaf North-West Ground, King City
22 August 2008	Scotiabank Tri-Series 2008	Canada v West Indies	Maple Leaf North-West Ground, King City
24 August 2008	Scotiabank Tri-Series 2008	Canada v West Indies	Maple Leaf North-West Ground, King City

Other Career Matches

Date	Match	Venue
24th October 1988	Sydney Gregory Cup	New South Wales Colts v Queensland Colts	Village Green, Sydney
27th December 1988	Pakistan in Australia and New Zealand 1988/89	New South Wales Invitation XI v Pakistanis	No 1 Sports Ground, Newcastle
30th October 1989	Other matches in Australia 1989/90	New South Wales Second XI v Victoria Second XI	Village Green, Sydney
14th January 1990	England Young Cricketers in Australia 1989/90, 1st Test	Australia Young Cricketers v England Young Cricketers	North Sydney Oval, Sydney
11th December 1990	England in Australia 1990/91	Bradman XI v England XI	Bradman Oval, Bowral
18th February 1992	Benson and Hedges World Cup 1991/92 Warm-up	New South Wales v Australians	North Sydney Oval, Sydney
18th January 1994	South Africa in Australia 1993/94 Bushfire Relief Fund	New South Wales Invitation XI v South Africans	Sydney Cricket Ground
18th December 1994	Other matches in Australia 1994/95	Bradman XI v World XI	Sydney Cricket Ground
20th September 1997	Transvaal in Australia 1997/98	New South Wales v Transvaal	Drummoyne Oval, Sydney
7th May 1999	ICC World Cup 1999 Warm-up	Sussex v South Africa	County Ground, Hove
10th May 1999	ICC World Cup 1999 Warm-up	Middlesex v Bangladesh	John Walker's Ground, Southgate
11th May 1999	ICC World Cup 1999 Warm-up	Middlesex v South Africa	John Walker's Ground, Southgate
8th June 2002	Pakistan in Australia 2002	Queensland Invitation XI v Pakistanis	Allan Border Field, Brisbane
4th September 2002	New Zealand in Australia 2002/03	Tasmania v New Zealanders	Alan Davidson Oval, Sydney
6th September 2002	New Zealand in Australia 2002/03	New South Wales v New Zealanders	Caringbah Oval, Sydney
4th February 2003	ICC World Cup 2002/03 Warm-up	Boland Invitation XI v South Africa	Boland Bank Park, Paarl

Other Career Matches continued.

6th February 2003	ICC World Cup 2002/03 Warm-up	Boland v Netherlands	Boland Bank Park, Paarl
14th June 2005	Tsunami Relief Fund 2005	Marylebone Cricket Club v International XI	Lord's Cricket Ground, St John's Wood
2nd October 2005	Johnnie Walker Super Series 2005/06 Warm-up	Victoria v ICC World XI	St Kilda Cricket Ground, Melbourne
11th February 2008	ICC Under-19 World Cup 2007/08 Warm-up	Ireland Under-19s v Papua New Guinea Under-19s	Selangor Turf Club, Kuala Lumpur
14th February 2008	ICC Under-19 World Cup 2007/08 Warm-up	Bermuda Under-19s v Namibia Under-19s	Selangor Turf Club, Kuala Lumpur

ACKNOWLEDGEMENTS

Thinking about who to thank always raises the embarrassment of leaving out someone who deserves to be acknowledged. There are so many people who have been instrumental in shaping my life and later on my career as a cricket umpire and I offer my thanks to them for their involvement and guidance through what have often been trying times.

In Robert Griffiths QC, Stephen Whale QC, from 4-5 Gray's Inn Square, employment lawyers Carolyn Brown and Paul Gilbert along with Mark Stephens and Daniel Marks from Finers Stephens Innocent, I could not have asked for better advice or commitment to a cause they firmly believed in. I am forever in their debt for doing such a fine job and achieving the result I thought would be forever beyond fruition — returning to umpire Test cricket.

John Beveridge QC played a major part in supporting me when I most needed his advice. My early trips to his St James Chambers in London in the weeks following The Oval Test match where I gained inspiration for the battle ahead were instrumental in helping me move my life forward in the face of adversity. Thanks John and Rebecca.

The guidance and advice I received from Nigel Plews and John Jameson was an integral part of my learning, not just about the more recent events but along the way in our discussions about the Laws of Cricket and how they should be implemented and improved. I thank them for mentoring me and making a difference.

To Graham and Di Morris, thanks for your hospitality and confidentiality in the lead-up to the Employment Tribunal hearing in London and for supplying many of the photographs used in this book. Thanks also to UK journalists Ivo Tennant, Jamie Jackson and Patrick Kidd for writing it as it happened during the Employment Tribunal, rather than what people may have wanted to hear.

I thank my former neighbours from Mill Road, Lincoln for keeping the peace when a circus load of media personnel camped outside our house. A special thanks to Maggie and Alan, my hosts at the Lincoln Strugglers Inn, for always pouring the perfect pint of Black Sheep Bitter and for handling the persistent reporters with style and panache — they almost believed you when you said you had never heard of me!

Australian journalists Robert Craddock and Malcolm Conn wrote insights about the lack of ethics of cricket and supported me with encouragement to see it through and not back down. Thanks for your very public support, which helped so much in getting this story told.

The New South Wales Cricket Umpires Association and all its members through their then Executive Officer Peter Hughes never gave up the public battle to have me reinstated and provided great support through their public statements, made while others within the game remained silent. A special thanks to you all.

To all the cricketers from the Orange City Cricket Club and the Molong District Cricket Association, I am grateful for the opportunities you presented to me all those years ago. Playing cricket at such an early age with those who placed the integrity of the game so very high on the list was something I have never forgotten and learned a lot from. In particular thanks go to Carl Sharpe for his encouragement all those years ago and his friendship and support through the tough times. Terry Rayner with his no-nonsense approach to cricket and how it should be played along with the endless jokes and wisecracks, provided so many of the lighter moments about cricket and life that made us laugh when we sometimes felt like crying. Terry's list of jokes would fill several books.

To my wife, Amanda, who assisted with much of the research for this book and put up with many tantrums along the way when things just wouldn't come together as I wanted them to, I thank you with all my heart. It would never have been possible without your strong support and encouragement.

To Graham Reed and Ian Thomas, two of the greatest blokes in the game and exceptional umpires, I thank you for your guidance, support and teachings throughout the formative years of my career. If not for you, it would never have happened for me. To each and every umpire I have stood with: each day has been a pleasure and 'just another day in paradise' as I often said on our way out to call 'play'.

I say thanks to Ric, Pat, Murph, Jude, Rob, Jo, Paul, Howard, Maureen, Jenny, Bryan and Margaret for making our Friday evenings at The Strugglers with the perfect pint so memorable and enjoyable.

I thank Kathy, Tony and Emma for their kind assistance when we returned to Australia slightly bruised and battered. They helped us get back on with normal business.

I thank the many supporters who believe in the true spirit of the game and who offered me encouragement through emails, phone calls and letters. And finally, thanks to Ron and Doreen for the sacrifices they made to enable me to live such a full life and achieve my dreams.